Effective Healthcare Leadership

Effective Healthcare Leadership

by
Melanie Jasper
and
Mansour Jumaa

Blackwell
Publishing

© 2005 by Blackwell Publishing Ltd

Editorial offices:
Blackwell Publishing Ltd, 9600 Garsington Road, Oxford OX4 2DQ, UK
   Tel: +44 (0)1865 776868
Blackwell Publishing Inc., 350 Main Street, Malden, MA 02148-5020, USA
   Tel: +1 781 388 8250
Blackwell Publishing Asia Pty Ltd, 550 Swanston Street, Carlton, Victoria 3053, Australia
   Tel: +61 (0)3 8359 1011

First published 2005 by Blackwell Publishing Ltd

Library of Congress Cataloging-in-Publication Data

Jasper, Melanie.
   Effective healthcare leadership /Melanie Jasper and Mansour Jumaa.
      p. ; cm.
   Includes bibliographical references and index.
   ISBN-13: 978-14051-2182-8 (pbk. : alk. paper)
   ISBN-10: 1-4051-2182-3 (pbk. : alk. paper)
   1. Health services administration–Great Britain. 2. Leadership–Great Britain.
   [DNLM: 1. Health Services Administration–Great Britain. 2. Leadership–Great Britain. 3. Evidence-Based Medicine–organization & administration–Great Britain. 4. Models, Organizational–Great Britain.
5. Organizational Case Studies–Great Britain. W 84 FA1 J39e 2005] I. Jumaa, Mansour. II. Title.

   RA971.J37 2005
   362.1'068–dc22

                     2005005882

ISBN 10: 1-4051-2182-3
ISBN 13: 978-14051-2182-8

A catalogue record for this title is available from the British Library

Set in 10/12.5pt Palatino
by SPI Publisher Services, Pondicherry, India
Printed and bound in India
by Replika Press Pvt Ltd

The publisher's policy is to use permanent paper from mills that operate a sustainable forestry policy, and which has been manufactured from pulp processed using acid-free and elementary chlorine-free practices. Furthermore, the publisher ensures that the text paper and cover board used have met acceptable environmental accreditation standards.

For further information on Blackwell Publishing, visit our website:
www.blackwellpublishing.com

Contents

Contents

Foreword

Donald H McGannon wrote that leadership is an action not a position. I agree with this statement wholeheartedly. The National Health Service (NHS) is changing rapidly, it is now as concerned with health promotion and well-being as it is with sickness and curing. It is becoming truly patient led and everything we do as professionals is increasingly being measured by the impact it has on patients.

Today's NHS needs good leaders to ensure that services are delivered to a consistently high standard and are developed to meet the needs of individuals whilst not losing sight of the needs of the wider population. These leaders must be able to captivate, motivate and inspire their colleagues in order to respond effectively to the ever changing demands of healthcare.

This book explores the content and processes of leadership within today's NHS. Rather than being another textbook about the theory of leadership, it looks in depth at existing practice in clinical settings across the health service and identifies the key ingredients for and features of successful leadership.

I was particularly interested in the chapter identifying service challenges and how management and leadership techniques are used to solve them. By focusing on how the nursing profession has developed leadership strategies to deliver on the government's modernisation agenda, it is clear that nurses have been at the forefront of delivering many health reforms and policies.

Leadership is the art or process of influencing people so they willingly and enthusiastically move towards the achievement of a goal. The book rightly, in my view, concludes that strategic leaders are not superhuman with a clearer picture of the world than anyone else. Rather, they successfully create the right environments and understand their people to achieve successful outcomes.

Good leaders are aware of their strengths and weaknesses as well as those of others; they take responsibility for their actions and those of their teams; are able to set a clear direction of travel; use sound evidence to support decisions; keep their knowledge base current; and, through deploying all of these things, achieve and maintain the respect of colleagues across and beyond the organisation. Through the work they do on a daily basis and from the leadership they have shown in delivering on healthcare reforms, it is clear that many nurses already have a substantial range of these skills. For those looking to further develop their management skills and expertise, this book will be a valuable and inspirational resource be they nurses or other healthcare professionals.

Professor Chris Beasley CBE
Chief Nursing Officer
Department of Health

List of Contributors

Dr Jo Alleyne, Principal Lecturer in Nursing and Healthcare Management, School of Health and Social Sciences, Middlesex University, London
Jo is the current Chartered Management Institute's Programme Director for the Institute's Approved Centre at Middlesex University. She devised and successfully applied a model of Group Clinical Supervision as part of her doctoral studies, through a co-operative inquiry approach, which used focused management and leadership interventions. She is an RCN and National Association for Teachers in Further and Higher Education (NATFHE) activist, a member of the RCN Education Forum and the negotiating secretary for the Middlesex University NATFHE branch. She is Chair of the Health Educators Forum. Jo combines her management and leadership knowledge and skills to support her teaching and research and to contribute towards effective negotiations in her trade union activities.

Dr Nadia Chambers, Consultant Nurse for Older People, Southampton University Hospitals NHS Trust
Nadia qualified in 1982 and gained extensive experience in medicine and care of older people. She has led both practice and service developments for older people, including influencing the development of a staff support system for victims of violence experienced at work, developing quality standards for care of the older person, developing the care of the older person in an acute medical assessment unit and developing a rapid access Transient Ischaemic Attack Service. In addition to this, her experience as a teacher in higher education has included innovative curriculum developments such as post-graduate studies in clinical governance and clinical leadership.

Christopher M.A.D. Gbolo, Charge Nurse, Mental Health, Barnet, Enfield and Haringey Health Care NHS Trust, London
Christopher is a charge nurse/team leader in the psychiatric intensive care unit in Barnet, Enfield and Haringey Health Care NHS Trust in north London. He trained as a psychiatric and general nurse in Ghana and migrated to the UK in 1999. He progressed in his nursing career and became a charge nurse by 2003. He studied at Middlesex University and obtained an advanced diploma in healthcare, ethics and law and an advanced diploma in health and social care management. He is currently studying to obtain a BSc Honours

degree in nursing studies and a professional diploma at Middlesex University and Chartered Management Institute respectively.

Lindsey Hayes, Senior Fellow, Leadership for Primary Care, Royal College of Nursing Institute, London

Lindsey brings many years of knowledge, skills and experience as a community nurse, teacher and trainer to the world of leadership in primary care. Her passion for primary and public health developed when she was working as a health visitor in an inner city multicultural and ethnically diverse area. Then she chose to work with disadvantaged community groups, specialising in the homeless, a fairly unique health visiting role. Her interest in individual and group behaviours led her to undertake a period of ante-natal teaching and then go on to further education, where she managed and taught a large child care course in one of the most deprived inner London boroughs. Her passion for health and understanding of behaviour was further enhanced through counselling and more recently completing an MSc in health psychology. She is now Senior Fellow, Leadership for Primary Care at the Royal College of Nursing Institute in London.

Mark Hodder, Head of Organisational Development, Mid and West Wales (NHS Secondment from Centre for Health Leadership, Wales)

Mark is a training and development professional working to improve organisational and individual performance in NHS Wales through the implementation of the balanced scorecard approach to performance management. Mark gained his leadership experience as a Royal Air Force Officer developing and delivering officer training both in the UK and overseas. He is also a qualified performance coach, master practitioner of neuro-linguistic programming and hypnotherapist, skills that he uses to develop excellence in others.

Professor Melanie Jasper, Professor and Head of Health and Social Welfare Studies, Canterbury Christ Church University College

Having practised in the community as a midwife and health visitor for a number of years post-qualification, Melanie moved to the University of Portsmouth as a senior lecturer in 1990. She led the Masters curriculum and the Professional Doctorate in Nursing, as well as developing her academic field in critical reflection, reflective practice and reflective writing, until her appointment at Canterbury. She was appointed Editor of the *Journal of Nursing Management* in 2002, and holds an honorary appointment with Thames Valley University as Visiting Professor in the Adult Nursing subject group.

Helen Julu, Senior Practitioner, Health Visiting, London Borough of Enfield

Helen trained as a nurse in Uganda and migrated to Great Britain in 1983, elevating her nursing career to the level of a Ward Sister by 1998. Her ambition carried her further and she obtained an Honours degree at the University of

South Bank in Specialist Community Nursing Public Health/Health Visiting in 2000 and an advanced diploma in Management in 2003 with the Chartered Institute of Management and Middlesex University, London.

Dr Mansour Jumaa, Chartered Manager and Executive Coach, Chief Emeka Anyaoku R&D Centre for Work Based Learnig and Leading. Anyaoku Centre, West Sussex

A Florence Nightingale Foundation Scholar in Evidence-Based Practice in Healthcare and Nursing Management, Academic Group Chair (Healthcare Management), and former Chartered Management Institute Programme Director at Middlesex University, London. Mansour is now a Chartered Manager and Executive Coach at the Anyaoku Centre, West Sussex. He is the first nurse, the first West African, the first Nigerian and the first black person of African origin resident in the UK to be awarded Chartered Manager status, the hallmark of the professional manager. His award was based on his ability to use knowledge management processes for performance improvement within organisations. Mansour has over 30 years of experience within the NHS and the higher education sector in the UK. Since 1987 he has taught, facilitated and supervised management and leadership courses from doctorate and masters levels to single study days at many universities in the UK – the Middlesex, the London School of Economics, and the Universities of Sussex, Surrey, and Wales in Swansea. He is committed to widening management and leadership access to first- and middle-line managers, particularly managers from black and minority ethnic communities. It is for this reason that he has established L4T – Leadership For Today (www.leadershipfortoday.com).

Dr Ilkka Kunnamo, Editor-in-Chief, EBM Guidelines, Finland

Ilkka, a specialist in general medicine, wrote his doctoral thesis in the field of paediatrics. Since 1986 he has worked as a general practitioner at Karstula in central Finland. He developed the idea of Evidence-Based Medicine Guidelines (www.ebm-guidelines.com) and has served as its Editor-in-Chief since 1988. He is the author of about 30 research papers. He has been involved in several projects in primary care computing and medical informatics. He is a member of the Editorial Board of Clinical Evidence (BMJ Publishing Group, London) and the core reviewer group of BioMed Central.

Stuart Marples, Former Chief Executive, Institute of Healthcare Management, London

Although Stuart has now moved on in his career, at the time of writing he was Chief Executive of the Institute of Healthcare Management. The Institute is the professional body for managers working in healthcare. He is also a Fellow and Companion of the Institute. His 38-year career has been mainly in the NHS, including a long period as Chief Executive Officer of a large NHS Trust. He is a Business Studies Honours graduate and NVQ assessor and verifier. His personal interest is in management.

Dr Janet McCray, Principal Lecturer, Portsmouth Institute of Medicine, Health and Social Care, University of Portsmouth
Throughout her career, Janet has always maintained a connection with learning disability services. This has been broad, ranging from leading one of the first community care projects in North West England in the 1980s to taking forward the validation of the first joint prequalifying programme in nursing and social work in the learning disability field in the 1990s. Recently she has explored further practice roles in the field, gaining her PhD in 2002, and from this developing a conceptual framework for practice. At present she is beginning further testing of the framework and exploring its potential as a leadership tool.

Robert McSherry, Principal Lecturer, Practice Development, School of Health and Social Care, University of Teesside, Middlesbrough
Rob's current post is Principal Lecturer in Practice Development at the School of Health and Social Care, University of Teesside, Middlesbrough. His long-term aim is to develop and strengthen practice development within the School of Health and Social Care, local community and NHS Trusts locally, regionally and nationally. Rob has facilitated and supported the advancement and evaluation of many innovative practice developments by focusing on the promotion of multiprofessional collaboration and teamworking in delivering evidence-based practice. Rob's main concern is seeing research being utilised at a clinical level, whereby nurses, midwives, nurse specialists and other allied health professionals are equipped with the essential skills and knowledge to aid this process. Rob has shared and disseminated his work on practice development in three key areas – practice development, healthcare governance and evidence-informed practice – nationally and internationally through publications, conferences, consultancy and workshops.

Paddy Pearce, Head of Healthcare Governance, Hambleton and Richmond-shire Primary Care Trust
Paddy is the Head of Healthcare Governance for Hambleton and Richmond-shire Primary Care Trust and is responsible for the integration of clinical and corporate governance. He trained as an RGN, practised in orthopaedics and has established clinical audit, clinical effectiveness and clinical governance in secondary and primary care trusts. Paddy holds a BSc (Honours) in Professional Studies in Healthcare and an MSc in Social Research Methods. He is a Health Care Commission Clinical Governance Reviewer and Cochrane Reviewer.

Janice Phillips, Service Manager for Learning Disability Services, Glen Care Organisation, Epsom, Surrey
Janice was a ward manager with the North London Forensic Service when she wrote her chapter. She has a specialist interest in risk assessment and risk management, and also self-harm and suicide. This has led to a number of

clinical practice publications, where she has sought to challenge and test current clinical thinking, based on her own interpretation and application of research findings within the clinical environment. Much of her development in the clinical arena has been driven by clinical-based problem resolution, which has identified the need for a systematic strategy to improve the management of staff, resources and information systems.

Gülnur Salih, Patient Advocate and Language Interpreter, Camden PCT Advocacy and Interpreting Services, St Pancras Hospital, London
As a Health Advocate, Gülnur has worked for the NHS for 13 years, undertaking a range of duties providing help, advice and support for patients from the Turkish communities. She has established and run health education groups for Turkish communities and also devised and delivered training on Turkish culture to clinical and non-clinical staff. Achieving management and leadership qualifications has given Gülnur a new perspective on healthcare provision, which has allowed her to extend her effectiveness and interactions with patients and other health and social care staff. She has recently been seconded to work on a project involving healthcare provision to children and will be undertaking work to do with public consultation of the recommendations.

Theresa Shaw, Chief Executive, Foundation of Nursing Studies, London
Theresa Shaw is the Chief Executive Officer of the Foundation of Nursing Studies (FoNS), a small charity committed to supporting nurses to lead and develop innovative ways of working that improve patient care. Theresa successfully combines her role of charity manager with that of practice development facilitator, a role she believes is key to enabling development and research in practice. Prior to joining FoNS 6 years ago, she had been working in the NHS for 17 years. Her experience spanned clinical nursing, education and practice development, and whilst her clinical expertise lies in cardiothoracic nursing, she has worked with a variety of nurse-led teams. Theresa is currently undertaking the Doctor of Nursing Programme at Nottingham University, with specific focus on the impact of practice development.

Alyson Wadding, Senior Lecturer for Leadership Development, School of Health and Social Care, University of Teesside, Middlesbrough
Alyson is a Senior Lecturer for Leadership Development, responsible for leading the development and delivery of multiprofessional leadership programmes for all health and social care staff. She is a registered practitioner in the use of the Myers Briggs Type Indicator and is experienced in using this tool for individual and team leadership development. She is a registered feedback facilitator and trainer for the NHS Leadership Qualities Framework 360-degree diagnostic tool for leadership development and has integrated this framework into the design of leadership programmes. She is a licensed

facilitator of the Leading an Empowered Organisation Programme, with a wide range of experience of delivering this programme to various groups. Alyson is also experienced in providing mentorship to clinical leaders in practice.

Introduction

Several certainties can be taken for granted when considering healthcare in Britain today. We can assume that there will be a population generating an ever-increasing demand for healthcare, founded within developments in medical science. These developments arise from the need, within an affluent Western society at least, to move from a front-line service where emergency and acute care is paramount, to a demand-led service providing access to secondary and further care for long-term and enduring conditions, and services beyond life-saving, such as preventive and palliative care. Many of these latter services arise from changes in perceptions of quality of life and perceived 'rights' of access within a publicly funded organisation; for instance, the demand for reconstructive surgery, organ transplant, termination of pregnancy and infertility treatment.

Another assumption that can be made in Britain, for the near future at least, is that there will be a publicly funded National Health Service (NHS) that is free at the point of delivery, providing healthcare to the majority of the population. As a public service this is subject to political whim and the blunt instrument of a general election every four to five years, resulting in a certain lack of stability, consistency or long-term focus in terms of priorities, structure and direction. Arising from this is the assumption that resources for the NHS are not infinite but limited through the Exchequer and public taxation, and allocated through recourse to political priorities, albeit those arising from a detected and quantifiable need.

Finally, and key to the successful delivery of healthcare, are those who provide the services – the people at the centre of the organisation. In order to be effective at both an organisational and an individual level, they need effective and efficient leadership.

The purpose of this book therefore is to explore both the content and processes of leadership within the British NHS today. The intention was not to create yet another textbook about leadership – there is already a vast selection of these available, providing different perspectives on how to achieve successful leadership in myriad settings and circumstances. Rather, the intention of this book was to consider the NHS today through the reality of *what* is already happening and explore the features of successful leadership through *where* and *how* it is happening.

Hence, although theoretical perspectives are provided throughout the book, they are inextricably linked to the context in which they are presented. There is no neat boundary between theory and practice; there are no 'off-the-peg' solutions. Rather, we present a series of chapters, in Sections 2 and 3, which focus on individual problems and utilise a selection of management and leadership strategies to solve them. These nine chapters are drawn from real-life case studies across England and one from Finland, where practitioners have used strategies arising from different theoretical starting points to effect change in their areas of service. They are not presented as perfect examples – rather they describe and demonstrate the need for intelligent flexibility and critical thinking in order to utilise the tools and resources available to work through and solve problems in order to improve services for their users.

The brief provided to our contributing authors was to present an example of how a particular strategy for leadership was used to solve a problem within their practice. They were asked to consider the principles behind this approach and show, through their case study, how this had enabled them to solve their problem or move their practice forward. As leadership was the focus for these, this inevitably meant enabling other people to consider their practice and make a conscious decision to change it, thus facilitating practice development.

Section 1 – The Challenges of Leadership in Healthcare

These sections are, of course, set within the context of the British NHS at the beginning of the twenty-first century, and shaped by the politics of the 'New Labour' Government first elected in 1997 following 18 years of Conservative policies. The purpose of Section 1 of this book is to set the background and context for the focus on leadership within the restructuring and modernisation of the NHS heralded by the change in political focus and driven by the following:

- the internal and external environment required for effective healthcare leadership
- the critical success factors for managing strategic linkages between healthcare leadership activities and
- the consequent challenges posed for effective healthcare leadership during the first decade of the twenty-first century.

Chapter 1 presents and explores the central tenets driving the Labour government's policies, exploring in particular the significance of strategies for leadership within this by considering in-depth how one particular healthcare profession – nursing – has been facilitated to develop leadership strategies. Melanie Jasper concludes, in this chapter, that leadership as a central feature of the modernisation agenda is presented as everyone's concern and not just a role of those charged with a management function. Chapter 1 therefore establishes the context for leadership set at governmental level, within which the rest of the chapters in the book are located.

Chapter 2 presents a critical overview of theories and perspectives of leadership over time. Leadership theories, Mansour Jumaa contends, will always be set within the political, economical, sociological and technological structures existing at the time. This chapter provides a useful summary for readers who want a 'potted history' of the ways in which ideas and styles of leadership have developed over the past 50 years. Leadership styles do not happen by accident, rather they emerge in response to cultural imperatives within a specific sociotemporal context. This chapter identifies these trends and how they have, at various times in the history of the NHS, been adopted for use.

Chapter 3 builds on this foundation by considering what effective leadership means in the NHS today through five strategic questions. These questions explore the goals of leadership, its location and how effective it is perceived to be. Finally, the chapter considers what pathways would be preferred for leadership, who and what could sustain it and when it could be sustained.

Intrinsic to all perspectives on leadership is the use of emergent concepts, which are part of the presentation of initiatives as 'new' (where some might cynically consider that nothing is new, rather that old ideas are repackaged and resold in another temporal context). The identification of these concepts provides the structure for this book, as we wanted to see them in action. Two of these concepts, *strategic leadership* and *healthcare governance*, apply generically across the NHS and are therefore part of the context within which leadership development is perceived. The conclusion of this chapter, according to Mansour Jumaa, is that the new NHS is on the way to a full recovery, a view shared by both patients and staff within the NHS. This chapter also confirms that leadership is in a state of flux and that irrespective of perspectives taken to describe or define this concept, it is about relationships, and it has undergone a series of transformations over the 100 years of modern management.

Chapter 4 considers strategic leadership as the 'ultimate unbounded problem, full of complexity and uncertainty, where cause and effect can be difficult, if not impossible, to see clearly'. Mark Hodder and Stuart Marples explore the need for creating an environment where strategic leadership can work, identifying issues of diversity, influencing people, identifying a management code and embracing transformational leadership styles as key concepts within this. They conclude that 'strategic leaders are not superhuman with a clearer picture of the world than anyone else. Rather they have created an environment and an understanding of their people that allows success to take hold'. This is very much the message promoted by Government rhetoric, and exemplified in the individual case studies in the next two sections.

Finally, we end this section with a consideration of the strategies for leadership required to ensure effective healthcare governance. Rob McSherry, Alyson Wadding and Paddy Pearce suggest that 'leadership development must be linked to both personal and organisational aspirations where clearly defined measurable objectives impact on performance for modernisation and service improvement'. Using case studies to illustrate their argument, these authors explore the drivers for modernisation and service improvement, and define, compare and contrast healthcare governance and leadership in order to demonstrate their integration. In common with many authors in this book, they identify transformational leadership as the most effective style to achieve the Government's agenda for change.

Section 2 – Using the CLINLAP/LEADLAP Model for Effective Healthcare Leadership

This section is driven by the work of one of the editors of this book, Dr Mansour Jumaa; it presents the CLINLAP/LEADLAP model and how this has been developed and used in a variety of healthcare and nursing practice contexts. It:

- explains and demonstrates that leadership is a process of *living as learning*, a process of sense-making in a community of practice
- presents a full exposition of the CLINLAP/LEADLAP model and its applications in various contexts for strategic nursing management performance in management and leadership activities
- proposes that, through the CLINLAP/LEADLAP model, leaders become the pathway travelled in order to enter the world of the community of practice and the external broader communities that sustain and keep them going. It demonstrates how, through a well structured model, such as the CLINLAP/LEADLAP model, the complexity of healthcare leadership activities and processes could be 'reduced' to observable and repeatable actions. Such an approach will always help to plan, implement and sustain effective service delivery.

In Chapter 6, Mansour Jumaa presents the CLINLAP/LEADLAP model, which he developed while he was a Principal Lecturer (Healthcare and Nursing Management) and the Programme Director of the Chartered Management Institute Accredited Centre at Middlesex University in London. The CLINLAP/LEADLAP model is both wide-ranging and specific. The essence of the model iterates around at least four main areas of responsibility and accountability, namely:

- Specific goals – deciding what is to be achieved in the collective interest and planning to put the decisions into action to meet most of the stakeholders' expectations.
- Explicit roles – good decision-making processes about the agreed specific goals and about who does what with the available resources so that patients, clients and/or customers are pleased with the available services.

- Clear processes – ensuring that the best is being done in terms of effectiveness and efficiency to keep on target for the agreed specific goals.
- Open relationships – implementing agreed specific goals through partnership and collaborative working with other stakeholders.

This is followed, in Chapter 7, by a case study illustrating the model's use in facilitating policy change within a clinical practice environment, presented by Janice Phillips, Helen Julu, Gülnur Salih and Chris Gbolo. Janice was a ward manager with the North London Forensic Service when this chapter was written. Helen is a Senior Practitioner, Health Visiting, with the London Borough of Enfield. Gülnur was a Patient Advocate and Language Interpreter within the NHS, providing help, advice and support for patients from the Turkish communities. Chris is a charge nurse/team leader on a psychiatric intensive care unit in Barnet, Enfield and Haringey Health Care NHS Trust in north London. They conclude, in this chapter, that current managers are expected to implement strategy, influence change and meet stakeholder expectations, and that the CLINLAP model can assist strategic thinking without neglecting clinical practice. This is contrary to beliefs that the creation of such a 'toolbox' can imply that management is just a series of 'tricks' that anyone can perform.

Chapter 8 presents the use of the CLINLAP/LEADLAP model in group clinical supervision for managing change in district nursing practice. Dr Jo Alleyne co-writes this chapter with Dr Mansour Jumaa. Dr Alleyne is the current Programme Director of the Chartered Management Institute Accredited Centre at Middlesex University in London and has devised and successfully applied a model of Group Clinical Supervision as part of her doctoral studies, through a co-operative inquiry approach, which used focused management and leadership interventions. This inquiry concluded that the challenge for practitioners wishing to apply the group clinical supervision approach will be achieved when 'good nursing' is accepted as being synonymous with 'good management'.

Chapter 9, written by Mansour Jumaa, Dr Ilkka Kunnamo, who developed the idea of Evidence-Based Medicine (EBM) Guidelines (www.ebm-guidelines.com) in Finland and has served as its Editor-in-Chief since 1988, and Melanie Jasper, presents the results of a post-doctoral study[1] that explored the leadership successes of the 'Finnish way' to evidence-based practice by general practitioners in Finland. It illustrates, using the LEADLAP model for analysis, how the problem of tackling healthcare delivery to a diverse population, geographically and culturally, was implemented successfully. The main lesson from this study is that survival in the workplace of the future demands that the nurse, midwife, health visitor and all other healthcare practitioners become capable of converting their many years of *tacit* knowledge to *explicit* knowledge for the benefit of their organisations, professions and themselves. This was the main strength behind the success of the 'Finnish way'.

---

[1] This post-doctoral travel study was possible through a Florence Nightingale Foundation Scholarship sponsored by the St Mary's Hospital League of Nurses, London, UK.

The final chapter in this section, authored by Mansour Jumaa, considers the use of emotional intelligence as a leadership strategy. The chapter concludes that the emotional intelligence attributes required are practical and rooted in everyday activities. They are feelings: awareness; ownership; identification; discrimination; acceptance; choice; transmutation; expression; control; and catharsis.

Apart from using the CLINLAP/LEADLAP model, these case studies have in common the need for ordinary people to lead their teams in solving problems in their everyday practice. This section focuses on the ways in which everyone can utilise leadership skills and management tools available in order to be involved in leading small parts of their own, others', professional and service development. Whilst these may be seen as minute cogs in a very large wheel, it is a combination of all of these initiatives that will be contributing to change in our health service, improving patient care and leading towards the future. These case studies are clear examples of New Labour's strategy of leadership at all levels within the health service that will 'make a difference' for the NHS and the people it serves.

Section 3 – Strategies for Making a Difference in Healthcare Leadership

Section 3 provides a collection of case studies driven by the notion of transformational leadership. If any one theory of leadership has achieved dominance within New Labour's modernisation policy it is this one. Using the features of idealised influence, inspirational motivation, intellectual stimulation and individual consideration, transformational leadership seeks to win the hearts and minds of those being led to effect wholesale changes owned and developed by those involved in them. We are beginning to see the devolution of the power to effect change across far more levels of the NHS hierarchy, as well as dissemination to more professional groups. The chapters in this section illustrate this policy effectively, showing the effect of collaborative rather than competitive working within services. They are driven by the concepts of primary and community care, transformational leadership, practice development and interprofessional working. This section:

- considers different enactments of transformational leadership
- presents four case studies illustrating how transformational leadership can work in practice
- identifies how leadership can occur at all levels of the health service hierarchy.

In Chapter 11, Lindsey Hayes, working within the Royal College of Nursing as a senior fellow in leadership for primary care, explores the leadership skills required to influence the development of primary and community care services strategically, ensuring that the views of all healthcare professionals are clearly articulated and that their voice is heard. She presents features of the Primary Care Leadership Programme, concluding that 'central government expects professionals to embrace change, challenge existing professional boundaries and reflect on existing practice to enable change to happen'. Training for healthcare leadership must therefore take place within the context of change in both the health and social care domains.

Just such an example of change is presented through the work of Dr Nadia Chambers, who has undertaken one of the new Nurse Consultant roles introduced by the Government. Working with a multidisciplinary team, she instigated an older person's outreach and support team, negotiating the delicate boundaries and shifting sands of enabling and facilitating interprofessional teamwork in order to provide a service responding to the service users' needs. The results and evaluation of the initial pilot project enabled a successful bid to be made to the Department of Health, securing full funding for a further 2 years for the project.

In Chapter 13, Theresa Shaw, Chief Executive of the Foundation of Nursing Studies, suggests that 'whilst practice development needs effective and supportive leadership it also has the potential to enable the development of leaders', and she goes on to consider the role of leadership in practice development. In presenting five case studies she identifies the flexible nature of styles of leadership within different roles and considers the features and advantages of each.

Finally, in Chapter 14, Dr Janet McCray presents a grounded theory model of how interprofessional working can be facilitated. Arising from a learning disabilities perspective, Dr McCray suggests that recent policy changes have resulted in a 'role shift for community-based RNLDs [Registered Nurses for People with Learning Disabilities], where leadership skills and teamwork facilitation roles are increasingly at the forefront of their practice across the boundaries of health and social care'. As a result she concludes that RNLDs are in a prime position to facilitate interprofessional working, presenting a model of how this can be accomplished. She suggests that 'in highlighting the attributes needed for contemporary interagency teamwork, with reflection as a central element of change, the tool acts as an iterative mechanism for all those who wish to develop their skills as transformational leaders further'.

These chapters demonstrate that responsibility for change and development is indeed filtering down through the hierarchical ranks of the NHS, as more and more people are being charged with leading developments within their own services. New roles and new responsibilities are located within those charged with providing the services rather than those managing them. Leadership is no longer the purview of the few, a fact that recognises the increasing levels of academic preparation for those working within the NHS, and seeks to utilise the knowledge and skills developed as a result.

Section 4 – Challenges for Leadership in the Future

This section consists only of Chapter 15 written by Professor Melanie Jasper. It anticipates the challenges that need to be addressed if the Government's vision of 'leadership-for-all' is to become a reality in the next decade. Four challenges are discussed: gaining hearts and minds – the challenge of culture change; leadership-for-all; overcoming traditional boundaries or barriers; and education for leadership. Melanie Jasper concludes that this final chapter has been a personal reflection and deliberation on what the future of leadership within the NHS means to her; this involves recognising and valuing the importance of the individual at all levels, and providing leadership within a culture that maximises the talents of all those individuals.

Melanie Jasper and Mansour Jumaa

Section One

The Challenges of Leadership in Healthcare

1 The Context of Healthcare Leadership in Britain Today

Melanie Jasper

Introduction

Avery's textbook on leadership (Avery 2004) attempts to draw together the many and varied perspectives and theories that have developed as our (capitalist) societies become more fluid and rapidly changing than at any other period in history.

> The speed of change on multiple fronts seems to be pushing humankind to the limits of its adaptability. People have no sooner adapted to one change than the next one is upon them, bringing more uncertainty and complexity. The challenge is for leadership to operate under rapidly mutating circumstances, which requires a rethink of paradigms of leadership both in theory and in practice. (Avery 2004, p. 7)

The development of healthcare provision in Britain is a perfect example of this frantic need for increasing efficiency in service sector industries, where the traditional public service ethos is being influenced, and often replaced, by the ethos and ethics of business and the marketplace.

For many who have grown up in the post-war years of the welfare state, and who have spent their working lives in public services directed and run by it, this is an uneasy alliance of competing sets of beliefs and values. Alongside managerial concepts and strategies imported from successful business organisation runs a whole vocabulary that those working in health and social care are having to embrace and adapt to. As with many instances of social change, the reorganisation and adoption of new directions and challenges in healthcare is a political response to fundamental problems in sustaining the basic premises envisaged at the creation of the welfare state. British society is simply unable to continue to fund a state-financed health-care system where demands on it are infinite, where the changing demography over the next 30 years will result in an increasingly elderly and dependent population and where the working population will generate insufficient taxation to meet demand. Hence, it is reasonable that government strategies are directed towards the fundamental premises of the welfare state, whilst at the same time attempting to introduce concepts from business and the marketplace to take it into a sustainable future, and to seek innovative approaches to funding healthcare, which under another name would be labelled 'private sector'. As the Government White Paper *The New NHS: Modern and Dependable* (DH 1997, p. 8) identified:

> It is clear there are tough choices facing the NHS. It has to improve its performance if it is to deliver the sort ozzf services patients need.

The context of leadership within the British National Health Service

In short, the New Labour Government created a vision of 'a new NHS for a new century' (DH 1997, p. 8), expanded in a number of governmental papers over successive years (e.g. DH 1998, 2000, 2001, 2002a, 2002b) and still progressing. The message in these was clear – that a central plank of governmental vision was the need for leadership as well as efficient management throughout all areas of activity in the NHS. As Liam Donaldson (2001), Chief Medical Officer, said:

> Implementing this major programme of change will require active leadership at all levels in the NHS and an inclusive approach. If it is successful the pay-off for the patients and staff will be huge.

This is reinforced by Nigel Crisp, NHS Chief Executive:

> We must lead change as well as manage it. We need leadership in setting out the vision and working with and through people to achieve it. We need excellent management in systematic and tested approaches to secure delivery and improvement. (DH 2002a, p. iv)

Leadership per se is a relatively new (and inclusive) concept for the British NHS. As a result there is a dearth of published material relating to its nature and content over and above that in government papers and policies. These, by their very nature, take a particular view of leadership, influenced by the vision and direction of healthcare delivery at the beginning of the new century. The concept of leadership adopted has to be set within the social, cultural and environmental context of its time. Outmoded notions of leadership equated with authority, traditional and hereditary power are not commensurate with the values espoused by the New Labour Government, seeking equality throughout society. Rather, the definition of leadership adopted needs to reflect the values inherent within the socialist paradigm, and reflect increasing participation in policy-making and decision-making at all levels within the NHS. This latter point is perhaps one of the most important – transformation of the NHS will not occur unless the majority of employees at all levels within it are empowered to lead in new directions and espouse the values inherent within the policies. To this end, a blueprint has been created through government policy; what is missing is exactly how this can be achieved, given the lack of an evidence base relating to effective leadership styles of the type envisaged within public services – the evidence does not exist for the very reason that this is wholesale change of a type never before witnessed in state-funded organisations.

However, a plethora of literature from successful businessmen (e.g. Charles Handy, John Harvey Jones, Geoff Smith), prominent leaders (e.g. Winston Churchill) and self-styled leadership gurus (e.g. Adair 1998, 2002, Bennis 1998, Goleman 1995, Goleman *et al.* 2002) has influenced the ways in which leadership is framed and conceived. Hence, there are many theories about leadership, and many theorists writing about it, but little solid work to link these to the realities of the challenges of leading a modernised NHS where little remains the same. Whilst we can draw lessons and wisdom from the insights and experiences of others, we desperately need to encourage and develop the vision and skills of those leading from the inside and at all levels of the organisation. Whilst we need to be aware of published (and publicised) notions and models of leadership, we also need to be able to critique and evaluate them, with a view to making intelligent selection of strategies and building upon models that have been seen to be effective.

A culturally specific concept of leadership

What is significantly different in the approach of the New Labour Government is that leadership is not regarded as the preserve of the powerful few, but as being a function of people's roles throughout the NHS. Hence, the concept of leadership is key to the modernisation of the NHS and has been enshrined in the work of the NHS Leadership Centre, created in 2001 as part of the NHS Modernisation Agency (*The NHS Plan*, DH 2000). The Centre launched the NHS Leadership Qualities Framework in 2002 (NHS Leadership Centre 2003). The components of this framework (shown in Table 1.1) comprise 15 qualities, organised into three clusters of setting direction, personal qualities and delivering the service.

Table 1.1 Components of the NHS Leadership Qualities Framework.

Setting direction	Personal qualities	Delivering the service
Broad scanning	Self-belief	Empowering others
Intellectual flexibility	Self-awareness	Holding to account
Seizing the future	Self-management	Leading change through people
Political astuteness	Drive for achievement	Effective and strategic influencing
Drive for results	Personal integrity	Collaborative working

It can be seen clearly that these qualities reflect the values and beliefs inherent within the Government's political stance. They reflect a 'here and now' snapshot of public values, which, it could be suggested, would be unrecognisable to both political and military leaders 50 years ago, and certainly are unlikely to be those identified by a different political party whose values derive from capitalism and the marketplace. The emphasis is on personal attributes and qualities, as opposed to traditional sources of authority and power or target-driven incentives derived from a business culture.

These qualities are considered to be a 'set of key characteristics, attitudes and behaviours that leaders should aspire to in delivering the NHS Plan':

- setting the standard for leadership in the NHS
- assessing and developing high performance in leadership
- individual and organisational assessment
- integrating leadership across the service and related agencies
- adapting leadership to suit changing contexts
- benchmarking – by enabling the development of a database on leadership capacity and capability

The framework is the result of a consultation exercise with NHS Chief Executives and Directors of all disciplines and 'sets the standard for outstanding leadership in the NHS' (www.nhsleadershipqualities.nhs.uk). It is considered to have the following applications:

- Personal development
- Board development
- Leadership profiling for recruitment and selection
- Career mapping
- Succession planning
- Connecting leadership capability
- Performance management

Jean Faugier (2003), project director of the NHS Modernisation Agency's national nursing leadership project, suggests that 'effective leadership should embrace cultural, social, economic and organisational challenges and changes if it is to play a part in improving patient care', and suggests that this is reflected in three themes:

- developing and strengthening nursing leadership
- breaking down the boundaries between professional groups
- national nursing leadership programmes and the developing work of the NHS Leadership Centre.

This recognises that change, and leadership for change, is multifactorial, emphasising the need for wholesale, organisation-wide refocusing, rather than dependence on individual change. Government strategies, to this end, identify strategic, organisational, managerial and educational elements of the modernisation of the NHS, and task 'leadership' as the mechanism by which these will be effected.

There is further emphasis on the notion of interprofessional collaboration and development, particularly across both health and social care settings, and between primary and secondary care. Indeed, central to the vision of effective healthcare services premised upon local needs is the movement of funding to primary care services from secondary care and the strengthening of the role played by Primary Care Trusts in the new-look NHS (DH 1997, 2000).

Transformational leadership – the latest trend?

Central to all policies, and coherent throughout the NHS modernisation documents, is the notion of 'transformational leadership', as opposed to 'transactional leadership', as being the way in which the workforce will be led through service developments and change. Transformational leadership is identified by Burns (1978) as a process where 'one or more persons engage with others in such a way that leaders and followers raise one another to higher levels of motivation and morality'. It is characterised by leaders motivating their followers by transcending their own self-interests, elevating their needs, and making them aware of the mission of the larger entity of the organisation to which they belong (Bass 1995). This is in contrast to transactional leadership, which is seen as a process whereby leaders identify the needs of their followers and 'transact' with them in relation to objectives to be met – in other words, it is conceived as a social exchange process based on a power and reward system. Transformational leadership styles appear to be seen as superior to transactional styles on the basis that the whole workforce is developed as part of the process and is seen as 'on message' in delivering the organisation's objectives. This is achieved by going 'beyond simple leader–follower transactions by envisioning a future, fostering identification, and developing and intellectually stimulating employees' (Vandenberghe *et al.* 2002, p. 16), resulting in increased levels of effectiveness within the organisational culture. In short, transformational leaders are seen to use 'emotional intelligence' to direct their leadership of others. In contributing to this, the individual feels valued and at the same time enabled to develop, provided that his/her developmental needs coincide with the mission and direction of the organisation.

One of the features of transformational leaders is that they can 'inspire others to follow their clear vision' and that 'they demonstrate self-confidence in their ability to articulate the vision and promote change' (Mullally 2001). Indeed, the idea of a transformational leader has much in common with what has previously been called 'charismatic' leadership and which went out of fashion as an attribute because of the individual power seen to be wielded. For instance, people such as Mao Tse Tung, Hitler, Mussolini, The Reverend Moon and Winston Churchill have all been perceived as charismatic leaders in the past – but one would hesitate to afford them the label of 'transformational' leaders. This leads us to question the difference between charismatic leaders and transformational leaders, especially where the leader is instrumental in forming an organisation's vision as well as leading towards achieving it. Sarah Mullally, Chief Nursing Officer (CNO) at the Department of Health 1999–2004, suggests that it is the moral element identified in the notions of service that protects against the dangers of charisma, with emphasis on the developmental and motivating aspects that are significant. She says:

> I make no apology for asserting my belief that there is a moral dimension to leadership. In a public service such as the NHS, and a profession such as nursing whose ethos is concerned with care, support and protection, there can be no dispute that the ends we pursue and the means by which we achieve them must be ethically defensible. (Mullally 2001, p. 24)

Throughout this book, many authors will address perspectives of transformational leadership, paying homage to its centrality within government and thinking in terms of the prescribed mode for leadership of the NHS. We asked the authors to adopt an analytical and discursive style throughout their chapters in terms of the fundamental questions of *who, why, when, how* and *what* in relation to the leadership focus being taken, either explicitly or implicitly. Case studies are presented describing initiatives that have been effective in 'transforming' elements of service delivery. It is left to the reader to decide whether these case studies demonstrate effectively the characteristics of transformational leadership in terms of:

- idealised influence
- inspirational motivation
- intellectual stimulation
- individualised consideration

We take the view that if there are transformational leaders out there effecting change at all levels of the NHS, we must shout it from the roof tops! Clearly, there are superb initiatives transforming care delivery and enabling a move from a traditional custom and practice approach; if so, we need those to be critiqued and presented to a discerning audience from a conceptual basis.

We have to ask, however, to what extent transformational leadership has been uncritically accepted as the leadership style to be aspired to; to what extent it is realistic in terms of a publicly funded service, albeit with devolved delivery, but of centrally determined vision and outcomes; and, indeed, what value system it is that supports this style as the most appropriate. Sarah Mullally offers another style of leadership, which she sees as having increasing credibility – that of 'servant' leadership:

> Servant leaders make serving their employees a priority. They inspire, create collaboration, coach, are consistent, are confirming, promote continuous development and improvement. Servant leaders create matrix organisations and promote reconciliation and have a genuine concern for others. They recognise the possibility of

human failure and see discipline as part of the developmental process. (Mullally 2001, p. 24)

This appears to complete the transition from authoritarian modes of leadership to those that are truly democratic; it presents a vision of collaboration and equality, where everyone's opinion is valued, and employees are respected for the contributions they can make[1, 2]. Brave new world indeed!

However, one test of government policy is how it is translated in reality, and the following section demonstrates how one healthcare profession is being moved in the direction of the 'new' leadership styles of the NHS.

Leadership in nursing – a case study for healthcare

Significant emphasis has been placed on the roles that nurses, midwives and health visitors can play in terms of leadership within the NHS. The Government says:

> We need nurse, midwife and health visitor leaders who can establish direction and purpose, inspire, motivate and empower teams around common goals and produce real improvements in clinical practice, quality and services. We need leaders who are motivated, self-aware, socially skilled, and able to work together with others across professional and organisational boundaries. (DH 1999, p. 52)

The issues involved, elements identified and approaches taken can be seen as a case study for other healthcare professions in achieving equality in influencing NHS service delivery. Nursing leadership (nursing will henceforth be used as a generic term for all three professional groups) attracts such attention because nurses make up such a large proportion of the NHS workforce – over 397 515 in 2004 (DH 2005). They are seen as key to the reconfiguring of services to enable more effective use of resources and skills, and the redistribution of power and decision-making away from other professional groups. Perhaps most importantly, however, nursing's contribution is considered as 'crucial to the Government's plans to modernise the NHS and to improve the public's health' (DH 1998, p. 4). We see here an acknowledgement of the key role nurses play in public health, marking a 'step change' in focus of health services away from secondary care to care based in and for the community as a whole. However, for the majority of nurses this notion of being the leaders rather than the led is a huge change in focus, involving fundamental changes to the power balance and power-holding of the past, and also requiring other professions and the public to refocus the ways in which they perceive nursing itself.

---

[1] It must be acknowledged, however, that Sarah Mullally was an ordained minister of the Church of England and moved from her post as CNO to become a parish priest in 2004. The notion of 'servant leadership' is clearly enshrined in Christian ethics and must be considered within that context.

[2] However, this idea of servant leadership could also be seen as a return to authoritarian leadership, as the 'leader' has many attributes of the 'parent' figure, deriving authority for nurturing and benevolent discipline from his or her appointment to the leadership role.

In *Making a Difference – Strengthening the Nursing, Midwifery and Health Visiting Contribution to Health and Healthcare* (DH 1999, p. 52), the Government presents a vision for empowering nurses, midwives and health visitors in their roles in terms of leadership, establishing four key points:

- The Government's modernisation programme means that more nurses, midwives and health visitors need better leadership skills.
- Work to equip them with these skills will be part of the wider programme to boost leadership and management across the NHS.
- A new career framework and introduction of nurse, midwife and health visitor consultants will provide a stronger focus for clinical leadership.
- Greater emphasis is needed on leadership development for Sisters and Charge Nurses.

Furthermore, the Government most importantly states:

> Aspiring leaders need to be identified, supported and developed. Senior colleagues have an obligation to spot and nurture talent, to encourage and develop leadership qualities and skills to create a professional and organisational climate that enables the next generation of leaders to challenge orthodoxy, to take risks and to learn from experience. (DH 1999, p. 53)

Education for nursing leadership

The first key to this is the education needed to enable nurses to take up the challenges of leadership at all levels. In the past, nurses moving into management have been given 'management' training, often in the absence of the development of leadership skills, or indeed developing their clinical skills over and above that required for everyday care delivery (Antrobus 2003, DH 2001, Jasper 2002). This is a far cry from the skills needed for leadership in the new NHS, which require a nurse to be:

- a powerful influential operator
- a strategic thinker
- a developer of nursing knowledge
- a reflective thinker
- a process consultant

(Antrobus & Kitson 1999)

As Fergusson (2004, p. 8) suggests:

> To be effective, nurse leaders of today should understand the nature and impact of health service reform. They must be visionaries, strategic thinkers, effective planners and managers of change, and should contribute to policy development and work effectively in teams, partnerships and alliances. They also require a range of business and interpersonal skills in areas such as resource management, media and marketing, communication, negotiation and motivating and influencing others.

In recognition of this, several leadership development programmes, some specific to nurses but others aimed at a multidisciplinary audience, have been created in order to address the knowledge and skills needing to be developed, for instance:

- the Leading an Empowered Organisation programme (Cooper 2003, DH 2001, Miller & Wright 1999, National Leadership Centre 2000)
- King's Fund Leadership programmes for: clinicians; executives and general managers; clinical leaders; and board leadership (www.kingsfund. org.uk/leadership)
- National Nursing Leadership Programmes delivered by the Royal College of Nursing, e.g. the Political Leadership Programme (Antrobus 2003, Antrobus & Kitson 1999), Clinical Leadership Programme (Beech 2002), Primary Care Leadership Programme (Hayes 2002) and Ward Manager Leadership Development (DH 2001) (www.rcn.org.uk)
- the International Council for Nurses Leadership for Change programme (Fergusson 2004) (www.icn.ch)
- Management Education Scheme by Open Learning (MESOL) programmes, delivered in partnership by the Open University and the NHS Leadership Centre

These have all been supported by the Government, often with significant funding and commitment, to ensure that policy is enacted rather than consigned to the black sack of good ideas. These, of course, are in addition to programmes leading to formal educational qualifications delivered through institutions of further and higher education and specifically addressing leadership development, such as the MSc Clinical Leadership and Professional Doctorate Programmes in Strategic Leadership and Management at Middlesex University.

There is often tension between the aims for multidisciplinary and generic leadership skills and the need for discipline-specific development. As Antrobus & Kitson (1999) point out:

> Lack of consensus on nursing leadership has led to leadership development programmes for nurses which have emphasised the development of corporate or political skills, often to the detriment of nursing knowledge.

Arising from their study exploring the broader sociopolitical factors impacting upon nursing leadership, they draw attention to three key areas:

- educating leaders to become practice and policy shapers
- translating nursing knowledge to the broader health picture
- developing mechanisms to acquire greater political influence.

This emphasises the need for both generic and discipline-specific preparation, where the 'leader-in-training' can be encouraged to see both the large and small pictures, to develop the skills to fight the corner for his or her own profession, as well as setting this within the wider context of whole service provision.

The Government equates poor leadership with poor standards of care, which they consider 'unacceptable and will be highlighted more readily by the new arrangements for clinical governance' (DH 1999, p. 54). Hence, there is a drive towards educational preparation for clinical leadership focused at the Ward Sister/Charge Nurse level. Faugier (2003) said that:

- Since 2000, the NHS Leadership Centre, incorporating the national nursing leadership programme, has put 45000 nurses through leadership development courses.
- Thirty-two thousand nurses have taken part in the Leading Empowered Organisations (LEO) course.
- A further 1200 have been trained through the Royal College of Nursing.
- Two thousand have gone through regional programmes linked to national service framework priorities.

Hence we see that not only has development of courses been supported, but also nurses have been facilitated to attend, emphasising the commitment outlined by the Government in policy documents.

Political leadership – where do nurses fit in?

The second key concept in the Government's vision for nursing leadership is about empowering nurses to play a full part in both creating and delivering the service. Antrobus (2003, p. 40) suggests that:

> (a) clinical leader's main aim is to deliver improved patient outcomes, while creating an environment and culture at micro (clinical) and meso (strategic/executive) levels that enables a patient-centred perspective. Political leadership in nursing, however, has a different purpose. Political leadership aims to deliver improved health outcomes for patients and communities by creating and influencing public policies at a macro-level, on a larger scale that takes account of the evidence and experience of caring for patients and the perspectives of users.

Central to the notion of a role for nurses in terms of political leadership therefore is the idea that nurses have valuable skills, expertise and experience to be able to contribute to policy-making and service development at both local and national levels. As Antrobus (2004, p. 227) later says:

> It is vital that as the political environment is changing, as nurses we learn how we can effectively lead and shape policy at a local and a national level and that as a profession we invest in developing political leaders.

This is evidenced in the July 2004 issue of the *Journal of Nursing Management*, an issue devoted to a focus on political leadership from multiple perspectives, including editorial comments from all four countries of the UK (Andrews 2004, Clark 2004, Ishmael 2004, McKenna 2004). These authors demonstrate the effectiveness of nursing in exercising political influence within devolved governmental structures where the needs of the local, regional population can be addressed if they are given a voice. However,

Davies (2004, p. 235) cautions against a focus on political leadership that is 'inward-looking and individualising', instead suggesting 'an alternative perspective starting from an assumption that nursing operates in a position of cultural and structural disadvantage'. She suggests that three issues arise from this stance, in terms of the concept of political leadership in nursing:

(1) Leaders at all levels need to acknowledge and understand the complex and ambiguous position that nursing continues to occupy in healthcare.
(2) Political leaders need political analysis.
(3) Political leaders need to work with others as co-producers of change.

To be 'Poliskilled', Ishmael (2004) suggests that nurse leaders need to have the following characteristics:

* the skill to encourage others to believe they have the power to make a difference
* an understanding of the 'big health picture'
* a combination of the right level of clinical skills and well-honed interpersonal, technical, corporate, professional, organisational and communication skills – referred to as akin to a 'Masters in Political Prowess'
* the ability to get on with people at various levels and from different nationalities and backgrounds
* an understanding of other people's points of view, being able to speak out clearly against injustice and inequalities, and to write cogently
* an understanding of current issues and their implications and ramifications
* the ability to help others to arrive at sensible decisions whilst maintaining the 'primacy of nursing'
* the ability to remain focused but flexible
* an understanding of the difference between attitude and aptitude
* the ability to share and extend their skills and expertise, to underpin their knowledge and vision by practice and innovation, and to outweigh their foibles by strength and constructive action
* the vision, values and versatility that form a key part of self-belief and purpose, and skills that range from practical to strategic.

Fradd (2004) suggests that these characteristics can be condensed as key leadership competencies:

* political astuteness
* the ability to work independently
* effective collaboration
* the ability to develop high trust relationships
* self-confidence, tempered with humility
* respect for the process of change, as well as the content
* the ability to work across business functions and units.

Arising from these two lists of leadership attributes is a clear need for leadership development, only part of which can come from educational strategies. As leaders function in the real world, dealing with everyday challenges, problems and obstacles, and focus their practice on delivering a service to their clients, leadership development must arise from within the culture and environment of that practice. Perhaps this is one of the major challenges being faced within nursing today – that of enabling and facilitating those with the potential for leadership to do so in a culture embedded within traditional authority, hierarchy, practice and relationships with other professions.

Part of the Government's vision for the future is that leadership will occur at all levels within the NHS; this seems to beg three questions:

(1) Do leaders at all levels need all of these political leadership skills – are we envisioning a 'one-size-fits-all' model?
(2) Is it realistic to aim for leadership at all levels?
(3) If leaders are to be seen at all levels, who is left to be led?

These questions inject an element of caution into the debate, in that we are in danger of diluting the impact of the 'leader' if leadership is perceived as a generic function. Could it be that many of the functions encompassed in the broad definition of leadership within the current environment are not 'trad-itional' leadership functions at all, but may be perceived as professional and practice development which includes an element of facilitating and enabling others to move forward within their practice? This seems a little less daunting than the label of 'leadership', which brings with it the notions of high-level decision-making and strategic planning which are often out-with the parameters of everyday practice. This is not to suggest, however, that nurses do not have the right or duty to attempt to influence strategy and decision-making, and perhaps it is these skills that need the most development at the grassroots level.

Recognising clinical nursing expertise – the creation of consultants

Finally, the creation of nurse, midwife and health visitor consultants, and a new career framework to support and develop professional expertise and leadership skills, is central to government plans to value and develop the roles of nurses in the NHS. It is envisaged that these initiatives will help to retain expert practitioners within practice and provide a stronger focus for clinical leadership, thus helping to improve quality and shape services to make them more responsive. However, it must not be forgotten that a strong driver for the increasing use of nurses to deliver services within their own authority was the need to reduce junior doctors' hours and find a cost-effective way of replacing the work done by them; nurses, even at consultant level, are cheaper to employ than the cost involved in strengthening the contribution of junior doctors. Moreover, there are simply not enough doctors to provide the service envisaged, whereas the career structure for nursing has long been in need of revitalisation to ensure that those with the greatest levels of clinical expertise and experience are not lost to the delivery of care.

The move to more community-led care was also an influence, where there is a dearth of GPs willing to deliver the increased range of services envisaged.

As a result, the Government has acted on the recommendation of the profession to create consultancy posts for nurses, outlined in *Making a Difference* (DH 1999). These posts have four core functions:

- Expert practice
- Professional leadership and consultancy
- Education and development
- Practice and service development

Charged with ensuring that clinical care is developed within current guidelines of good practice, including evidence-based decision-making and informed care, consultants need to be at the forefront of the triad of practice, education and research, and address all three within their role. Manley (1997), in an action research study, identified the consultant nurse role as multidimensional, comprising a number of functionally derived components (Manley 1997):

- an expert practitioner in nursing, either as a generalist or within a specialism
- an educator, enabler and developer of others, thus enabling the development of practice
- a researcher with specific expertise in practice-based research methodologies
- an expert and process consultant from the clinical to executive and strategic levels
- a transformational leader, who enables a culture to develop where everyone can develop their leadership potential.

Moreover, the study identified core outcomes that would be achieved when a consultant nurse is working within a conducive and supportive context:

- Transformational culture
- Empowered staff
- Practice development (Manley 1997)

This work was the first attempt, within a British context, to identify features of advanced nursing practice and the key roles and processes that would lead to practice development and change through effective leadership. In later stages of the study (Manley 2000a) the features of the organisational context that facilitated the consultant nurse roles were explored, and emphasised 'the importance of the use of approaches that clarify values and highlight the contradiction between espoused culture and culture in practice' (Manley 2000a, p. 34). Finally, the work presented consultant nurse outcomes (Manley 2000b), linking these very clearly with the impact of a transformational style of leadership within an effective organisational culture. She concludes that:

if consultant nurses are appointed with the skills and processes described, they promise to be extremely influential in terms of the impact they will have on organisational culture and the subsequent positive effect on performance of individuals, teams and organisations. (Manley 2000b, p. 38)

This ensures that consultants influence care at the point of delivery, and indeed have to spend a significant proportion of their time in the clinical environment. Chapter 12 presents a case study of how it was envisaged that consultants would influence strategies for care utilising the premises of transformational leadership.

Messages from this case study

This case study demonstrates the movement made by one professional group within the NHS and illustrates how traditionally perceived occupational roles can be shifted to empower the practitioners within that group. The combination of policy vision and change, changes to the professional body and professional regulation, involvement of professional organisations together with commitment by employers within the NHS has made the rhetoric of leadership development into a reality.

This is starting to happen within the allied health professions too; the Health Professions Council is now established as the professional body tasked with central registration of healthcare practitioners from the previously divergent professional groups such as physiotherapists, speech therapists, pharmacists, occupational therapists, radiographers, operating department practitioners, etc. Many of the professional organisations have previously played a regulatory and registration function; these will now transfer to the Health Professions Council. These organisations also play a key role, like the Royal College of Nursing above, in providing professional education and development for their members. However, many of the leadership programmes available are intentionally multidisciplinary in nature, with the specific intention of breaking down traditional professional boundaries and breaching barriers to effective patient care.

Nursing has traditionally been viewed as a 'handmaiden' occupation, and as such it has often been perceived as low status and disenfranchised from the policy-making, strategic and leadership echelons of the NHS. The ways in which nursing has responded to the calls by New Labour to reinvent the NHS is a model that all professions can emulate, in setting specific targets for improvement, empowering those who deliver the care and establishing strategies where initiative is valued and encouraged.

Small steps – giant strides

The vision for this book was to gather together a collection of chapters that address the key concepts outlined within the leadership strategies espoused by the Government, in order to explore where and how leadership at all levels is making a difference to service delivery, patient care and outcomes. This first section provides perspectives on the 'big issues' challenging leadership today. We explore the notion and history of leadership in the next chapter to set the scene and context in theoretical and developmental terms. This is followed by three chapters exploring the meaning of leadership in the contemporary context established by the Modernisation Agency.

Section 2 introduces and develops the CLINLAP/LEADLAP model developed by one of the editors of this book, and presents four case studies describing the implementation and effect of different aspects of it.

Section 3 presents four more perspectives on leadership that are being effective in managing change and transforming practice in a variety of healthcare settings. Finally, Section 4 consists of one chapter that attempts to gaze into a crystal ball and anticipate the challenges of leadership for healthcare in the future.

However, we wanted this book to be more than simply another 'how-to-do' textbook on leadership. Rather, we scanned the country for examples of where leadership at whatever level, from grassroots ward managers and community nurses to strategic leaders in government departments, has been effective. Hence, it is an eclectic book presenting visions and strategies and the enactment of those from the perspective of those involved in them. However, every chapter presents an aspect and example of leadership that includes lessons that can be learnt.

The brief for our authors was to demonstrate how one key concept or theoretical perspective has gone from rhetoric to reality through a case study. We asked them to focus specifically on the elements of leadership that made their case effective, and also to provide a critique, in some way, of that concept. This latter was to be either explicit in terms of context, sociopolitical or cultural factors or against theoretical perspectives, or implicit in terms of establishing a need for change. Hence, there is no formula for the chapters in this book, each author has interpreted the brief in his or her own way and presents his or her perspective and what he/she considers to be significant. What we believe has been achieved in this collection is a broad perspective of the leadership issues of today, set in the context of governmental policy in twenty-first century Britain for modernising the NHS. Most importantly, what the case studies demonstrate is the interdisciplinary nature of leadership concepts. Whilst the case studies themselves may be located within particular professional disciplines, the ways in which leadership has been enacted are generic and can be seen as exemplars for other disciplines, and for multiprofessional working. So, from the small steps presented by these authors today, great strides may be taken in positive leadership for healthcare in Britain tomorrow.

Leadership is about influencing what happens tomorrow today

Of course, the future is about tomorrow, and working towards tomorrow requires leaders with a vision of what this might look like. Gone are the days of stability and predictability that required efficient management (in reality did they ever exist, or are they a feature of false memory syndrome, asking us to believe it was all better in the olden days?). Welcome to the world of leadership, where those tasked with taking health and social care forward need to be constantly crystal-ball gazing in order to motivate and facilitate others to respond to the challenges of constant change.

References

Adair, J. (1998) *The Action Centred Leader*. The Industrial Society, London.

Adair, J. (2002) *Effective Strategic Leadership*. Pan Macmillan, Basingstoke.

Andrews, J. (2004) The Scottish Parliament. Editorial. *Journal of Nursing Management*, **12**, 229–230.

Antrobus, S. (2003) What is political leadership? *Nursing Standard*, **17** (4), 40–44.

Antrobus, S. (2004) Why does nursing need political leaders? Editorial. *Journal of Nursing Management*, **12**, 227–228.

Antrobus, S. & Kitson, A. (1999) Nursing leadership: influencing and shaping health policy and nursing practice. *Journal of Advanced Nursing*, **29** (3), 746–753.

Avery, G.C. (2004) *Understanding Leadership*. Sage, London.

Bass, B.M. (1995) Theory of transformational leadership redux. *Leadership Quarterly*, **6**, 463–478.

Beech, M. (2002) Leaders or managers: the drive for effective leadership. *Nursing Standard*, **16** (30), 35–36.

Bennis, W. (1998) *On Becoming a Leader*. Arrow Books, London.

Burns, J. (1978) *Leadership*. Harper and Row, New York.

Clark, J. (2004) Political leadership: a Welsh perspective. Editorial. *Journal of Nursing Management*, **12**, 232–233.

Cooper, S.J. (2002) An evaluation of the Leading and Empowered Organisation programme. *Nursing Standard*, **17** (24), 33–39.

Davies, C. (2004) Political leadership and the politics of nursing. *Journal of Nursing Management*, **12**, 235–241.

Department of Health (1997) *The New NHS: Modern and Dependable*. The Stationery Office, London.

Department of Health (1999) *Making a Difference – Strengthening the Nursing, Midwifery and Health Visiting Contribution to Health and Healthcare*. The Stationery Office, London.

Department of Health (2000) *The NHS Plan: A Plan for Investment, a Plan for Reform*. The Stationery Office, London.

Department of Health (2001) *Working Together – Learning Together*. The Stationery Office, London.

Department of Health (2002a) *Managing for Excellence in the NHS*. The Stationery Office, London.

Department of Health (2002b) *Shifting the Balance of Power*. The Stationery Office, London.

Department of Health (2005) Staff in the NHS 2004: on overview of staff numbers in the NHS. Prepared by the Government Statistical Services www.dh.gov.uk.

Donaldson, L. (2001) Quotes from the CMO, accessed from website. *Journal of Clinical Excellence*, **2**, 199–202.

Faugier, J. (2003) Paper presented at the *Effective Nursing Leadership Conference.* www.dh.gov.uk/newshome/conferenceandeventreports/conferencereportsc

Fergusson, S. (2004) Developing nurse leaders for today and tomorrow. *Nursing Management*, **10** (9), 8–9.

Fradd, L. (2004) Political leadership in action. *Journal of Nursing Management*, **12**, 242–245.

Goleman, D. (1995) *Emotional Intelligence: Why it Can Matter More Than IQ.* Bantam Books, New York.

Goleman, D., Boyatzis, R. & McKee, A. (2002) *The New Leaders – Transforming the Art of Leadership into the Science of Results.* Little, Brown, London.

Hayes, L. (2002) A primary care leadership programme: why leadership skills are so essential to nurses working in primary care. *Primary Health Care Journal*, **12** (10), 22–25.

Ishmael, N. (2004) Political leadership in England. Editorial. *Journal of Nursing Management*, **12**, 230–231.

Jasper, M. (2002) Nursing roles and nursing leadership in the New NHS – changing hats, same heads. *Journal of Nursing Management*, **10** (2), 1–3.

Manley, K. (1997) A conceptual framework for advanced practice: an action research project operationalising an advanced practitioner/consultant nurse role. *Journal of Clinical Nursing*, **6** (3), 179–190.

Manley, K. (2000a) Organisational culture and consultant nurse outcomes: part 1, organisational culture. *Nursing Standard*, **14** (36), 34–38.

Manley, K. (2000b) Organisational culture and consultant nurse outcomes: part 2, nurse outcomes. *Nursing Standard*, **14** (37), 34–39.

McKenna, H. (2004) Trouble with the troubles: a reflection on nursing and politics in Northern Ireland. Editorial. *Journal of Nursing Management*, **12**, 231–232.

Miller, D. & Wright, D. (1999) (eds) *Leading an Empowered Organisation.* Creative HealthCare Management, Minneapolis.

Mullally, S. (2001) Leadership and politics. *Nursing Management*, **8** (4), 21–27.

National Leadership Centre (2000) *Leading Empowered Organisations: Evidence of the Success of the Programme.* Unpublished report. The National Leadership Centre, Manchester.

NHS Leadership Centre (2003) *The NHS Leadership Qualities Framework.* www. nhsleadershipqualities.nhs.uk. Accessed 21 July 2004.

Vandenberghe, C., Stordeur, S. & D'hoore, W. (2002) Transactional and transformational leadership in nursing: structural validity and substantive relationships. *European Journal of Psychological Assessment*, **18** (1), 16–29.

2 What is Leadership? A Critical Overview of Frameworks, Models and Theories

Mansour Jumaa

Introduction

Understanding leadership, according to Rost (1993), is a perennial task. It has been so for well over the last hundred years because it is a fundamental, universal and pervasive part of what goes on in human organisations. In this book, as Chapter 1 established, many authors will address perspectives of leadership, paying homage to its centrality within government thinking in terms of the prescribed mode for leadership of the NHS. The authors were asked to adopt an analytical and discursive style throughout their chapters in terms of the fundamental questions of who, why, when, how and what in relation to the leadership focus being taken, either explicitly or implicitly. Case studies are presented describing initiatives that have been effective in 'transforming' elements of service delivery. It is left to the reader to decide whether these case studies demonstrate effectively the characteristics of leadership.

Consequently no particular definition of leadership is prescribed. Despite this approach, it is, nevertheless, important to present what have been the dominant approaches to the study and problem of leadership. Four key areas are reviewed: *trait*, *style*, *contingencies* and *transformational leadership*. Three of these – trait, style and contingencies – tended to dominate in the past. It is important to recognise that these three theories are not totally 'obsolete'. However, when critically analysed, they failed to provide a comprehensive, consistent and congruent account of leadership activities. It is not the intention here to review all past leadership theories because they are so numerous, but to demonstrate an awareness of the existence of these theories and explore the possibility of their application in order to assist with the improvement of effective nursing and healthcare leadership within the UK National Health Service (NHS). This chapter will, therefore, discuss these theories briefly as well as examine current approaches to leadership activities and studies.

Significant leadership approaches from the early twentieth century to present day

Handy conducted a useful review of *trait theories, style theories* and *contingency theories* (Handy 1999). In the 1920s, the first serious research started with the first leadership theory – *trait theory* – which attempted to identify the common characteristics of effective leaders. The advocates proposed that leaders were weighed and measured and subjected to a battery of psychological tests. However, no one could identify what effective leaders had in common. Most studies singled out *intelligence, initiative*, and *self-assurance*. This approach has two kinds of advocates: the prescriptive theorists and the descriptive theorists. Barnard (1938) is perhaps the most noteworthy of the 'prescriptives', while Ghiselli (1963) and Wald & Doty (1954) are the most worth studying of the 'descriptives'. These studies are to be found in Hun=eryager & Heckmann's (1967) book of readings for managers. Trait theory fell into disfavour soon after expensive studies concluded that effective leaders were either above average height or below.

Trait theory was replaced by *style theory* in the 1940s, first in the USA. One particular style of leadership was singled out as having the most potential. Style theorists are best studied by referring to their original works, e.g. Likert (1961), McGregor (1960) and Blake & Mouton (1964). A good review of many of the studies in this field is provided in Vroom & Yetton's (1970) book of readings. Although many of the style theorists pay lip service to the impor=tance of the task and situational variables, they tend to be advocates or 'prophets' of the participative culture. There is too little critical evaluation of when leadership works and when it does not – and most of the studies are primarily concerned with establishing that it is correlated overall with satisfaction or with productivity and are insensitive to explanatory condi=tions. On reflection, Handy (1999) thinks that the influence of some of these 'prophets' has been great but can be better explained on a cultural basis than using an efficiency criterion. They represented a more democratic humanistic approach to the use of man in organizations and came at a time of reaction against scientific management.

Contingencies approaches to leadership studies are more specific in relation to the *task, work group* and the *position* of the leader within that work group. Fiedler (1967), a leading contingency theorist, has suggested that leaders who differentiate highly between co-workers have a differentiated approach to style. Under stress they show consideration, under favourable conditions they show high initiation of structure. This notion of a *differentiating* leader is one that was fully discussed by Schein (1980). Two leading leadership researchers, Vroom and Yetton, carried the contingency theories of leader=ship even further. They looked at two aspects of a decision, its quality and the likelihood of its implementation, in terms of the nature of the task, the quality of the subordinates and their relationship to the leader. They then produced a formal decision tree, which minimizes the time taken for a decision after consideration of these other factors. What, in effect, they did was to make the full contingency idea operational, hence making it testable and teachable. So far they have found much pragmatic evidence to validate it, although it is perhaps too mechanistic and limited in that it deals only with formal decision-making acts of the leader. Details are available in their book *Leadership and Decision-Making* (Vroom & Yetton 1973).

Handy concludes from his review that a more 'integrative way of looking at the subject' was needed (Handy 1999, p. 117). What he proposed is the *best fit approach*. Effective leadership performance, he suggested, will depend on the environment, which includes:

- the power or position of the leader
- the relationship with his or her group
- the organisational norms
- the structure and technology
- the variety of tasks and
- the variety of subordinates.

Could it be that Handy was describing the new paradigm leader, sometimes referred to as a transformational leader (Bass & Avolio 1993)? Transformational leaders have been characterised by four separate components: '(1) idealized influence; (2) inspirational motivation; (3) intellectual stimulation; and (4) individualized consideration' (Bass & Avolio 1993). Schuster (1994) compares transactional and transformational leadership as follows: transactional leadership is found wherever power is the rule; transformational leadership, however, appeals to people's higher levels of motivation to contribute to a cause and add to the quality of life. The advent of total quality management, flattened hierarchies and empowered staff is a sign of transformational leadership at work. Major qualities of the transformational leader include: (1) holding a vision for the association that is intellectually rich, stimulating and true; (2) being honest and empathetic; (3) having a well-developed character without ego power; (4) evincing a concern for the whole; and (5) being able to share power. Of all the qualities, the capacity to envision is probably the most important.

Leaders may wish to employ the following strategies for organisation-wide learning and transformation: (1) tap into the deepest held values; (2) articulate a bold vision and communicate it repeatedly; (3) invite others to participate in the realisation of the vision; (4) become comfortable with and adept at managing resistance; and (5) refrain from holding individuals accountable for the system. Most of these theories originate it appears from the USA. There are, however, key leadership theorists from other parts of the world. Handy reminds us that in Britain, Mant (1984) cast an iconoclastic Australian eye on Anglo-Saxon leadership habits and assumptions. Peters & Waterman (1982) have added to the folklore of American business leaders with some perceptive comments, and Adair raised the flag for England through Action Centre Leadership (Adair 1978).

Kotter (1982), writing perceptively about American business leaders, and Bennis's (1992) study *On Becoming a Leader* are as valuable for their insights into the minds of particular leaders as they are for their general conceptual conclusions. These two books convey a good feel of what it means to be a leader. Both these it appears are a transformation of our world view. Is this change in leadership perception sweeping the world, at least the industrial world and are many individuals, leaders and managers (particularly nurses) espousing this new belief system? The trouble is evidencing the behavioural consequences of this so-called transformation. Where are the transformed organisations? Where are the reflecting transformed nurse leaders, managers and individuals? The best examples are small, transient and fragile. They, nevertheless, exist, in higher numbers, within the NHS post 1997. Stories of the NHS Beacon organisations are a testimony to this new positive development.

Commitment is needed to make transformational leadership work. Being a transformational leader is more than a technique that perseverance alone can establish. It is a way of being. At its best, it suggests an individual with a very clear vision and the ability to convince others of its value. It is a style and a personality and a quality of character that is quite different from the contrasting transactional leader who is more a manager than a leader, an administrator or functionary, albeit a good one – even a motivational one. Thus commitment is not enough. It must be accompanied by deliberate conceptual training and coaching if it is not a natural part of the nurse or healthcare leader's personality. Such commitment is demanded from the leadership development process of the Middlesex University's innovative Strategic Clinical Leadership module within the MSc Clinical Leadership programme. Leadership, notes Handy (1999), has been a subject of specula-tion and research for centuries. As Warren Bennis once pointed out, it is remarkable that we should know so little about something on which so much has been written. We still do not really know in any detail how effective leaders should behave or how they are best developed. There are still many exceptions to any theory.

Leadership, power, style and culture of the organisation

It is becoming more and more difficult to talk about leadership without also talking about power, about the style and culture of the organisation and about its politics. Both Mintzberg's (1973) and Pettigrew's (1974) contribu-tions on *politics* and change are of use in this review. One of the 'classic' management books is that of Mintzberg (1983), *Power in and Around Organ-isation*, in which he gives a comprehensive review of power and politics in organisations, which is still relevant for use today.

For the purpose of this chapter I have drawn upon the work of Johnson & Scholes (2002) and their cultural web analysis, which can provide a descrip-tion, analysis and understanding of the relationship between culture and an organisation's leadership strategies. An observation of the cultural artifacts (the routines, rituals, stories, structures, systems, etc.) not only gives some clues to the way the NHS and its organisations is/are operating, but also indicates how power is perceived within the organisation, through a consideration of the current dominant paradigm. More on the relationship between culture and leadership in organisations appears later in this chapter.

Significant general leadership approaches from the early twentieth century to 2004 are discussed above and summarised in Table 2.1. The table is presented in three columns: the first column shows the time period of the particular theory of leadership, the second shows the leadership perspective, while the last column is about the specific focus of the leadership approach. The middle column states some of the 'theories' of leadership: trait; style; contingencies; post-contingencies; transformational leadership; and 'people's leadership'. People's leadership approaches cut across the others.

Understanding leadership particularly in nursing and in healthcare

A review of the leadership literature on nursing and healthcare in the Cumulative Index to Nursing and Allied Health Literature (CINAHL) database of 287 articles published from March 1982 to July 2003 found less than 20 articles based on research. Similar literature reviews arrived at similar conclusions (Cook 1999, Girvin 1996). Clarification or evidence of the effectiveness of clinical leadership is sparse at present and the evidence itself is not necessarily quantifiable (Cook 1999). However, the situation described by Cook is changing in a positive direction. There is a significant amount of literature, in the UK and the USA, which concentrates on understanding the concept of leadership as applied to nursing (Girvin 1996). The comprehensive literature review found in Girvin (1996) provides an adequate background and critical review for research studies in leadership and nursing and confirmed that much nursing literature relating to leadership was *opinion-led* and *anecdotal*. Some discussed training and preparation for leadership roles. While these 'expert' opinions are legitimate views on leadership in their own right, the paucity of research-based articles on leadership by nurses and from nursing would appear to weaken nurses' claims to act as an authority in this area compared with acclaimed scholars and 'seasoned' practitioners.

A more realistic model for understanding leadership situations

This book is concerned with what takes place that counts as effective healthcare leadership within the UK NHS. Chapter 1 has made explicit the mode, style and culture of leadership the government would like to see within the new NHS. Overall, the government's view is enshrined in the various White

Table 2.1 The 'history' of leadership theory from the early twentieth century to 2004.

Time period	Theory	Focus
1920s	**Trait theory** Barnard (1938) for the 'prescriptives'; Ghiselli (1963) and Wald & Doty (1954) for the 'descriptives'; see Huneryager and Heckmann (1967) for more details	Intelligence, initiative and self-assurance
1940s	**Style theory** Blake & Mouton (1964), Likert (1961) and McGregor (1960); see Vroom and Deci's (1970) book of readings for more details	Advocates or 'prophets' of the participative culture. Represented a more democratic humanistic approach to the use of man in organisations and came at a time of reaction against scientific management
1960s	**Contingencies approaches** Fiedler (1967), Schein (1980) and Vroom & Yetton (1973) (Handy 1999)	More specific in relation to the task, work group and the position of the leader within that work group. A 'differentiating' leader. Formal decision tree. An integrative way of looking at leadership. A best fit approach
1980s	**Post-contingencies approaches** Bennis (1992), Kotter (1982), Mant (1983) and Peters & Waterman (1982)	Iconoclastic Australian eye on Anglo-Saxon leadership habits and assumptions. The folklore of American business leaders with some perceptive comments. On American business leaders. The minds of particular leaders

Continued

Table 2.1 *Continued*

Time period	Theory	Focus
1990s	**Transformational leadership** Bass & Avolio (1993), Cunningham & Kitson (2000a, 2000b) and Schuster (1994)	Four separate components: (1) idealised influence; (2) inspirational motivation; (3) intellectual stimulation; and (4) individualised consideration. Flattened hierarchies and empowered staff. Comparison of transactional and transformational leadership
Late 1990s and the 2000s	**People's leadership** Goleman (1999) Jumaa (2001) Alleyne (2002) Goffee & Jones (2000) Adair (1978) Klenke (1996)	Emotional leadership Strategic leadership and strategic learning Clinical leadership Myths of leadership Three cycles of leadership Feminist perspectives

Papers introduced in some of the chapters in this book. This includes statements such as:

> Aspiring leaders need to be identified, supported and developed. Senior colleagues have an obligation to spot and nurture talent, to encourage and develop leadership qualities and skills to create a professional and organisational climate that enables the next generation of leaders to challenge orthodoxy, to take risks and to learn from experience. (DH 1999, p. 53)

These sentiments are reflected in the NHS approach to leadership development expressed in the work of the NHS Leadership Centre, created in 2001 as part of the NHS Modernisation Agency (*The NHS Plan*, DH 2000). Key stakeholder statements supporting this approach include those of the NHS Chief Medical Officer, Liam Donaldson: 'Implementing this major programme of change will require active leadership at all levels in the NHS and an inclusive approach. If it is successful the pay-off for the patients and staff will be huge'; and Sir Nigel Crisp, NHS Chief Executive: 'We must lead change as well as manage it. We need leadership in setting out the vision and working with and through people to achieve it. We need excellent management in systematic and tested approaches to secure delivery and improvement' (DH 2002).

It is evident from the statement above that a radical culture change is a key aspect of this type of leadership development in the new NHS. The approach taken by Alleyne (2002) and Jumaa (2001) in their research studies on strategic leadership and learning and clinical leadership, respectively, represents practical visible leadership demonstrating the politics of strategic learning. I have captured this perspective of leadership in Table 2.2.

What, in effect, Alleyne (2002) and Jumaa (2001) did was to make the full contingency idea operational through the CLINLAP and LEADLAP models (CLINLAP – Clinical Nursing Leadership Learning and Action Process; LEADLAP – Leadership Learning and Action Process), hence making it quantifiable, testable and teachable. This approach has so far found much pragmatic evidence to validate it, which has led to two doctorate awards in leadership studies. One significant theme that runs through this approach is the management of the dominant cultural paradigm in the workplace. This approach pays particular attention to: stakeholder issues; the roles of leaders and their followers; the processes relating to the task in hand; and the relationships needed based on the organisational context of the leader, the followers and the importance and urgency of the task. This is what is contained in the column entitled '*Politics of strategic learning*' in Table 2.2. Enhancing the strategic learning of individuals and also promoting organisational capability could only become a reality within an appropriately supportive and sensitively managed cultural environment. This is where the work of Johnson and Scholes (2002) was useful. It contributed to our understanding of the cultural process through the *cultural web*. The web demonstrates how managers and others in the healthcare organisation, including nurses, heavily draw on frames of reference they have accumulated over

Table 2.2 Practical visible leadership and the politics of strategic learning.

Practical visible leadership	Politics of strategic learning
Specific agreed desired goals by stakeholders for the organisation, department or unit	*Tell* others about the agreed goals *Involve* others in the agreed goals *Others decide* about the agreed goals
Explicit disciplined roles for stakeholders to achieve the agreed goals	*Tell* others what to do about the agreed goals *Involve* others in what to do about the agreed goals *Others decide* what to do about the agreed goals
Clear disciplined processes for the roles of stakeholders to achieve the agreed goals	*Tell* others how to go about the agreed goals *Involve* others in how to go about the agreed goals *Others decide* how to go about the agreed goals
Open active relationships amongst stakeholders to achieve the agreed goals through explicit roles and clear processes	*Tell* others what open relationships mean to implement the agreed goals *Involve* others in what open relationships mean to implement the agreed goals *Others decide* what open relationships mean to implement the agreed goals

time. The implications of these frames of reference are that they tend also to be important at a collective organisational level (a dominant paradigm). They may, therefore, be protected by different aspects of organisational culture. Gaining insight into the paradigm is possible by analysing the elements of the cultural web, which are: stories; routines and rituals; symbols; organisational structures; control systems; and power structures

Leadership, according to the approaches of Alleyne (2002) and Jumaa (2001) also requires vision. The leader must have a strong sense of mission and the ability to develop a sense of community based on shared values. These together provide the meaning, value and the platform for action at work. One of the particular strengths of the CLINLAP/LEADLAP model is that as a strategic performance implementation model, it allowed the analysis, choice and implementation of management and leadership strategies to pursue the vision and mission that is consistent with shared values in a given context, the new NHS, for example.

Conclusions

This chapter has presented a brief review of the main theories on leadership. It also suggested a more realistic model for understanding leadership situations. Four key areas on theories on leadership were reviewed. They are trait, style, contingencies and transformational leadership. Handy (1999) proposed the best fit approach. Effective leadership performance, he suggested, will depend on the environment, which includes:

- the power or position of the leader
- the relationship with his or her group
- the organisational norms
- the structure and technology
- the variety of tasks and
- the variety of subordinates.

This suggestion is not far removed from what, in effect, Alleyne (2002) and Jumaa (2001) have done, which was to make the full contingency idea operational through the CLINLAP/LEADLAP model, hence making it quantifiable, testable and teachable. This approach pays particular attention to: stakeholder issues; the roles of leaders and their followers; the processes relating to the task in hand; and the relationships needed based on the organisational context of the leader, the followers and the importance and urgency of the task. Both Handy's best fit approach and the CLINLAP/LEADLAP model are in keeping with the NHS approach to leadership development expressed in the work of the NHS Leadership Centre, created in 2001 as part of the NHS Modernisation Agency (*The NHS Plan*, DH 2000).

According to a Department of Health publication, *The NHS Plan*, reforms and investment are transforming the NHS, with dramatic improvements in key areas. Tackling the two biggest killers, cancer and coronary heart disease, has been a priority over the past 4 years and mortality rates are already falling rapidly.

Less than 4 years into the period covered by the 10-year NHS Plan, the new delivery systems and providers are expanding capacity and choice. As these new ways of working really take hold across the whole system, the dividend will be a higher-quality service with even faster access to care. A new spirit of innovation has emerged, centred on improving the personal experience of patients as individuals, and this is now taking root in the NHS. Details of this publication are available at: http://www.publications.doh.gov.uk/nhsplan/nhsimprovementplan-execsum.htm (accessed 2 August 2004).

Leadership, whether it is nursing, medical or healthcare leadership, is about knowing how to make visions become reality. The vision that many nurses hold dear to their hearts is one where patients are treated with dignity and respect at all times; where systems are designed for the benefit of individual needs; and where the work performed by nurses and other carers is valued and respected. Achieving such a vision will require a paradigm shift in the philosophy, priorities, policies, and power relationships of the health service. (Kitson 2001)

To what extent do the claims by the Department of Health and the positive sentiments of Professor Kitson represent a reality?

The next chapter in this book provides a platform to explore these issues through a case study of effective healthcare leadership in action from the leadership activities of the new NHS in England.

References

Adair, J. (1978) *Effective Leadership*. Gower, Aldershot.

Alleyne, J. (2002) *Making a Case for Group Clinical Supervision Through Management and Leadership Concepts.* Unpublished Research Project Report, part of a Doctor of Professional Studies (DProf), through work-based learning in clinical nursing leadership, Middlesex University, London.

Barnard, C.L. (1938) *The Functions of the Executive*. Harvard University, Cambridge, Massachusetts.

Bass, B.M. & Avolio, B.J. (1993) Transformational leadership and organizational culture. *Public Administration Quarterly*, Spring, 112.

Bennis, W.G. (1992) *On Becoming a Leader*. Business Books, London.

Blake, R. & Mouton, J. (1964) *The Managerial Grid*. Gulf, London.

Cook, M.J. (1999) Improving care requires leadership in nursing. *Nurse Education Today*, **19** (4), 306–312.

Cunningham, G. & Kitson, A. (2000a) An evaluation of the RCN clinical leadership development programme: part 1. *Nursing Standard*, **15** (12), 34–37.

Cunningham, G. & Kitson, A. (2000b) An evaluation of the RCN clinical leadership development programme: part 2. *Nursing Standard*, **15** (13), 36–39.

Department of Health (1999) *Making a Difference: Strengthening the Nursing, Midwifery and Health Visiting Contribution to Health and Healthcare*. The Stationery Office, London.

Department of Health (2000) *The NHS Plan: A Plan for Investment, a Plan for Reform*. The Stationery Office, London.

Department of Health (2002) *Managing for Excellence in the NHS*. The Stationery Office, London.

Fiedler, F.E. (1967) *A Theory of Leadership Effectiveness*. McGraw-Hill, Hemel Hempstead.

Ghiselli, E.E. (1963) Managerial talent. *American Psychologist*, **18**, 631.

Girvin, J. (1996) Leadership and nursing (part 4). Motivation. *Nursing Management*, **5**, 16–18.

Goffee, R. & Jones, G. (2000) Why should anyone be led by you? *Harvard Business Review*, **78** (5), 62–69.

Goleman, E. (1999) *Working with Emotional Intelligence*. Bloomsbury, London.

Handy, C. (1999) *Understanding Organisations*, 6th edn. Penguin, London.

Huneryager, S.G. & Heckmann, I.L. (eds) (1967) *Human Relations in Management*. Arnold, London.

Johnson, G. & Scholes, K. (2002) *Exploring Corporate Strategy; Text and Cases*, 6th edn. Prentice Hall, Hemel Hempstead.

Jumaa, M.O. (2001) *Enhancing Individual Learning and Organisational Capability Through Learning Projects and Developmental Interventions*. Unpublished Research Project Report, part of a Doctor of Professional Studies (DProf), through work-based learning in strategic leadership and strategic learning in nursing and healthcare, Middlesex University, London.

Kitson, A. (2001) Nursing leadership: bringing caring back to the future. *Quality in Health Care*, **10**, 79–84.

Klenke, K. (1996) *Women and Leadership: A Contextual Perspective*. Springer, New York.

Kotter, J. (1982) *The General Managers*. The Free Press, New York.

Likert, R. (1961) *New Patterns of Management*. McGraw Hill, Maidenhead.

Mant, A. (1984) *Leaders We Deserve*. Blackwell, Oxford.

McGregor, D.V. (1960) *The Human Side of Enterprise*. McGraw-Hill, New York.

Mintzberg, H. (1973) *Nature of Managerial Work*. Harper and Row, New York.

Mintzberg, H. (1983) *Power in and Around Organisation*. Prentice Hall, Hemel Hempstead.

Peters, T. & Waterman, R.H. (1982) *In Search of Excellence*. Harper and Row, New York.

Pettigrew, A. (1974) The influence process between specialists and executives. *Personnel Review* (http://lysander.emeraldinsight.com/vl=1248475/cl=16/nw=1/rpsv/cw/www/mcb/00483486/contp1-1.htm).

Rost, J.C. (1993) *Leadership for the Twenty-First Century*. Praeger, Westport, Connecticut.

Schein, E.H. (1980) *Organizational Psychology*, 3rd edn. Prentice-Hall, Englewood Cliffs, New Jersey.

Schuster, J.P. (1994) Transforming your leadership style. *Association Management*, January, 39.

Vroom, V.H. & Yetton, P. (1970) *Management and Motivation*. Penguin, London.

Vroom, V.H. & Yetton, P. (1973) *Leadership and Decision-Making*. University of Pittsburgh.

Wald, R.M. & Doty, R.A. (1954) The top executive – a first hand profile. *Harvard Business Review*, **32** (4).

Further reading

Department of Health (1997) *The New NHS: Modern and Dependable*. The Stationery Office, London.

Department of Health (2000) *Quality and Performance in the NHS. Performance Indicators*. The Stationery Office, London.

Department of Health (2002) *Shifting the Balance of Power*. The Stationery Office, London.

Jumaa, M.O. (1997) *Strategic Clinical Team Learning Through Leadership*. Unpublished Research Project Report, part of an MA-WBLS (Strategic Nursing Leadership and Management), Middlesex University, London.

Mink, O.G. (1992) Creating new organizational paradigms for change. *International Journal of Quality and Reliability Management*, **9** (3), 21.

3   What is Effective Healthcare Leadership? A Case Study of the NHS in England

Mansour Jumaa

Introduction

An unfortunate reality is that more than half of the people who aspire to leadership roles fail. Generally, they fail not because of lack of technical expertise, nor because of an inability to conceptualise the job that needs to be done. Mostly the failures have to do with individuals not knowing how to bridge the gap between who they are as a person and what type of behaviour is expected of them in the job. This lack of knowledge and understanding is more significant than being deficient in highly specialised expertise. To most organisations that are continually searching for individuals who have competencies beyond expertise in a specific discipline, this fact comes as no surprise. The competencies organisations are looking for in individuals are often referred to as human behaviour skills, which include the ability to understand oneself and others. When leaders do have that personal knowledge and ability, they are instinctively aware of it (Fandt & Quirk 2000).

In this chapter, five strategic questions are posed in order to explore the perennial and complex question, 'What is effective healthcare leadership?'. The five questions are as follows:

(1) What is the goal of effective leadership in healthcare in the NHS?
(2) Where is leadership currently located generally and particularly within healthcare?
(3) How effective is healthcare leadership currently perceived to be?
(4) Which are the preferred pathways for effective healthcare leadership?
(5) Who or what could sustain effective healthcare leadership and when?

Three of these questions, which form the focus of this chapter, are discussed in relation to the National Health Service (NHS) in England as a case study of effective healthcare leadership. Answers to the other two questions are explored elsewhere in this book. Chapter 1 has already addressed question two, while the fourth question is explored in the case studies provided in the various chapters of this book.

What is the goal of effective leadership in healthcare in England?

The NHS Improvement Plan

The NHS Improvement Plan (DH 2004) is an essential document for any discussion about the provision of effective healthcare leadership in the NHS between now and 2008. It is about the goal of effective leadership in health-care in England. It is the document that portrays, publicly, the Government's ongoing commitment to a 10-year process of reform first set out in *The NHS Plan* (DH 2000). The NHS Improvement Plan affirms the Government's wish for the NHS. It reads:

> Our vision is one where the founding principles underlying the NHS are given modern meaning and relevance in the context of people's increasing ambitions and expectations of their public services. An NHS which is fair to all of us and personal to each of us by offering everyone the same access to, and the power to choose from, a wide range of services of high quality, based on clinical need, not ability to pay. (DH 2004, Preface)

It is difficult not to notice the radical reforms that have been sweeping through the NHS over the past 7 years. After decades of underinvestment, the NHS has begun to turn itself around, with unprecedented increases in the money it can spend. As its budget has grown from £33 billion to £67.4 billion, the average spending per head of population has gone up from £680 to £1345 per year (www.dh.gov.uk). Has this made a difference to the patient's experience? The Government believes so.

The Government's aim has been to reshape the NHS, building on the NHS Plan. This chapter will show the extent to which this has been and is being continuously achieved. A very bold aim of the Government which may be overlooked by many is the ambition to 'give' the health service dual names: a national health service *and* a personal health service for every patient in England. This has very serious implications for the nature of healthcare leadership to achieve this very humanistic and desirable aim. It means, at the least, ensuring that the activities and services listed in Box 3.1 are available to each taxpayer when he/she needs it.

It is clear from this that the answer to the question 'What is the goal of effective leadership in healthcare in England?' would be to make sure patients always come first by implementing and sustaining the current radical reforms and changes to the way the NHS works. Therefore, the chosen leadership approach must understand how the NHS works internally as well as externally (see Fig. 3.1).

Internally, how the NHS works could be made sense of through a simple approach called the *7Ss* (Peters & Waterman 1983): i.e. knowing and

Box 3.1 A national health service (NHS) *and* a personal health service (PHS) for every patient in England (synthesised from *The NHS Improvement Plan* (DH 2004).

- More choice for all patients, irrespective of the money in their pockets.
- A continuing commitment to the founding principles of the NHS.
- The provision of quality care based on clinical need, irrespective of the patient's ability to pay.
- Meeting the needs of people from all walks of life.
- A resolve to ensure that the NHS meets the expectations of all people in England.
- Enabling and supporting people in improving their own health.
- Meeting the challenge of making a *real* difference to inequalities in health.
- Staying the course and supporting those with conditions that they will live with all their lives.
- Quickly treating people with curable problems so that they can get on with their lives and live them to the full.

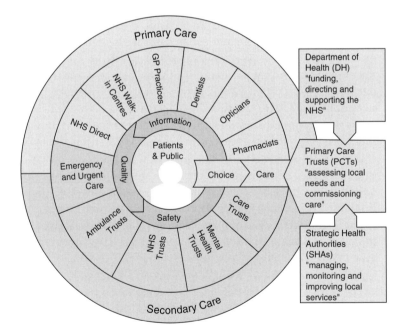

Fig 3.1 How the NHS and its organisations are organised (source: www.NHS.uk). (Crown copyright is reproduced with the permission of the Controller of HMSO and the Queen's Printer for Scotland.)

understanding what is the NHS *strategy* (the direction and goals of the NHS); the *structure* (the boundary and the stakeholders who will deliver the strategy); its *systems* (the processes, i.e. the policies, protocols and procedures that will assist in delivering the strategy); the *staff* (who may be permanent or interim, internal as well as external, and at all levels of healthcare organisations, who have to deliver the strategy); the *skills* of the staff [skills covering all aspects of resource utilisation – THEIMM (time, human, equipment, estates and energy, information, material and money)]; the *style* of management (using the appropriate mode of communication with the staff and all stakeholders); and the *shared* values (creating an environment for trust, loyalty and solidarity in order to work towards achieving the strategy). All of these activities must be perceived as having relevance to the needs of the many stakeholders of the NHS. While it is necessary to understand the internal factors impacting on the NHS, it is not sufficient in itself. A working understanding of the external environmental factors influencing activities throughout the NHS is mandatory. These external factors are described as PESTELI by Johnson & Scholes (2002) and PEST'O' by Jumaa (2001). The application of PEST'O', to make sense of how outside forces are impacting on the workplace, is further explained in Chapter 7. It would be difficult and possibly impossible to consider the purpose and objectives of the NHS in England without pondering on the relevance of questions such as 'Why does the NHS exist?', 'What does the NHS believe in?', 'What are its strategies and distinctive competencies to assist the NHS to meet the objectives which reflect NHS values?', 'What behavioural standards exist for the NHS to achieve its strategies based on the purposes and objectives?' (Campbell & Yeung 1990). Figure 2 in the Government's publication *A First Class Service: Quality in the New NHS* (DH 1998a) made explicit how these questions would be answered. Although the shape of the quality performance framework in this publication is continuously modified, it captured three significant aspects of how the NHS in England would achieve its purposes and objectives: through setting quality standards, delivering quality standards and monitoring quality standards. The implementation process expects a focus on patient and public involvement, professional self-regulation, clinical governance and lifelong learning, with a deliberate intention that the service will lead to dependable local delivery.

A significant part of the implementation of the purposes and objectives of the NHS therefore relies on the primacy of stakeholder objectives and relationships. Unfortunately, though, the powers of these many stakeholders are unequal, irrespective of what some authors on transformational leadership would have us believe. It would be naïve for general managers, professionals and others within the NHS not to constantly remember that despite public commitment by the Government, there are, overall, political strategies driving these objectives and purposes. The control of scarce resources and other forms of power is at the heart of effective stakeholder assessment, management and evaluation (Jumaa & Alleyne 2002).

The nature of the stakeholder relationship

As Jumaa (2001) argues, knowing, conducting an analysis and assessing the sources of power of the various stakeholders will help the new strategic nurse leader and healthcare practitioners to appreciate that stakeholders bring different resources to the organisation. Hence, the NHS's ability to prosper and survive depends on its ability to continue attracting those stakeholders and their resources to the activities of the NHS. In order to do so, the NHS must continue to use the resources in such a way as to add value for its variety of stakeholders. Stakeholders contribute resources in the full expectation of claiming some reward from the organisation's value-adding activities. Indeed, stakeholder analyses might be more correctly termed 'contributor and claimant' analyses. Stakeholder relationships are characterised by interdependence and exchange, a process of flux and mutual adjustment.

Managing within an environment of trust

One of the problems encountered when dealing with the model of strategy that emphasises the primacy of stakeholder objectives and collaboration, as is the case with the new NHS, is how to deal with the large number of organisations within the NHS, where ownership and the right to residual benefits cannot be easily determined, naturally, in a quantifiable way. For our purpose, both the health and the social services sectors are prime examples. In the NHS organisations, for example, there is usually a significant purpose of trust and 'benefit for others' in their activities, explicitly made in purpose statements, and explicit and implicit in their relationships. Legally, NHS organisations exist to fulfill the wishes of the Government on behalf of the citizens, who are tax payers (DH 1997). The return to the providers of resources is the fulfillment of their wishes, rather than an economic reward such as a 'shareholders' dividend.

Managing stakeholder relationships from this analysis and discussion appears to be a complex exercise, but a key requirement if effective healthcare leadership is the goal. In this section, we have explored the question 'What is the goal of effective leadership in healthcare in England?' We conclude that the purpose is to make sure patients always come first by implementing and sustaining the current radical reforms and changes to the way the NHS works. This needs a process of effective healthcare leadership that ensures a seamless and skilful integration of the NHS's purposes, values, strategies and agreed behaviour standards. However, could this competence and capability be developed in the strategic nurse leader and the healthcare practitioner for effective healthcare leadership? This leads to the second of our five questions, which has been discussed in Chapter 1: 'Where is leadership currently located generally and particularly within healthcare?' The overall message from Chapter 1 is that the concept of leadership in the NHS is key to the modernisation of the NHS and this has been enshrined in the work of the NHS Leadership Centre. The Centre launched the NHS Leadership Qualities Framework. It is within this framework that the answer to this question is located. This chapter will now explore the third question: 'How effective is healthcare leadership currently perceived?'

How effective is healthcare leadership currently perceived?

A series of authoritative research survey reports found that the NHS is firmly on the road to a full recovery with steady improvements in the quality of care delivered to patients. So there is 'some' cause for celebration. Policy evaluation of the provision of effective healthcare leadership in the NHS has to take place, at the very least, at two levels: the government level (the 'P' for political factors in the PEST'O' external environment analysis); and at the internal level [e.g. Primary Care Trusts (PCTs); NHS Trusts; Mental Health Trusts; Care Trusts]. It is difficult to imagine that either the government analysis would stop at the 'P' factors alone or that the NHS organisations would stop at the internal analysis. A full analysis for the achievement of effective implementation of any project must consider both the internal and the external factors impacting on any given organisation at a given period of time.

An example of one of the problems that could signal the onset or the presence of ineffective healthcare leadership, internally, is shown in Fig. 3.2, prepared by a lead nurse manager[1] working in a smear clinic. The most apparent barrier to this project in question, according to the lead nurse manager, is that of litigation. The lead nurse is concerned over the increased levels of autonomy that would be necessary for her to review and take action on smear results (see Fig. 3.2).

This approach works better when implemented with the key stakeholders involved in the project. A brainstorming technique facilitated this progress. While it is accepted from the analysis so far that effective healthcare leadership is making some contribution to progress in the new NHS on the road to full recovery, caution is needed to ensure that NHS organisations who might be implicated by the findings of two recent and relevant management and leadership studies are taking necessary remedial actions.

One of the research's findings is that professions lag behind in management and leadership skills. This research, carried out by the Council for Excellence in Management and Leadership (CEML), set up by the Government, was reported to be the most comprehensive study ever conducted into the supply of and demand for management and leadership capability in the UK (CEML 2002). The report stated that current management and business

---

[1] The lead nurse successfully completed a Chartered Management Institute degree level Diploma in Management and Leadership at the Middlesex University. This extract is from the project report which was part of the summative assessment.

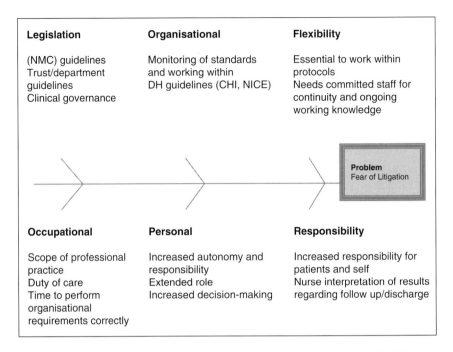

Fig 3.2 Isikawa's fish bone (cause and effect) diagram and the LOOP Factors Framework (Jumaa 2001) used to make sense of a 'fear of litigation'.

leadership development is 'a dysfunctional system', and that the UK's economic performance is being held back by a shortage of appropriate and practical leadership skills. The second report, *Leading Change in the Public Sector: Making the Difference*, was sponsored by the Department for Education and Skills, Defence Leadership Centre, Improvement and Development Agency for Local Government, National College for School Leadership, Metropolitan Police Service and the Training Group Defence Agency. According to the Chartered Management Institute (the Institute), it follows on from a major study into the nature of leadership in UK organisations in 2001 by the Institute in association with the think-tank Demos, on behalf of CEML. In that report, *Leadership: The Challenge for All?* (Horne & Jones 2001), the quality of leadership in UK organisations did not receive high ratings and public sector organisations received the lowest ratings of all.

Leading Change in the Public Sector: Making the Difference, a report by the Chartered Management Institute (2003), claims that the Government's public sector reform agenda is in danger of stalling due to the lack of good quality leadership within the public services. As the public sector attempts to realign itself to satisfy rising customer expectations and engage its communities, managers want their leaders to 'ditch a skill set that is ten years out of date'. This is the key finding of the Institute's in-depth survey, examining current leadership performance based on the views of 1900 public sector managers as they face the daily pressures of the public reform agenda.

Managers talk of a 'blame culture', where all too often priorities are blurred and targets are the 'raison d'être'. Leaders need to foster a culture of trust, with increased focus on customers. As one panel member explained: 'we're not going to get better just by getting better at measuring performance'.

Managers refer time and again to the current emphasis on standards, targets and procedures as a barrier to imaginative management and leadership. Initiative overload is common: almost two-thirds of managers cite the sheer pressure of work, while almost half say insufficient finance and the time-consuming and bureaucratic nature of such initiatives are the key barriers to implementation of public sector reform. Nearly six in ten managers say that while the billions of pounds already invested in the public sector have brought major reforms in the past 3 years which have directly improved service delivery, further reforms will only be brought about if their leaders refocus on what is really important. The findings of these two key studies should serve as 'wake-up' calls for health and social care organisations and should assist them to make the minimum of management and leadership mistakes. For discussion and answers to the fourth question 'Which are the preferred pathways for effective healthcare leadership?' readers will find these in the discussions and presentations in the various case studies throughout the chapters of this book. Our final question for discussion is 'Who or what could sustain effective healthcare leadership and when?'

Who or what could sustain effective healthcare leadership and when?

As we explore this fifth and final strategic question, we reflect on the following sub-questions: to what extent are the contents of the chapters of this book a reflection of what happens or has happened in organisations in the NHS? What are the essential things required to achieve the next stage of development? Who, for example, is already implementing some of the good practice in this book, and maybe much more? The next step, therefore, would be to explore how and what could make this local (tacit) knowledge become explicit and be shared with the rest of the healthcare professions through publication in an appropriate journal, the *Journal of Nursing Management*, for example.

To explore the fifth strategic question demands putting in place a system to manage and lead work culture in a practical and pragmatic way. A tried and tested approach to do this is through the day-to-day implementation and adaptation of Johnson & Scholes (2002) cultural web management and leadership approach. The web is an integrated feature of the Leadership Learning and Action Process Model (Jumaa & Alleyne 2002) and Chapter 7 demonstrates how this cultural web was applied at work for culture development and sustaining such changes.

Box 3.2 provides some questions that could be used to 'measure' the dominant cultural paradigm, through observation, within the new NHS – how the NHS field really behaves. We could add and expand these questions

Box 3.2 Exploring the *taken for granted* assumptions of healthcare leadership in the NHS.

Stories
- What core NHS beliefs do stories you hear reflect about healthcare leadership?
- Do these stories relate to:
  - strengths and weaknesses of the NHS?
  - NHS successes or failures?
  - NHS staff as conformers or mavericks?
- Who are the heroes and villains in the NHS?

Routines and rituals
- Which routines are emphasised within the NHS?
- Which of these routines and rituals will look odd if changed?
- How easy are routines and rituals to change in the NHS?

Symbols
- What common language and jargon are used in the NHS?
- What status symbols exist within the NHS?

Organisational structures
- How mechanistic/organic are NHS structures?
- Do NHS structures encourage collaboration or competition?

Control systems
- Does the NHS put emphasis on reward or punishment?
- Are there many/fewer controls in the NHS?

Power structures
- How is power distributed within the NHS?
- What are the core beliefs of the leadership in the NHS?
- Where are the main blockages to change in NHS nursing?

Overall dominant culture
- What is the dominant culture in the NHS?
- How easy is this dominant culture in the NHS to change?

---

to suit our purposes. When this analysis is concluded, we should be able to declare, justifiably, whether the overall dominant culture reflects one of the following types of culture: *defender, prospector* or *analyser* (Miles & Snow 1978); or *role culture, task culture, power culture* or *personal culture* (Handy 1993). We could, of course, make a case for a combination of these types of culture. The dominant cultural paradigm of the NHS as perceived by managers in the 1990s, for example, was that the NHS is a 'good thing'; a public service; free at point of delivery; 'ours'; composed of clinicians' values; that providers know best; acute sector superior. This is a powerful measurement of the prevailing dominant paradigm at that time (Johnson & Scholes 2002, p. 232).

On reflection, in over 30 years of working within and with the NHS and applying the legal, organisational, occupational and personal factors (the LOOP factors framework) (Jumaa 2001) as points of reference, I appreciate the immense positive growth within the NHS that has taken place since the start of the twenty-first century, and I am very proud of and celebrate the significant contributions of nursing and nurses to these achievements. Irrespective of our different political perspectives, we will find it difficult not to notice these improvements, some of which are described in Table 3.1. This table uses the THEIMM approach (resources analysis) (Jumaa 1997) to present an overview of strengths and opportunities facing the new NHS.

Despite all these successes it is inevitable that there are still areas for improvement due to systems failure or 'perverted' machinations of some staff within the NHS or related organisations. The word 'perverted' is used to mean interventions that are 'deliberately malicious, that intentionally seek to do harm to another person' (Heron 1990, p. 9), and degenerate interventions 'that fail in one, and usually several, of these respects, because the practitioner lacks personal development, or training, or experience, or awareness, or some combination of these' (Heron 1990, p. 9).

The growing case for improvements within the new NHS is supported by both patients who use the service and the staff who provide these services. Healthcare Commission Chief Executive Anna Walker said:

> More than 200,000 people have told us what it is like to work in the NHS. Many said they were generally satisfied with their jobs, but further analysis of the results show that some groups of staff are more likely to experience violence and bullying, have a poorer work–life balance and report higher levels of work related stress and injury.... People who care for everyone's health needs should not have to endure violence or harassment as part of their daily working life. We urge NHS organisations to investigate and address these issues and examine the scope to improve work–life balance and reduce work pressure for staff. We will continue to assess and monitor the way staff are managed, including how issues of harassment and bullying are handled, as part of our annual ratings of NHS performance.

The NHS staff survey was conducted in October 2003 and is probably the largest workforce survey in the world. A total of 203 911 NHS employees responded and 572 organisations took part. (See www.healthcarecommission.org.uk for more details.)

The Healthcare Commission conducted five surveys during 2004 on how patients experience the NHS. These were published in the first week of August 2004. The Commission reported that a consistent positive theme across the NHS is the patients' high opinion of the care they receive. They say they have trust and confidence in the clinical staff, they are listened to and they are treated with respect and dignity. The Healthcare Commission's Chairman, Professor Sir Ian Kennedy, said:

Table 3.1 A SWOT analysis of the NHS in England, showing its strengths and opportunities mapped against its resources.

Resources (THEIMM, Jumaa 1997)	Strengths	Opportunities
Time (reputation, culture)	Quality is also improving; a track record of success; the maximum waiting time for an operation has fallen from 18 months to less than 9 months	The range of services available to the public is widening; gives the confidence to support further investment and reform
Human	Access to GPs; steady increases in the number of NHS staff; the Healthcare Commission inspects NHS services	Accident and emergency (A&E) care, operations and treatment are improving with every passing year; more focused on the personal care of individual patients and better enabled to do so
Equipment, estates and energy	Expansion and modernisation of buildings, equipment and facilities; dozens of new hospitals; spending on buildings and equipment has increased from £1.1 billion to £3.4 billion	The NHS is enabled to provide better quality care for patients, with safer and more effective treatment, better surroundings and services that better suit their lives
Information	A series of positive authoritative reports; death rates from cancer and heart disease are sharply down; development and delivery of National Service Frameworks	Found that the NHS is firmly **on the road** to a **full** recovery; improvements in the quality of care
Material	NHS Direct and NHS Walk-in Centres	Growing numbers of patients are taking advantage of new services such as Walk-in Centres
Money	More, in real terms; investment has increased from £33 billion in 1996/1997 to £67.4 billion in 2004/2005	Increased capacity of the NHS to serve patients; it has helped give faster and more convenient access to care

In general, patients have given a 'thumbs up' to the care they receive from the NHS. However, those patients who do not feel completely involved in decisions about their care and treatment are not able to consent to treatment in any meaningful sense.... While there has been a great improvement in communication between NHS staff and their patients there is still much to be done to ensure that patients understand the information they are given and can influence decisions.... Asking patients what they think about the care and treatment they have received is an important step towards improving care for patients in hospitals and other health services.

The questionnaires and methodology were developed by the NHS Surveys Advice Centre at Picker Institute Europe. Each trust that took part identified 850 eligible people. Patients were sent questionnaires and up to two reminders. A total of 568 NHS organisations and 312 348 patients took part in the surveys. Response rates to the surveys varied from 63% for the adult inpatient survey to 42% for the mental health survey. (See www.healthcare commission.org.uk for more details.)

Enhancing the strategic learning of individual nurses and other healthcare practitioners as well as promoting NHS organisational capability could only become a reality within an appropriately supportive environment. The transformational leadership approach would appear to be very popular with nurses and others within the new NHS. However, if all the positive things that are written about transformational leadership are to be realised, I am in agreement with Bass (1995) that the future learning organisation, like the new NHS, will need such leadership at all levels of the organisation. Success will not be realised nor sustained unless the following processes (see Box 3.3) are addressed in all the leadership activities within the new NHS.

Box 3.3 Sustaining Transformational Leadership Achievements in the NHS.

Inspirational leadership
Articulate what is missing and the changes required. Share a vision of the style of TL you need. Receive and provide mentoring and coaching. Become competent in giving and receiving feedback. Practise open communications, careful listening and create an environment of trust. Encourage a consultative mode of leadership. Desired leadership role models regularly shown by the NHS organisation's Chief Executive Officer and his/her team and are encouraged at each level below. Behaviours of the leaders at the top act as symbols of the new organisational culture.

Continued

> **Box 3.3** *Continued*
>
> **Intellectual stimulation**
> Bring forth the expert knowledge of the members of the organisation. Stimulate thinking at all levels about the organisation's objectives and the means to meet them. Actively encourage airing of problems. Stories about successful problem solving are passed on and made public to everyone. Mechanisms for upward communication are developed, transparent and consistent. Creativity, innovation, calculated risk-taking and careful experimentation are fostered by real and visible examples.
>
> **Individualised consideration**
> As a considerate leader, take part in more acculturation activities with your people and within your NHS organisation. Treat each individual follower as having different developmental needs, but do not talk down to him or her. Give and accept feedback as part of the continuous, living, learning and leading process. Provide mentoring and coaching for members of your NHS organisation.
>
> **Contingent reward**
> Foster organisational learning by introducing changes into the daily practices of the NHS organisation following suitable education and training efforts. Praise individuals and departments publicly. Provide earned promotions and pay increases for trying and succeeding in introducing learning approaches into everyday activities. Provide rewards sometimes, even for failing after trying.

Summary and conclusions

This chapter has attempted to provide a view of effective healthcare leadership in action within the new NHS. To do so the NHS in England was used as a case study to illustrate *effective healthcare leadership in action*. This chapter demonstrates an example of one approach with a focus on the use of relevant management and leadership concepts, frameworks and techniques to assist with the evaluation and make sense of the NHS as a case study of effective healthcare leadership. It has been shown in this chapter that the new NHS is improving its services to patients. The new NHS is on the way to a full recovery, a view shared by both patients and staff within the NHS. This chapter has also confirmed that leadership is in a state of flux and that irrespective of perspectives taken to describe or define this concept, it is about relationships, and it has undergone a series of transformations over the last one hundred years of modern management. Leadership, as a universal idea, has been defined variously by almost every writer contributing to this ferment (Fairholm 1997). We have intentionally not given a prescriptive definition of leadership. It is my opinion from the analysis and evaluation of this case study that effective healthcare leadership within the new NHS has to adopt a 'balanced' approach, focusing on: financial perspectives; customers', patients' and clients' perspectives; internal conversion process perspectives; and innovation and learning growth perspectives (Kaplan & Norton 1996). I have also come to the conclusion in my research and development activities in healthcare management and leadership that the key questions the effective healthcare leader must focus on and find answers acceptable to key stakeholders are as follows:

- How do we appear in the perceptions of our commissioners, sponsors and key stakeholders in relation to our healthcare leadership activities?
- How do our external and internal customers, our patients and our clients value our services and products?
- What are our organisation's core internal processes and how are they performing to meet our agreed or politically 'imposed' goals?
- How do we develop, nurture and grow the talents of our staff to meet the challenge of turbulence and the constantly changing environment of the new NHS?

Effective leadership is seen here as getting things done without excessive 'pressure' from the manager. Stakeholder agreement and consent are the essence of the leadership learning and action process approach favoured in this chapter. In the current environment of the twenty-first century, an effective organisation has to combine efficient management with the best of leadership processes. Either is necessary but not sufficient on its own. The presentation in this chapter was based on the CLINLAP/LEADLAP model, which is presented in more detail in Chapter 6.

References

Bass, B.M. (1995) Theory of transformational leadership redux. *Leadership Quarterly*, **6**, 463–478.

Burns, J. (1978) *Leadership*. Harper and Row, New York.

Campbell, A. & Yeung, S. (1990) *Do You Need a Mission Statement (Ashridge Mission Model)?* Special Report no. 1208. The Economist Publications Management Guides, London.

Chartered Management Institute (2003) *Leading Change in the Public Sector: Making a Difference*. CMI, London.

Council for Excellence in Management and Leadership (CEML) (2002) *Managers and Leaders: Raising our Game*. DTI, London.

Department of Health (1997) *The New NHS: Modern and Dependable*. The Stationery Office, London.

Department of Health (1998) *A First Class Service: Quality in the NHS*. The Stationery Office, London.

Department of Health (2000) *The NHS Plan: A Plan for Investment, a Plan for Reform*. The Stationery Office, London.

Department of Health (2004) *The NHS Improvement Plan*. The Stationery Office, London.

Fairholm, G.W. (1997) *Capturing the Heart of Leadership: Spirituality and Community in the New American Workplace*. Praeger, Westport, Connecticut.

Fandt, P.M. & Quirk, M.P. (2000) *The 2nd Language of Leadership*. Preface. N.J. Lawrence Erlbaum Associates, Mahwah, www.questia.com.

Handy, C. (1993) Trust and the virtual organisation. *Harvard Business Review*, May–June, 40–50.

Heron, J. (1990) *Helping the Client. A Creative Practical Guide*. Sage, London.

Horne, M. & Jones, D.S. (2001) *Leadership: The Challenge for All?* Chartered Management Institute, London.

Johnson, G. & Scholes, K. (2002) *Exploring Corporate Strategy; Text and Cases*, 6th edn. Prentice Hall, Hemel Hempstead.

Jumaa, M.O. (1997) *Strategic Clinical Team Learning Through Leadership*. Unpublished Research Project Report, part of an MA-WBLS (Strategic Nursing Leadership and Management), Middlesex University, London.

Jumaa, M.O. (2001) *Enhancing Individual Learning and Organisational Capability Through Learning Projects and Developmental Interventions*. Unpublished Research Project Report, part of a Doctor of Professional Studies (DProf), through work-based learning in strategic leadership and strategic learning in nursing and healthcare, Middlesex University, London.

Jumaa, M.O. & Alleyne, J. (2002) Strategic leadership in health care, in challenging times. In: *Strategic Issues in Health Care Management: Efficiency, Quality and Access in Health Care* (eds M. Tavakoli *et al.*) (2001). University of St. Andrews Press, Fife.

Kaplan, R.S. & Norton, D.P. (1996) *The Balanced Scorecard: Translating Strategy into Action*. Harvard Business School Press, Cambridge, Massachusetts.

Miles, R.E. & Snow, C.C. (1978) *Organizational Strategy, Structure, and Process*. McGraw-Hill, New York.

Peters, T.J. & Waterman, R.H. (1983) *In Search of Excellence*. Harper and Row, New York.

Further reading

Alleyne, J. (2002) *Making a Case for Group Clinical Supervision Through Management and Leadership Concepts*. Unpublished Research Project Report, part of a Doctor of Professional Studies (DProf), through work-based learning in clinical nursing leadership, Middlesex University, London.

Cook, M.J. (1999) Improving care requires leadership in nursing. *Nurse Education Today*, **19** (4), 306–312.

Department of Health (1998) *Making a Difference: The Nursing Contribution to Healthcare*. The Stationery Office, London.

Department of Health (2001) *Working Together – Learning Together*. The Stationery Office, London.

Department of Health (2002a) *Managing for Excellence in the NHS*. The Stationery Office, London.

Department of Health (2002b) *Shifting the Balance of Power*. The Stationery Office, London.

Goleman, D. (1995) *Emotional Intelligence: Why it Can Matter More Than IQ*. Bantam Books, New York.

Goleman, D. (1999) *Working with Emotional Intelligence*. Bloomsbury, London.

Goleman, D., Boyatzis, R. & McKee, A. (2002) *The New Leaders – Transforming the Art of Leadership into the Science of Results*. Little, Brown, London.

Handy, C. (1993) *Understanding Organisations*. Penguin, London.

Heron, J. (1989) *The Facilitator's Handbook*. Kogan Page, London.

Jumaa, M.O. & Alleyne, J. (2001) Learning, unlearning and relearning: facilitation in community nursing for delivering the new primary care agenda. In: *Organisation Behaviour and Organisation Studies in Healthcare: Reflections on the Future* (ed. L. Ashburner). Palgrave (Macmillan), Basingstoke.

4 Strategic Leadership for Healthcare Management

Mark Hodder and Stuart Marples

Whole-picture leadership

Strategic leadership is the ultimate unbounded problem, full of complexity and uncertainty, where cause and effect can be difficult, if not impossible, to see clearly. Compare this with medicine where tests lead to diagnosis, diagnosis informs treatment and treatment leads to an outcome. In strategic leadership, cause and effect are rarely so well defined. Rather the analogy of a chess game helps to give some understanding of the daily pressures. Imagine trying to define a winning strategy where your own pieces not only have their own agendas, ideas and views, but also the issues you seek to overcome. In this environment just getting your own pieces moving in the same direction is a challenge in itself. Comparison can be drawn with the challenges of managing any team that has star players. People with exceptional talent, whether footballers or consultants, must first be committed team members. No matter how talented, it is unlikely they will achieve even their own aims without the support of the team. Healthcare is a team game. The environment we are operating in is becoming more and more complex; not only are we trying to influence our own chessboard to a positive outcome as our target moves, but also we impact on related sectors such as social care and public wellbeing. Further adding to the complexities are the unrelenting rule changes with the impact of European and UK legislations, rapidly changing technology, demographics, expectations and the onset of globalisation. All these add extra pressures and change the territory daily. With the pieces, the board and the game rules all in motion, your reality is to try to win when even knowing how to score points is uncertain.

The ideas we want to explore in this chapter are how to create the environment in which strategic leadership works in reality, looking particularly at taking a balanced approach, and how the stakeholders must provide the check and balance for strategic solutions. The inclusion of diversity in all our thinking is now essential rather than desirable. Today's health service must mirror the society it operates within – 'one size fits all' solutions are no longer appropriate. Getting the chess pieces moving in the right direction or influencing staff to want to take strategic goals forward underpins this environment. While a strategy may be well founded, if the people we ask to implement this do not have the skills, knowledge and behaviours to turn the blueprints into reality the initiative will be doomed to failure before it leaves the boardroom. Setting a clear culture from day one and encouraging staff to adhere to this is the key. How much can we influence our people to provide continuous quality performance?

We want to explore this while looking at why we need a managerial code and how that in turn leads to the need for lifelong learning. To be successful, new thinking is required. Our current thinking can provide a foundation to work from, yet it is already out of date. Making those new neural connections work is what strategic leadership is all about – defining the future, being able to see what is important through the minefield of options and communicating this vision to others. Success also requires personal determination, motivation and the ability to engage others, along with luck. What, therefore, are we saying? Is strategic leadership impossible to define? In some ways it is. It is fluid and it constantly changes.

There are, however, a number of ways in which we can create the environment for success. The move towards transformational leadership (Bass 1994, developed by Alimo-Metcalfe 1998) and away from transactional management leads us to an idea we want readers to think about throughout this chapter. We believe that the majority of people are desperate for leadership; they need direction, purpose and goals, yet they would prefer not to feel controlled or manipulated. The growth in personal choice and diversity means that healthcare staff want freedom in how they achieve these goals. They want the objectives of their organisation to accord with their own personal beliefs. A strategic manager, therefore, must maintain the basic controls of transactional management but at the same time provide this inspiration. This is what we will define here.

Vision, goals and targets

Establishing a clear culture from the start and encouraging staff to adhere to this is the key. A vision will work best where it is challenging and desirable. Furthermore it is essential that it is not just empty dreaming but is backed up with a clear idea of what is to be achieved, by when, by who and with what – 'how' should remain the remit of the individual within the boundaries of the behavioural code. Staff will seek advice, develop and grow as they need to, but the 'monkey' of authority and responsibility remains firmly with them. As long as the efforts of individuals are heading towards the objectives, small deviations from the most direct course should be expected and allowed to flourish; after all, this is often how new thinking comes about. The skill, of course, is knowing when to allow staff to run and when to step in. This requires a balance for which there are no hard and fast rules, although we can offer some guidance. Metaphorically, give everyone a blank sheet of paper to begin with, regardless of what you already know or the 'baggage' they come with. Based on their performance with you, begin to allow them more deviation from the standard thinking, more opportunity to show you their true potential. As they see their most senior leaders value their efforts towards corporate goals and also the individualism they bring, they will achieve and go the extra mile to make that intangible difference a great performer has over a competent one. We believe this can only be achieved by knowing and valuing the individual. The best leaders at this level will also realise their ability to lead and the impact they have is like throwing pebbles into a pond. If you stick to a few well-chosen initiatives and reinforce these regularly the ripples through the system are the same and repeated, staff can learn the behaviour and work towards the goals. Evaluation of the impact of the initiative also remains at least a possibility. As soon as the leader starts to bombard the pond with initiatives the ripples quickly become lost in one another, and this is akin to the confusion staff feel. What was the message? What should they be doing next? The realistic ability to evaluate the effects is also lost or at least made more complex. To give people a chance, make your goals few and clear and celebrate successes when they are achieved. Start with a balanced approach.

Changes to the scenery of healthcare provision

The new structure of the NHS is based on local commissioning. Local organisations are working closely with local authorities and, while there are still national political imperatives, the main planning document will be through some form of locally negotiated health, social care and well-being strategy. The boards of these organisations will need to include health professionals, local authorities, patients and carer representatives. Whatever their composition their role will be to commission services that meet the needs of the local population, while also being a part of a cohesive national system. This is a complex task in itself. Chairs and board members must be subject to goal setting and appraisal against a required set of competencies, just as we expect this of other staff. The challenge is to develop all board members so that all voices are heard and all views represented; this will ensure that the diversity becomes part of mainstream activity. There are many barriers to overcoming the traditional medical model and the large acute hospital focus will not be the focus of the future. Here the local organisations will encounter many of the tests of strategic leadership. They will have to deal with the power base of the large hospitals, agreeing priorities and the inevitable disagreement of groups whose issues are not defined as a priority, and they will have to have the strength to stand by their decisions when challenged by the media and politicians. The members will need to trust each other and support decisions that are maybe not their first priority. These organisations have a chance to use the Coca Cola inspired slogan 'Think global, act local'[1] where

---

[1] R. Goizueta, former Chief Executive Officer of Coca Cola, is credited with establishing the 'Think global, act local' philosophy in 1996.

they are part of a national whole but also responsive to local needs. The onset of technology and globalisation has made this an unavoidable priority. The Freedom of Information Act 2000 (http://www.informationcommissioner. gov.uk) will make even more details available and every decision open to scrutiny. Patients will now be able to compare their healthcare with that provided by the hospital next door, or one on the other side of the world. Their expectations need to be matched by the perception of the service they receive. The NHS cannot ignore the fact that informed customers now exist everywhere.

Training for strategic leaders

These are great ideals, but how can this be made a reality? Leaders need to lead by example, identifying their own needs and undertaking development programmes including visioning, goal setting and commissioning work-shops. There are already many assessment tools that allow boards to assess their own development needs and identify the knowledge and skills required. Simulation exercises are an excellent way to practise how the board will operate for real; using trained facilitators to watch and report on the behaviours they see, advising in a positive way on how communication and interaction can be improved. Chairs need to be developed to set targets and appraise their chief executive. Hence the objectives of the board are linked inextricably to those of the operational staff. Through this development programme these leaders will become more experienced at how to set the vision for their community and develop staff to meet that vision.

The 'move the big dot' (NHS Modernisation Agency; Bevan 2003) initiative is a good example of this growing competence. Simulation is an essential part of development, the chance to be creative, to try ideas and to receive constructive feedback. Simulation has been used for centuries by the military to good effect and is used in many other sectors, but we question if we have really grasped this in the NHS. Through simulation and then practice, a board can learn first-hand how to deal with the pressures of politics and the media. One note of caution concerns the current leaning towards transformational leadership (Bass 1994), with charisma at the top of the list of effective behaviours for strategic leaders. This is another reason why checks and balances are required. Charisma is required if you expect anyone to listen to your ideas and engage with them. History is, however, full of examples where charismatic leaders absorbed in their own view have led organisations to disaster. Hitler must of course be the most famous; a genius when he led by local command, and yet he caused a disaster when he later meddled in every decision, still convinced only he could be right. Are you prepared to challenge your beliefs with as much vigour as you support them? Take the example of Walt Disney; he was reputed to be a master at taking the first, second and third person perspectives about all his ideas. At board meetings he would present his ideas with vision, passion and determination, outlining exactly what people would see, hear and feel when the proposal was in place. Then he would switch to the second perspective and challenge his view with equal zeal, probing every what, why and wherefore. Finally he would look at the third perspective as if a total outsider and ask whether this would make sense to him. We are fortunate that we do not have to take on all these roles as we have board members and colleagues to provide them, a topic we will explore in more detail when looking at how to create the right environment.

Diversity

Diversity – true understanding and valuing of differences – is now a critical success factor for all health providers. In the public sector we have set the foundation stones, with diversity training and awareness well established in most organisations. Now we need to bring the diversity agenda into the mainstream. Using traditional measures it could easily be believed that the NHS has no diversity issues as the percentages of staff from minority groups are well in excess of UK averages. However, the black and minority ethnic group is beginning to form a poor view of the NHS as both provider and employer (AWEMA 2003), especially of our ability to communicate effectively and respect cultural differences. The current generation has been popularly labelled as the 'want it alls' in terms of less working hours, good salaries, more free time and fair treatment at work. At the same time the workforce is becoming smaller, with more competition for the best people, whatever their background. Globalisation, the acceptance of popular culture and systems, makes it easy for staff to compare the best employers world-wide and healthcare skills are in demand everywhere – why are we the employer of choice? We want to explore how diversity can become reality and the measures that can be taken at the strategic level to make this a mainstream issue.

The first step must be to make diversity a clear objective for all. Chairs and chief executives, director level and senior staff must set the example. We must also be able to measure and evaluate the effectiveness of diversity initiatives through the Balanced Scorecard (Kaplan & Norton 1992), which provides a system that measures the true impact of diversity initiatives throughout the organisation. To be truly effective, diversity must be woven into the fabric of four perspectives (quadrants):

- *Innovation and learning* – staff must be inducted into a system that is fair and that values all cultures and our innovations must consider all groups. When we benchmark our systems it must be against the best in the world, where the processes as well as the outcome are the measures.
- *Management processes* – the way we communicate with staff and service users must improve. Services provided by NHS Direct rely on verbal and written communication to get their message across, and help to diagnose,

advise and reassure patients. Our style of communication must be culturally aware. People need help to face any fear they have about contacting
the service. They need to feel safe in the knowledge that they will be
understood and treated with empathy and respect. Equally our own staff
must know that they will be managed fairly and that their employment
questions can be answered effectively. The trade unions have managed
this in attracting minority groups into their fold, yet employers seem to
find the same understanding difficult to achieve. Listening and acceptance of another's view often leads to a shift in perspective.

- *Resources* – looking at diversity in a positive way we can seek to recruit the
  right staff across sections of the society they live in. To do this our
  recruitment and selection procedures need to improve, the materials
  need to be available to all interested groups and we need to understand
  cultural barriers to joining the service.
- *Stakeholders* – we have already outlined the role of boards in commissioning services, and diversity must remain high on the agenda. Although in
  many areas the percentage of the population in minority groups may be
  small, this is no excuse to ignore the issues. The key strategic issue is
  partnership working. The solution is bigger than one health board or
  geographical region.

By driving innovation and learning we give staff the development opportunities and knowledge to embrace diversity and difference from the start and
encourage lifelong learning throughout their careers. In turn this will allow
them to appreciate the need for processes that encompass all groups; resources
will be used effectively as we will be treating individuals, not conditions or
prejudices. With staff that understand what is required of them, the wants and
needs of stakeholders – articulated by the board – can be achieved.

Transparent behaviour through the management code

Codes are as old as mankind; they are written ways to live and work together.
In the age of globalisation we have seen strategic leadership efforts that
include restructuring (or downsizing and delayering) and process approaches to change, such as business process re-engineering, which seek to
maximise the use of technology. In the NHS over 75% of our costs are related
to staff and again we come back to the thought we posed at the outset – that
people are desperate to be led but do not appreciate control and instruction.
They want to admire and trust the people charged with their leadership and
to know how best they can serve that end. Attitudes and values are notoriously difficult to change; at work we only see the behaviour or the tip of the
iceberg. Every decision we make is filtered through our own experiences
from childhood onwards about what happened last time we did something.
This is the rest of the iceberg, invisible below the waterline and which people
may be unwilling to show in a work environment. Therefore, trying to change

behaviour at work is where we can make a difference. When people talk about changing culture surely they really mean changing behaviour – after all, culture can be simply defined as 'the way we do things around here'. A behavioural management code underpins people-based change.

The Institute of Healthcare Management (IHM) code (see www.ihm. org.uk/managecode/ihmcode.cfm) is an example of developing a clear behavioural code that could impact on anyone involved in healthcare management, not just the professional management group. To be successful we must know what the success looks like – it must be clearly defined. The aim of the IHM code is to give managers clear guidance to what effective behaviour looks and feels like. It enhances the psychological contract between managers and staff; it defines the ways in which people can expect to be treated. If this is to be effective, top-level managers must sign up to and live the code. Most importantly it is a way of engaging the middle managers who will implement the strategic initiatives. It says to them 'If I behave in this way I can expect to be supported by my senior managers' and senior managers must be prepared to stand by their middle managers through both good and bad times if they display these behaviours. The code is only effective if leaders are strong enough to keep doing the right things, even when difficulties occur. The code, like any good vision, is about letting people know what they should see, hear and feel if they are doing the right things. Unlike attempts to change core attitudes or values, it does not stifle creativity or infringe diversity. On the contrary, it encourages difference. The code defines an outcome and something to strive for. How this is achieved is up to the individual and his or her manager.

Creating the environment

Still the question remains of how we can create an environment in which our strategic intentions motivate staff to carry them out. How can we give the feeling that we are leading and not instructing and controlling? Just as we have seen with leadership theorists, who in the early 1900s believed leaders were born and not made, it would be easy to believe that effective strategic leadership is the domain of a few gifted leaders. Rather, we believe it is the ability to create the right environment. To use our earlier analogy, this is to set the chessboard in your favour by knowing the rules and using the individuality of your pieces, or staff, to the full by using:

- *Strengths* – in this modern world no one leader can expect to have all the attributes required, although often we like to believe in the charismatic leader with all the answers. The reality is more likely to be that these people have identified their strengths and have used them to maximum effect. They have, however, acknowledged that others have complementary skills and have built their teams on that basis. Identifying the right team to lead leads us on to our next point.

- *Knowledge management* – to identify the strengths of a team you need to identify the tacit knowledge that makes your organisation work. Collecting this knowledge can be difficult, but a comprehensive skills and knowledge database can help identify the right person to deal with a project or incident. Knowing the behaviours that work also allows you to develop the next level of management. Knowing everything about anything is rarely possible in today's world and will be impossible in tomorrow's. We know more than we ever have about cancer; how much more will we know in 1 or 10 years time? What body parts will be replaceable by 2020?

- *Engagement and empowerment* – staff engagement and empowerment can be notoriously fickle. The NHS relies on good will and that extra commitment from staff; staff we might otherwise consider ordinary doing extraordinary things. The role of strategic leadership is to capture this enthusiasm and then turn it to improvement. Age is not a factor here and learning to accept responsibility and the challenges it brings must be introduced early. Just as we see with young children, so young managers are full of enthusiasm and willing to push the boundaries. Developing them takes time but can also give breathing space to your initiative-weary executives. Enthusiasm is highly infectious and new approaches can break down previously impenetrable barriers. Some of the factors essential for making this happen are as follows:

  - Clear leadership from the board and senior executives who welcome challenge.
  - Effective communication channels throughout the organisation, using the 'jungle drums' to the benefit of the organisation.
  - Use of important cultural symbols.
  - A focus on behaviour as well as values, which leads to my next point.

Intervention and risk

Knowing when to step in and when to allow staff to run with their ideas is probably the most difficult skill. If staff are displaying the right behaviours and their efforts are clearly towards the corporate objectives, risk and failure are part of the equation. Edison tried over 1000 ways to invent the light bulb and eventually succeeded because he had a clear goal and the drive and determination to achieve. We need to encourage people to challenge their own view of failure and regard it more as outcome, subject to the proviso that the outcome has been achieved using the right behaviours and with the right intentions. It is, after all, just a small deviation from the intended path. Allowing a seemingly negative outcome to occur can have positive benefits, a better solution may be stumbled across and it allows those who have achieved the outcome to learn how to brush themselves off and try again. If strategic managers step in too early they soon become operational managers and those they seek to develop learn nothing. If we never allow anything to go wrong on the path to success, how will we build the leaders of the future who are capable and have the skills and knowledge to deal with challenge and change? One final thought on intervention is the need for senior management to introduce change and instability within their own teams from time to time. Knowing when staff need to move on and gain a new perspective is essential. It is all too easy to load the same few competent people and hang on to them instead of questioning how the same extraordinary performance can be achieved by those currently considered ordinary.

The recipe for success

We hope that in this short chapter we have described and discussed some of the complexities leaders face at the strategic level. Strategic leaders are not superhuman with a clearer picture of the world than anyone else. Rather they have created an environment and an understanding of their people that allows success to take hold. They are determined advocates of ideas they think will work, but they also accept challenge of those ideas. If dazzling charisma is part of their armoury the challenge gains even greater importance. Having people follow is addictive and so being prepared to be challenged is essential to ensuring that others are being led in the right direction – *balance is the agent that binds this recipe.* Diversity and reflecting the changing needs of society is now a mainstream issue if we expect to staff and serve our communities. Strategic leaders must make this a priority in their organisations, leading by example.

Just knowing what you want to achieve and having agreement for that direction of travel will not get anything done. A truly effective strategic leader will create the environment where success is possible by developing:

- Vision – creating a clear and compelling vision to harness this power, and give the ordinary people a chance to prove they are extraordinary.
- Strengths – building a team based on individual yet complementary strengths.
- Knowledge management – understanding, recording and developing the tacit knowledge that makes the organisation work.
- Engagement and empowerment – being sensitive to the motivation of staff and considering what their decisions really say about the organisation.
- Behaviours – concentrating on developing and rewarding effective behaviours in staff that allow diversity and creativity to flourish.
- Risk – knowing when to step in and when to let staff run, when to shuffle the pack to reinvigorate.
- Sense – using intuition and fact, listening and weighing the anecdotes against the hard statistics, balancing views and using this to inform judgement.

Then when unleashing the next initiative the strategic leader will be able to answer the following questions:

- Why?
- What and with what resources?
- When?
- Who?
- How?

If the right environment has been created it will ensure your staff know and believe they have support. Now with the chessboard set in your favour, with an understanding of the rules and the strengths of your pieces, success for the organisation must follow in reality as well as in theory.

References

Alimo-Metcalfe, B. (1998) The crucial importance of leadership. *Health Service Journal*, 12 October, 26–29.

Bass, B.M. (1994) *Improving Organisational Effectiveness Through Transformational Leadership*. Sage, Thousand Oaks, California.

Bevan, H. (2003) *Move the Big Dot Idea*. Unpublished report from the Director of Modernisation, NHS Modernisation Agency, Institute of Healthcare Managers National Conference, 2003.

All Wales Ethnic Minority Association (AWEMA) (2003) *Mainstreaming from the Margins*. Research report by Ethnos Research and Consultancy, London.

Kaplan, R.S. & Norton, D.P. (1992) The Balanced Scorecard – measures that drive performance. *Harvard Business Review*, January–February, 71–79.

Further reading

Kaplan, R.S. & Norton, D.P. (1996) *Translating Strategy Into Action – The Balanced Scorecard*. Harvard Business School Press, Boston.

Robins, A. (1992) *Awaken the Giant Within*. Pocket Books, pp 187–189, 401.

5 Healthcare Governance Through Effective Leadership

Rob McSherry, Alyson Wadding and Paddy Pearce

The challenges of leadership for healthcare governance

This chapter attempts to address what appears to have been unanswered in much of the contemporary literature on leadership and healthcare governance, i.e. to outline the importance of leadership for healthcare governance and how the principles of healthcare governance enhance effective leadership. To achieve effective healthcare governance a decentralised approach to leadership is needed at all levels of the National Health Service (NHS) – nationally, regionally and locally – so that healthcare professionals feel empowered to modernise. Leadership development must be linked to both personal and organisational aspirations where clearly defined measurable objectives impact on performance for modernisation and service improvement. This approach to leadership could support the objectives of healthcare governance inferred in the publication *Building the Assurance Framework* (DH 2003a), whereby the objectives of the organisation are transcended to directorates and departments. These in turn need to be cascaded to individual healthcare professionals via appraisal systems linked to personal development plans. Such an approach will ensure that an organisation is able to prioritise and enabled to identify organisational objectives systematically and turn them into meaningful objectives for individuals. However, this approach will not be successful without strong leadership at all levels of an organisation.

To demonstrate the complex relationship between leadership and healthcare governance, the chapter aims to:

- outline the drivers leading modernisation and service improvement
- define, compare and contrast healthcare governance and leadership in showing the integrated nature of these key concepts
- use case studies directed at a local level to apply a practical approach, illustrating the importance of leadership and healthcare governance at an organisational, team and individual level, and demonstrating how ineffective leadership is the key barrier to the success of both concepts.

Setting leadership in the context of modernisation: key drivers

The drive for effective leadership within healthcare governance is primarily due to increasing political, professional and societal factors influencing and demanding healthcare professionals to provide care based on best evidence.

The NHS Plan (DH 2000a) identified the need for leadership development for all staff as central to the modernisation of the health service. Since then, documents and guidelines have emerged to give more direction for leadership and management in practice. *Managing for Excellence in the NHS* (DH 2002a) makes clear the need for health service managers to have effective leadership skills, and the simultaneous launch of the NHS *Code of Conduct for Managers* (DH 2002b) supports this. Crisp (2002) makes clear the need to develop a culture that is creative, challenging and supportive, highlighting the importance of working in modern ways through teams and networks, and the need to lead change as well as manage it. To realise all of this requires a cultural change for the health service as a whole, and leadership and management development need to be available to support this process and to achieve decentralisation. The NHS Modernisation Agency and Leadership Centre have devised a model for leadership development to establish a discipline of healthcare improvement science. This includes the three overlapping elements of leadership, care delivery systems and improvement science, thus emphasising that effective leadership should lead to improved patient services, as identified in Chapter 1. Related to this, the *NHS Leadership Qualities Framework* (Leadership Centre for Health 2002) was developed and can be used as a framework for individual, team and organisational leadership development (Fig. 5.1).

The three clusters of qualities are personal qualities, setting the direction and delivering the service. It is claimed that the qualities are applicable to all levels of leaders, but the combination of key qualities and the level of practice may differ according to the demands of the post. The five personal qualities in particular are congruent with those of transformational leadership and the emotionally intelligent leader. A 360-degree diagnostic tool has been devised as part of this framework to support leadership development. It is important that diagnostic tools such as these are used as part of a developmental process and not just as an assessment exercise, so that staff are supported and facilitated in the development of meaningful action plans to develop their leadership capability. This is an investment in individuals, which should also provide organisational benefits.

The government and professions have begun the modernisation and reforming process through the introduction of several important policies such as *Making a Difference* (DH 1999) and *Meeting the Challenge* (DH 2000b). In both, the emphasis of reform is targeted towards specific professional disciplines such as nursing and the allied health professions. Whilst these documents identify ways of modernising the professions it is the NHS Plan (DH 2000a) that provides a framework approach to NHS planning and policy.

Fig 5.1 NHS Leadership Qualities Framework.

The uniqueness of the New Labour Government health policy is that three main themes seem to run continually through all of these documents; that is the *desire* for healthcare professionals to *lead* and *develop* high quality local services for patient. However, it could be questioned whether the 10-year plan for reform is overambitious because it requires adequate resources and financial backing which to date do not seem sufficient for supporting such radical change.

Just as the government is encouraging and (debatably) supporting the healthcare professions to modernise, the professional bodies themselves recognise this need and have already begun the process of change. For example, the Nursing and Midwifery Council (NMC) replaced the United Kingdom Central Council for Nursing, Midwifery and Health Visiting in 2002. The main driver for this was modernisation. The new NMC is attempting to become more streamline, innovative, cost effective and evidence based whilst remaining responsible for regulation, registration and dealing with misconduct. We would argue that the NMC, Health Professions Council (HPC) and the General Medical Council (GMC) core values resonate with those of ethical leaders in encouraging creativity, innovation and vision, together with openness, honesty and transparency.

Other influencing factors can be traced back to a combination of societal changes associated with rising public expectations and a lack of confidence in the NHS due to a perceived decline in the provision of quality services and standards of healthcare and its technology. The public and healthcare professionals alike have exacerbated these concerns through facilitating the media in reporting major clinical incidents and declines in the standards of services within the NHS (Smith 1998). The public's growing lack of confidence in the NHS could be attributed to the lack of financial investment, poor management or because of unsuccessful reform through government policy (Ham 1986). However, it would appear that recent clinical disasters have only served to shock and horrify the public into thinking that this is a common occurrence and that the overall standards and quality of service are poor throughout the UK (McSherry & Haddock 1999). The impact of the Citizen's and Patient's Charters is only just being seen as effective because the public and healthcare professionals are better informed, educated and more interested in health and policy related issues (McSherry & Pearce 2002). Consequently they are not prepared to accept sub-optimal standards of practice, resulting in higher numbers seeking satisfactory outcomes through the courts (Wilson & Tingle 1999).

To tackle the rising political and societal factors directing health and social care professionals to provide evidence-based care, it is fundamentally important to define the terms healthcare governance and leadership.

Defining the terms healthcare governance and leadership

Healthcare governance

Healthcare governance is used in preference to 'corporate' or 'clinical' governance because it is a concept encapsulating all of these terms. In order to understand the meaning and value of healthcare governance and its relevance to leadership development it is essential to know where and why the concept originated. 'Healthcare governance' was first mentioned by McSherry & Pearce (2002) in their quest to demystify the meaning of clinical governance. Essentially healthcare governance is an amalgamation of the principles of corporate and clinical governance, which is about the continuous pursuit of excellence in clinical and non-clinical practice(s) or service(s). However, what do we mean by corporate or clinical governance and why are these terms so important to healthcare governance?

Corporate governance was introduced into the NHS in the publication *Corporate Governance in the NHS, Code of Conduct, Code of Accountability* (DH 1994). The focus of the document was directed at NHS Trust Boards in ensuring and demonstrating that the conduct of the board was exemplary. The code of conduct for NHS boards is based on three principles: accountability, probity and openness (DH 1994, p. 2):

- Accountability – everything done by those who work in the NHS must be able to stand the test of parliamentary scrutiny, public judgements on propriety and professional codes of conduct.
- Probity – there should be an absolute standard of honesty in dealing with the assets of the NHS: integrity should be the hallmark of all personal conduct in decisions affecting patients, staff and suppliers, and in the use of information acquired in the course of NHS duties.
- Openness – there should be sufficient transparency about NHS activities to promote confidence between the NHS authority or trust and its staff, patients and the public.

Essentially the code of conduct and accountability is about ensuring that each member of staff knows who he or she is accountable to and for what practices. This should occur in an honest and open environment. Basically this means telling the truth when things go right and when things go wrong. However, how do you know what is good or not so good practice? Establishing the latter is about ensuring that internal systems are working well throughout the organisation in highlighting good practice and areas in need of improvement; for example, periodic auditing of staff expenses claims and vetting the tendering process where external contractors are bidding for NHS work in order to gain the best possible quote and ensure value for money. To demonstrate best value for money requires the development of *controls assurance*.

Controls assurance can be viewed as part of governance and is described as 'a holistic concept based on best governance practice'(NHS Executive 1999, p. 2), that is meeting the codes of conduct and accountability as previously mentioned. Controls assurance is concerned with methods that enable healthcare organisations to provide evidence that they are doing their 'reasonable best' to manage risk and to demonstrate to the public and all stakeholders that they are doing so.

In brief, corporate governance within health and social care is concerned with the non-clinical aspects of healthcare provision, that is ensuring financial and operational success by demonstrating value for money. The link with achieving total healthcare governance (Table 5.1) is combining non-clinical with clinical aspects of healthcare provision. Perhaps this is the primary influence on the government's introduction of 'clinical governance'.

The term *clinical governance* can be traced to the White Paper entitled the *New NHS: Modern and Dependable* (DH 1997). Clinical governance is described as

> a system, which is able to demonstrate, in both primary and secondary care, that systems are in place guaranteeing clinical quality improvements at all levels of healthcare provision. Healthcare organisations will be accountable for the quality of the services they provide. (McSherry & Haddock 1999, p. 113)

Clinical governance is an umbrella term for all the issues and concepts that clinicians know and foster, including standard setting, risk management,

Table 5.1 Features of healthcare governance.

Corporate governance	Clinical governance
• Finances • Non-clinical systems, i.e. catering, maintenance • Open and honest decision-making and action trails • Dealing with risks effectively and proactively	• Patient focused • Quality services • Developing systems and processes to measure clinical efficiency and effectiveness, i.e. clinical audit • Being accountable for your clinical practice • User/carer and public involvement in clinical decision-making

training, reflection and professional development. Clinical governance is about instilling confidence in both the public and healthcare professionals by providing them with a safe clinical environment in which to accommodate the challenges identified at the start of this chapter. In a simple way clinical governance is about the patients and carers receiving the right care at the right time from the right person in a safe environment. To ensure that clinical governance is successfully implemented throughout the NHS the key components contained within its definition need to be available and achievable throughout the organisation, as the following section briefly explains.

The key components of clinical governance

The definitions of clinical governance highlight common themes that describe what clinical governance is and are summarised in Fig. 5.2.

This figure simply depicts the key components that make up clinical governance, which in turn could be considered as the building blocks for its success for either an individual or a healthcare organisation. For clinical governance to operate effectively the identified components need to be evident and operational. Clinical quality and continuous improvements in healthcare delivery can only be achieved in a culture and environment that supports, values and develops its staff. Likewise individual healthcare professionals need to continuously develop their professional standards whilst operating within the roles and responsibilities aligned to their contract of employment and codes of professional practice. Clinical governance is about providing good clinical care in an environment that places patient and staff safety as a priority.

It is evident from the above description of our interpretations of the definitions of clinical governance that their primary focus is on clinical practices, which few would disagree with, although within these definitions there appear to be no explicit links to the non-clinical aspects of healthcare,

Fig 5.2 Key components of clinical governance. [Adapted from McSherry & Pearce (2002) with permission from Blackwell Science; sources DH (1998), McNeil (1998), RCN (2000), Roland & Baker (1999), Scally & Donaldson (1998) and Sealey (1999).]

which are equally important in proving clinical quality; for example the abolition of the internal market that placed finance and activity above clinical quality, leading to fragmentation of services and the ideology of command and control. To resolve these failings the government's philosophy is that of partnerships and collaboration, where innovation is nurtured and staff are valued. The latter is to be achieved by the application of six key principles (adapted from DH 1997, p. 1; Crown copyright is reproduced with the permission of the Controller of HMSO and the Queen's Printer for Scotland):

(1) To re-establish the NHS as a national service for all patients throughout the country, where patients will receive high quality care, regardless of age, gender and culture, if they are ill or injured.
(2) To establish national standards based upon best practices, which will be influenced and delivered locally by the healthcare professionals themselves, taking into account the needs of the local population.
(3) Collaborative working partnerships between hospital, community services and local authorities where the patient is the central focus.
(4) Ensuring that the services are delivering high quality care and providing value for money.
(5) Establishing an internal culture where clinical quality is guaranteed for all patients.
(6) Enhancing public confidence in the NHS.

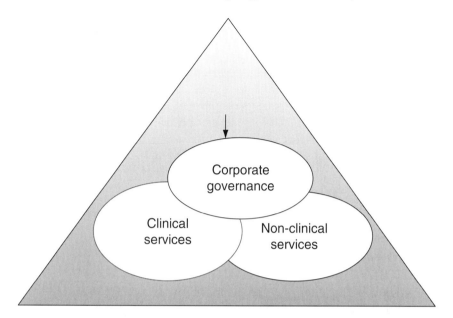

Fig 5.3 Healthcare governance in the NHS. [Adapted from McSherry & Pearce (2002) with permission from Blackwell Science.]

To ensure the unification of clinical and non-clinical services and the adoption of the six principles identified above healthcare governance comes into play as highlighted in the following section.

Corporate or clinical governance cannot be successfully implemented without the support of the clinical and non-clinical aspects of health and social care delivery. As most health and social care professionals are fully aware, healthcare provision and delivery is complex in nature. Successful healthcare delivery is dependent upon good teamwork, effective leadership and sound management in drawing together the non-clinical and clinical aspects of governance. Basically neither can work effectively without the other. The role of 'healthcare governance' is essentially about uniting the three elements of healthcare governance – corporate (management), clinical governance (clinical practice) and the non-clinical supporting services – into one. Basically none can work effectively without the other, as outlined in Fig. 5.3.

Having demonstrated what healthcare governance means it is essential to define the meaning of leadership and why transformational leadership is important for healthcare governance to become operational within health and social care practices.

The significance of transformational leadership within healthcare governance

McSherry & Pearce (2002) identified that ineffective leadership can be a barrier to achieving governance. This chapter argues that healthcare organisations can enhance success by taking an integrated approach to leadership development and governance in practice.

Many diverse views and theories of leadership currently exist, which can be confusing for leaders and professionals. Bennis (1994, p. 1) claims 'leadership is like beauty: it's hard to define, but you know it when you see it'. This chapter explores transformational leadership as a means of enhancing healthcare governance in practice and argues that the key elements of this leadership approach are fundamental to realising the modernisation of healthcare and are congruent with the aims and objectives of healthcare governance.

Burns (1978, p. 19) defines leadership as 'leaders inducing followers to act for certain goals that represent the values and the motivations – the wants and needs, the aspirations and expectations – of both leaders and followers'. Burns therefore takes a moral approach to leadership, where leaders and followers work together to achieve common aims. He refers to this type of leadership as transforming; 'such leadership occurs when one or more persons engage with the other in such a way that leaders and followers raise one another to higher levels of motivation and morality' (p. 20). In constantly changing and competitive environments (such as the current healthcare climate) transformational leadership should be fostered at all levels of the organisation (Bass 1990). Barker (1994) claims that transformational leadership involves the purpose of both the leader and follower becoming fused, creating unity and a collective purpose, all of which are necessary to realise service improvement.

Demonstrating the complementary and integrated nature of healthcare governance and leadership

It is evident from the arguments and debates so far that there is a limitation in the literature demonstrating the complementary and integrated nature of healthcare governance and leadership. This section aims to provide some preliminary work to address the latter. In Table 3.2 we outline the key components of governance and leadership, followed by an explanation of the findings under the headings of governance.

Achieving excellence

On examination of the concepts (Table 5.2) of healthcare governance and contemporary perspectives of leadership, shared elements immediately become apparent. A key element of governance is concerned with delivering the quality agenda and the pursuit of excellence. Leadership has been identified as central to the modernisation of the NHS. In order to transform the health service, a new kind of leadership is required, with the need for effective leadership at all levels of the organisation:

Table 5.2 Comparing and contrasting governance and leadership.

Governance	Leadership
Achieving excellence	• Leadership as fundamental to modernisation and service improvement • Development of leadership at all levels • The NHS Leadership Qualities Framework (LQF) sets a standard for outstanding leadership • Leadership competencies identified in the Knowledge and Skills Framework (DH 2003a)
Developing a transparent and open culture where: staff are supported, valued and developed; risk-taking is enabled; and learning from mistakes occurs	• Key elements of transformational leadership • Empowerment and growth and development • Personal qualities of the LQF • Emotional intelligence
Safety and accountability	• Empowerment and establishing boundaries • Patient/service user focused approach to leadership in practice • Quality of holding to account identified in LQF
Professional, personal and clinical outcomes (efficiency and effectiveness)	• Drive for improvement • Resilience and perseverance • Leadership within a framework of controls • Results orientated leadership

> Anyone working in the NHS, regardless of their position, grade, qualification or place of work, may be a leader or agent of change and improvement. (DH 2001)

The notion that leadership may be exercised at all levels of the organisation, offering opportunities that enable all practitioners to maximise their leadership potential, is supported in strategic health and social policy documents such as *The NHS Plan* (DH 2000a), *Making a Difference* (DH 1999) and *Meeting the Challenge* (DH 2000b). These documents also support the need for visionary leadership and the development of leaders who are self-aware, can empower others and appreciate a multi-agency approach to lead strategic change and improve service to patients/service users. This has been recently endorsed by the publication of the NHS *Leadership Qualities Framework* (Leadership Centre for Health 2002), which describes the key characteristics, attitudes and behaviours to which leaders in the NHS should aspire. This provides a clear structure for the design and delivery of leadership development programmes. The framework sets a standard for outstanding leadership in the NHS and can be used to support individual, team and organisational leadership development. Three elements or clusters of skills are identified: personal qualities; setting the direction; and delivering the service. The research from which the framework was devised demonstrated that the same leadership qualities were equally applicable across different levels of leaders; it is the level of skill that may differ (Hay Group 2003).

This perspective of leadership is one of enabling all professionals to maximise their contribution to service delivery, taking a patient/service user focus to service development. Decentralisation is required to release the full potential of individuals and teams. Covey (1992a) supports the concept of interdependent practice, where the paradigm of 'we' is always stronger than that of 'I' and achieves greater success. However, to work interdependently is a choice only independent people can make, again calling for effective leadership to support the growth and development of all team members. As Outhwaite (2003) highlights, an essential skill of a leader of an interdisciplinary team is to understand the history, values and goals of each professional in order to gain the commitment of team members. Each professional group will have expert contributions to make towards the pursuit of quality and excellence in the delivery of services. Effective leadership is required to provide direction and support for team members to collaborate effectively and to empower them to make service improvements.

Goleman *et al.* (2002) support the notion of the emotionally intelligent leader as crucial to effective leadership in modern organisations. Of various leadership styles they claim that visionary leadership is the most effective, an inspirational leader who can provide clear direction. They argue that leaders need to create resonance, 'a reservoir of positivity that frees the best in people'. When leaders genuinely believe in the vision they are able to guide others towards it. Olivier (2001, p. 19) defines vision as 'a desired future; something that can make a positive difference, does not yet exist, but is not impossible. When shared it helps to unify others around a goal and motivate them.'

Developing the right culture

An important element of this is for the leader to provide the right environment; that is an open and transparent culture. According to Goleman *et al.* (2002) transparency allows integrity, which is identified as one of five personal qualities within the first element of the NHS Leadership Qualities Framework:

- Self-belief – confidence not arrogance.
- Self-awareness – understanding own emotions and effect of behaviour on others.

- Self-management – manages own emotions in complex and demanding situations.
- Drive for improvement – a deep motivation to make a real difference.
- Personal integrity – a strongly held sense of commitment to openness, honesty, inclusiveness and high standards in undertaking the leadership role.

These qualities are supported by Goleman (1999) as integral to emotional intelligence. Writers such as Covey (1992a) and Kouzes & Posner (1995) emphasise the importance of trust and credibility. When these are present people are more likely to choose to follow their leader, and thus the leader is able to use legitimate power, leading to proactive and sustained influence (Covey 1992b). Leaders who possess these personal qualities are better able to provide this kind of open culture and an environment where staff feel valued and supported and able to take risks. As Kouzes and Posner (1995) identified, no trust leads to no risks, resulting in no change. To empower others, leaders must learn to let go of control. This requires a firm belief in the principle of empowerment and also a high degree of self-confidence.

Addressing safety and accountability

Healthcare governance is also concerned with safety and accountability. One problem with transformational leadership is the misconception that it is a 'soft' approach, where leaders want to be nice to everyone and strive for harmony. In fact transformational leaders do deal with issues as they empower within boundaries. This makes the difference between staff feeling empowered or enabled and not abandoned. This requires also that leaders know their team members and that they listen effectively. Transformational leaders have a high degree of self-knowledge, clear values and principles and are able to articulate their vision. These qualities are essential to provide direction and to set boundaries, making it easier to confront and deal with issues when they do arise. The Leadership Qualities Framework identifies the skill of holding self and others to account for delivering a high level of service (Leadership Centre for Health 2002). Leaders who operate at the highest level of this quality promote a high performance culture.

In the document *Governing the NHS* (DH 2003b), governance is identified as an essential prerequisite for all modernisation effort. With good governance arrangements in place clinical teams can be enabled to learn from failure as well as success, within agreed boundaries, that is, leadership within a framework of controls.

Leadership with a purpose: being results orientated

Whilst the processes of leadership are extremely important it should be remembered that effective leaders lead with a sense of purpose; they are results orientated. As discussed earlier, transformational leaders are vision driven. However, to be truly effective, the leader's vision must become a shared vision if it is to be turned into action. Landsberg (2000) suggests that leadership is the simple equation of vision × inspiration × momentum. The skill of inspiring others moves people to action, but a key quality or skill for the leader in health and social care is to be able to sustain the momentum of individuals and teams so that results can be achieved through energy and problem-solving skills. A key task for the healthcare leader is to align vision and mission, to keep reminding people of the greater vision and what can be when lack of motivation or disillusionment threatens. In the Hay Group research (2003), two features distinguished health service leaders from private sector leaders. These were the drive for improvement, wanting to make a difference, and the capacity for resilience, the ability to deal with setbacks. Part of the challenge for health and social care leaders is the complexity of the environments they work in and the situations they are faced with, such as an increasing number of stakeholders, competing priorities, achieving targets and transforming established ways of working.

Developing an integrated approach

It is evident that by taking an integrated approach to viewing healthcare governance and leadership, the potential for providing a culture in which excellence will flourish is realisable (Fig. 5.4). This figure summarises the key elements of the Leadership Qualities Framework and healthcare governance. The five personal qualities are essential to the development of an open culture. The qualities related to setting the direction are fundamental to a drive for improvement across the organisation, and the qualities related to delivering the service enable effective leaders to work with and empower others in order to achieve results.

Making it happen

To develop leaders with the qualities and skills discussed above, organisations must have a strategic and coherent approach to leadership development in order to realise the benefits for individuals and for the service. The NHS Leadership Qualities Framework provides a common structure to be used in all areas to provide a consistent approach and to make clear the desired standard of leadership. Leadership development needs to occur at all levels and be multiprofessional. Setting standards for leadership and providing the structures necessary to support development should be seen as essential elements of healthcare governance. To expect individuals, teams and organisations to deliver a quality service within a governance framework without recognising the fundamental nature of effective leadership will limit success.

In the authors' area, a collaborative partnership model has been developed to promote this approach across the region. A group comprising educationalists

Excellence and improved patient outcomes/service

Leadership qualities	Governance
Personal	Open culture
Setting the direction	Drive for improvement
Delivering the service	Results orientation

Fig 5.4 Harmonising the key qualities of healthcare governance and leadership.

and leaders and managers from service has used this framework to develop multiprofessional leadership development programmes at all academic levels, as demonstrated in the two cases studies.

Case study 5.1 Developing leaders who can meet the challenge of modernisation.

One such programme offers postgraduate study of leadership development contextualised within the health and social care modernisation and improvement agenda. The three modules that make up the postgraduate certificate programme are designed around the three elements of the national framework: personal qualities, setting the direction and delivering the service.

The programme enables professionals to examine their leadership roles and identify the key leadership qualities that are crucial to their role. This is then used as a basis for the 360-degree diagnostic tool feedback with facilitation of the development of personal action plans to develop leadership capability. Students also study health and social

Continued

Case study 5.1 *Continued*

care policy to develop skills of political astuteness and intellectual flexibility in order to take a proactive approach to service improvement. The final module draws this learning together using action learning and workplace learning to support leadership of real service improvement projects, approved by supporting managers. In this way the programme gives both personal and organisational benefits and contributes to the governance agenda. Service colleagues with expertise of leadership in healthcare practice contribute to the delivery of the programme, thus ensuring that the content is contemporary and grounded in the realities of current practice. This also provides a consistency of approaches between education and service developments so that any in-house programmes and developmental opportunities are complementary. Students will present their projects at a conference at the end of the programme in order to share success and disseminate their work.

Case study 5.2   Developing role-specific leadership competencies.

Accreditation of in-house programmes is also provided where leadership development for specific groups is required. Once again this promotes collaborative working and a consistency of approach. Such an organisational programme is currently being developed to integrate the Leadership Qualities Framework and the Knowledge and Skills Framework (DH 2003c) for a ward manager's programme. This meets the objectives of healthcare governance by using these frameworks to clearly identify the required leadership competencies for the post and importantly devising a developmental programme around these to enable staff to fulfil their potential as clinical leaders. This kind of programme acknowledges the important contribution of clinical leaders, and organisations prepared to value and invest in their staff in this way will reap long-term benefits.

Summary of making it happen

It is important that these programmes are contextualised within the wider organisational objectives and organisational support needs to be made available. This requires partnership, working at a strategic level and adopting a whole systems approach, as supported by Scally & Donaldson (1998).

Conclusions

Patient, public and professional demands are driving the need for efficient and effective healthcare which is of the highest quality. Leadership has been

Box 5.1 Features of leadership for healthcare govenance.

- A combination of societal, political and professional drivers has led to the introduction of healthcare governance and leadership development.
- Healthcare governance and leadership development requires an integrated approach.
- Transformational leadership is the most appropriate style and should be fostered across the healthcare organisation.
- The NHS Leadership and Qualities Framework provides a clear structure for a consistent approach to leadership development within and across organisations.

identified as fundamental to transforming the health service. Transformational leaders are essential in fostering the right culture and in empowering all professionals to maximise their full potential in the delivery of their services. Leadership development is an integral component of healthcare governance, which ultimately provides the public with an assurance that healthcare is of the best standard(s). To enhance the quality of healthcare, organisations must take a strategic approach to integrating leadership within healthcare governance across the whole organisation. It will be difficult to have healthcare governance without effective leadership and leadership development can be enhanced through having effective governance frameworks in place, thus highlighting the interconnectedness of these two essential concepts. Box 5.1 highlights the features of leadership for healthcare governance.

References

Barker, A.M. (1994) An emerging paradigm: transformational leadership. In: *Contemporary Leadership Behaviour: Selected Readings*, (eds E.C. Hein & M.J. Nicholson), 4th edn. JB Lippincott, Philadelphia.

Bass, B.M. (1990) From transactional to transformational leadership. Learning to share the vision. *Organisational Dynamics*, **18** (3), 10–31.

Bennis, W. (1994) *On Becoming a Leader*. Perseus Books, Cambridge.

Burns, J.M. (1978) *Leadership*. Harper and Row, New York.

Covey, S. (1992a) *The 7 Habits of Highly Effective People*. Simon and Schuster, London.

Covey, S. (1992b) *Principle-Centred Leadership*. Simon and Schuster, London.

Crisp, N. (2002) *Managing for Excellence in the NHS*. National Health Service Executive, London.

Department of Health (1994) *Corporate Governance in the NHS, Code of Conduct, Code of Accountability*. The Stationery Office, London.

Department of Health (1997) *The New NHS: Modern and Dependable*. The Stationery Office, London. http://www.archive.officaldocuments.co.uk/document/doh/newnhs/wpaper1.htm.

Department of Health (1998) *First Class Service, Quality in the New NHS*. The Stationery Office, London.

Department of Health (1999) *Making a Difference. Strengthening the Nursing, Midwifery and Health Visiting Contribution to Health and Healthcare*. HMSO, London.

Department of Health (2000a) *The NHS Plan: A Plan for Investment, a Plan for Reform*. DoH, London.

Department of Health (2000b) *Meeting the Challenge: A Strategy for the Allied Health Professionals*. HMSO, London.

Department of Health (2001) *Working Together–Learning Together, A Framework for Lifelong Learning in the NHS*. DoH, London.

Department of Health (2002a) *Managing for Excellence in the NHS*. DoH, London.

Department of Health (2002b) *Code of Conduct for NHS Managers*. DoH, London.

Department of Health (2003a) *Building the Assurance Framework: A Practical Guide for NHS Boards*. DoH, London.

Department of Health (2003b) *Governing the NHS*. DoH, London.

Department of Health (2003c) *The NHS Knowledge and Skills Framework (NHS KSF) and Developmental Review Guidance*, working draft. DoH, London.

Goleman, D. (1999) *Working with Emotional Intelligence*. Bloomsbury, London.

Goleman, D., Boyatzis, R. & McKee, A. (2002) *The New Leaders. Transforming the Art of Leadership into the Science of Results*. Little, Brown, London.

Ham, C. (1986) *Health Policy in Britain*. Macmillan, London.

Hay Group (2003) *NHS Leadership Qualities Diagnostic. EIS Facilitator Training Manual*. NHS Leadership Centre, London.

Kouzes, J.M. & Posner, B.Z. (1995) *The Leadership Challenge*. Jossey-Bass, San Francisco.

Landsberg, M. (2000) *The Tools of Leadership*. Harper Collins, London.

Leadership Centre for Health (2002) *NHS Leadership Qualities Framework*. Modernisation Agency, London.

McNeil, J. (1998) Clinical governance: the whys, whats, and hows for theatre practitioners . *British Journal of Theatre Nursing*, **5** (5), 209–216.

McSherry, R. & Haddock, J. (1999) Evidence based health care: its place within clinical governance. *British Journal of Nursing*, **8** (2), 113–117.

McSherry, R. & Pearce, P. (2002) *Clinical Governance. A Guide to Implementation for Health Care Professionals*. Blackwell Science, Oxford.

National Health Service Executive (1999) *Health Service Circular 1999/123. Governance in the New NHS: Controls Assurance Statements 1999/200: Risk Management and Organisational Control*. DoH, London.

Olivier, R. (2001) *Inspirational Leadership*. Spiro Press, London.

Outhwaite, S. (2003) The importance of leadership in the development of an integrated team. *Nursing Management*, **11** (6), 371–376.

Roland, M. & Baker, R. (1999) *Clinical Governance Practical Guide for Primary Care Teams*. The National Primary Care Research and Development Centre, University of Manchester and University of Leicester.

Royal College of Nursing (2000) *Clinical Governance: How Nurses Can Get Involved*. Royal College of Nursing, London.

Scally, G. & Donaldson, L.J. (1998) Clinical governance and the drive for quality improvement in the new NHS in England. *British Medical Journal*, 4 July, 317.

Sealey, C. (1999) Clinical governance: an information guide for occupational therapists. *British Journal of Occupational Therapy*, **62**, 6.

Smith, R. (1998) All changed, changed utterly: British medicine will be transformed by the Bristol case. *British Medical Journal*, **316**, 1971–1981.

Wilson, J. & Tingle, J. (eds) (1999) *Clinical Risk Modification: A Route to Clinical Governance*. Butterworth Heinemann, Oxford.

Further reading

Bennis, W. (1994) *On Becoming a Leader*. Perseus Books, Cambridge.

Covey, S. (1992) *The 7 Habits of Highly Effective People*. Simon and Schuster, London.

Goleman, D., Boyatzis, R. & McKee, A. (2002) *The New Leaders. Transforming the Art of Leadership into the Science of Results*. Little, Brown, London.

McSherry, R. & Pearce, P. (2002) *Clinical Governance: A Guide To Implementation For Healthcare Professionals*. Blackwell Science, Oxford.

Olivier, R. (2002) *Inspirational Leadership*. Spiro Press, London.

Useful websites

Commission for Health Improvement: *www.chi.gov.uk/eng/index.shtml*.

Department of Health: *www.doh.gov.uk*.

Leadership Qualities Framework: *www.nhsleadershipqualities.nhs.uk*.

Modernisation Agency: *www.modernnhs.nhs.uk*.

Nursing Midwifery Council: *www.nmc-uk.org*.

Section Two
Using the CLINLAP/LEADLAP Model for
Effective Healthcare Leadership

6 The CLINLAP Model – A Model for Nursing Management and Leadership Development

Mansour Jumaa

Introduction

There is evidence that effective leaders use a variety of distinct leadership styles, and that people perform well if leaders motivate them, create a sense of significance, a sense of community and a sense of excitement (Goffee & Jones 2000). We also know that an effective leader needs to be: a stakeholder manager; a strategic planner; a craftsperson; a strategy 'fixer'; a reflective 'leader'; a strategy 'fitter'; and a provider of continuous quality service (Jumaa 2001).

This chapter draws on 10 years' experience of developing health and social care managers to implement change and cope with uncertainties and on the author's leadership development experience as an accredited facilitator of group, personal and organisational development since 1988.

A significant influence on this chapter were the lessons learnt in the course of a doctorate in strategic leadership and strategic learning. One of the research and development methods used was in-depth executive coaching and developmental approaches, using pre-arranged individual coaching sessions over 2 years. The participants were: a principal lecturer at a British university; a district nurse team leader from one of the largest primary healthcare community National Health Service (NHS) organisations; and a ward nurse manager from a London teaching hospital. Coaching is presented in this chapter as a developmental disciplined activity, and with effective facilitation skills, the arrival at the participant's destination is greatly enhanced and assured.

A multiperspective modelling approach to leadership development in nursing and healthcare

This chapter introduces the Clinical Nursing Leadership Learning and Action Process model (the CLINLAP model), the name of the model when used for clinical nursing and midwifery. In a generic perspective the term Leadership Learning and Action Process model[1] (the LEADLAP model) (Jumaa & Alleyne 2002) is used. The CLINLAP model is a *learning* and *leading* nursing model for the workplace; a model that engages and encourages nursing systems to continue 'marching' within turbulent environments. This chapter argues the case for why nurses, midwives and others need this strategic nursing management performance implementation model for effective workplace activities. It indicates the extent to which the application of the CLINLAP model represents an example of good quality research and development for nurses, midwives and others in the healthcare industry and in the workplace (Ferlie *et al.* 2001).

The proposed approach has substantive implications for the study of leadership. If leadership is a process of *living as learning*, a process of sensemaking in a community of practice, as proposed in Chapter 2, then we must focus our attention on these communities – the team of individuals working towards the same purpose within hospitals, community care and in patients' homes. It is imperative that we do not focus just on the individual leaders, but pay attention to the relationships between leaders, the team and the broader community that they serve. Leaders, therefore, through the LEADLAP model become the pathway travelled to enter the world of the community of practice and the external broader communities that sustain and keep them going.

The shift from traditional NHS to the new NHS heralded by the NHS strategy – *The NHS Plan* (DH 2000a) is probably more fundamental than most nurses suspect. The new NHS requires radical transformation of working practices. It requires a sharing and a decentralisation of power and authority from the Strategic Health Authorities, NHS Trust/Primary Care Trusts and other similar institutions at the top, to the healthcare assistant at the bottom. There is every indication that we should not so much focus upon the development of *human resources* but shift our attention to that of *resourceful humans*. Resourceful people do not thrive in permanently bureaucratic organisations. Resourceful humans take power to act within the law on their own initiative for the benefit of the organisation, their profession and themselves.

This chapter provides a full exposition of the model used for strategic nursing management performance in management and leadership activities. It presents:

- the model's main assumptions
- the five strategic clinical questions used for its implementation

---

[1] For the rest of this chapter, the term the CLINLAP Model will be used. The LEADLAP Model will be used if this is necessary (Jumaa & Alleyne 2002).

- a diagram of the CLINLAP model and how it was developed
- the rationale for using this approach and a mini-case of its application
- its advantages and disadvantages
- the environment conducive for the use of the CLINLAP model.

The flexibility and versatility of the CLINLAP/LEADLAP model is demonstrated through its various applications in different contexts as shown in Chapters 7 through to Chapter 10. Chapter 7 presents an example of a detailed account of its application to a policy change within a clinical context. The result of the study featured in Chapter 8 sought to evaluate the application of the CLINLAP model as the major intervention for the facilitation of group clinical supervision for a doctorate in Clinical Leadership. Chapter 9 presents the results of a post-doctoral study[2] that explored the leadership successes of the '*Finnish way*' in evidence-based practice by General Practitioners. It illustrates, using the LEADLAP model for analysis, how the problem of tackling healthcare delivery to a diverse, both geographically and culturally, population was implemented successfully. Chapter 9 provides a real-life example of how effective leadership strategies can be adopted for large-scale changes in the fundamental ways that healthcare use information to inform their practice. Chapter 10 discusses how this model has been used to assist in the development of and the enhancement of emotional competence and capability in the workplace.

The CLINLAP model's assumptions

The CLINLAP model's original three assumptions are that:

(1) Health and social care staff need to believe in strategic (whole-picture) workplace learning for continuous quality improvement.
(2) The achievement of satisfaction for all stakeholders and practitioners involved in the processes of care, recipients and providers is paramount.
(3) Satisfaction is only possible through collaborative working amongst all health and social care practitioners, including patients, clients and users (Jumaa 2001).

However, according to Alleyne (2002) these assumptions do not address, comprehensively, the major cultural changes which are a central feature of the NHS Plan (DH 2000) and for the development of effective clinical leadership. She added the following assumption in relation to her studies with District Nurses (modified here for application to all practitioners):

- Rebalancing the power relationships within the workplace is necessary for the development of clinical, managerial and leadership competencies and capabilities.

---

[2] This post-doctoral travel study was possible through a Florence Nightingale Foundation Scholarship, awarded to Dr. Jumaa sponsored by the St Mary's Hospital League of Nurses, London.

It is these types of internal and external situations that are the driving forces creating demanding and increasing pressures on the workplace. They are the main reasons why an approach like the CLINLAP model is necessary for effective and continuous quality performance in the workplace[3].

How the CLINLAP model was developed

The CLINLAP model is a product of an Action Science Research Project over a period of 15 months. A progressive and forward-looking healthcare organisation initially commissioned Middlesex University in 1995 to provide management and leadership development activities for 46 District Nurse Team Leaders (DNTLs) (District Nurses may be called *Public Health Nurse* or similar names in other countries). It was later agreed that this commission could be used as a research project. The main purpose of the project was 'to discover what attitudes, skills, and knowledge are required for the DNTLs to perform their roles effectively, and to begin the development of these characteristics in these clinical team leaders'. A summary of the project is provided in Box 6.1.

Box 6.1 Summary of the original research for development of the CLIN-LAP model (Jumaa 1997).

The purpose of the project
- to discover what attitudes, skills and knowledge are required for 46 District Nurse Team Leaders (DNTLs) to perform their roles effectively, and
- to begin to develop these characteristics.

Theoretical framework
- Grundy's (1994) software for strategic learning was used to facilitate the DNTLs to begin to improve their clinical leadership skills, application and testing of strategic and creative management theories.

Methodology
- A 15-month Action Research Project.
- A multimethod responsive methodology, through triangulation, was used as follows:
  - questionnaire (pre- and post-workshops and focus groups)
  - open-ended interviews
  - one-to-one sessions

Continued

---

[3] More general information about the CLINLAP model and its application is available in Alleyne & Zack-Williams (2001), Jumaa & Alleyne (2000, 2001, 2002), and Jumaa *et al.* (2000a, 2000b).

Box 6.1   *Continued*

> – work-based periodic clinical assignments for praxis
> – workshops and focus groups
> – action learning groups
> – clinical service manager interviews
> – work book
> - The core of the investigation was a series of 2+1+1+1 day work-shops and focus groups, spread over the research duration.
>
> **Findings**
> The project found
> - that the main problems for the clinical team leaders revolved generally around clinical goals, roles, processes and relationships, and
> - that generally these problems could be resolved through specific goals, explicit roles, clear processes and open relationships.
>
> **Discussions**
> - The CLINLAP model, used effectively, was shown to enhance the ability to link theory with clinical practice and promote work-based learning.
>
> **Future activities**
> - Further research using the CLINLAP model is recommended to explore clinical leadership development patterns for 'generalisation' purposes.

The research (Jumaa 1997) that generated the model (Fig. 6.1) revealed that all of the key and significant problems within health and social care teams revolve around the following:

- problems with goals
- problems with roles
- problems with processes
- problems with relationships

This is confirmation of Moxon's (1993) work on how to manage teams and the 'hierarchy of team issues'. Both these aspects contributed significantly to this work-based research. The research revealed that these problems could generally be resolved through ensuring that health and social care education, research, practice and clinical environments have:

- specific and agreed goals
- explicit roles
- clear processes and
- open relationships.

A multimethod responsive triangulation methodology was used. This included pre-project diagnostic questionnaires, post-project evaluation

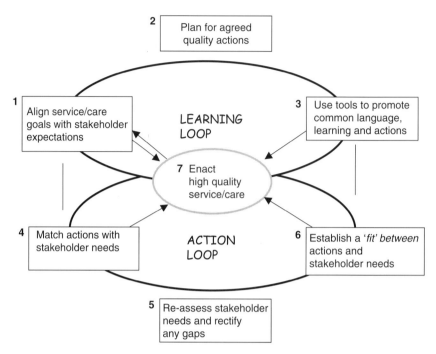

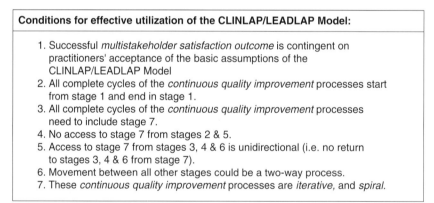

LEADLAP: Leadership Learning and Action Process (generic use)
CLINLAP: Clinical Nursing Leadership Learning and Action Process (clinical use)

Conditions for effective utilization of the CLINLAP/LEADLAP Model:

1. Successful *multistakeholder satisfaction outcome* is contingent on practitioners' acceptance of the basic assumptions of the CLINLAP/LEADLAP Model
2. All complete cycles of the *continuous quality improvement* processes start from stage 1 and end in stage 1.
3. All complete cycles of the *continuous quality improvement* processes need to include stage 7.
4. No access to stage 7 from stages 2 & 5.
5. Access to stage 7 from stages 3, 4 & 6 is unidirectional (i.e. no return to stages 3, 4 & 6 from stage 7).
6. Movement between all other stages could be a two-way process.
7. These *continuous quality improvement* processes are *iterative*, and *spiral*.

Fig 6.1 The CLINLAP/LEADLAP model (Jumaa 2001).

questionnaires, data, investigations, theory and methodological triangulation, as well as open-ended interviews with the clinical team leaders' line managers. The core of the investigation was a series of 2+1+1+1 day workshops and focus groups, spread over 15 months. This approach was appropriate, given that the Primary Health Care environment corresponds to Schon's (1983) concept of the *'situation'*, which he described as complex, full of uncertainty, instability, riddled with value-conflicts, yet one of uniqueness.

Why strategic leadership now?

In the book *Organisation Behaviour and Organisation Studies in Health Care: Reflections on the Future* (Ashburner 2001), the chapter *Learning, Unlearning and Relearning: Facilitation in Community Nursing for Delivering the New Primary Care Agenda* provides a detailed account of how and why CLINLAP was developed. The chapter in Jumaa and Alleyne's (2002) book also contains details about the history of the development of the model. Furthermore, in the NHS, radical changes were introduced which led to fundamental shifts in the delivery of healthcare. How will health and social care in the UK be delivered as we move beyond the beginning of the twenty-first century? How and where will patients receive their care; and what technological, organisational and demographic changes will influence and mould early twenty-first century health and social care practice? Clearly the future is uncertain, but it is already possible to see that the implications for effective healthcare management and leadership are potentially wide-ranging, uncertain and very complex.

What is clear, however, is that the government wants the many healthcare stakeholders – patients, clients and users; nurses; doctors; managers; pharmacists; radiographers; occupational therapists; etc. – within the NHS to work together in the delivery of efficient and effective healthcare (DH 1999b, 2000a, 2000b, 2001). The Labour Government has made many public announcements since coming into office in May 1997. Such a commitment was reaffirmed by the former Secretary of State for Health, Alan Milburn, in his Modernisation Agency launch speech in 2001. Many of these are a positive recognition of the role of the professions and healthcare managers, and particularly nurses, to 'really' manage the organisation and the delivery of care more efficiently and effectively.

The service delivery, organisational and management role of the new NHS requires that professionals and managers are explicitly and implicitly practising within the Clinical Governance Quality Performance Framework (DH 1998). Modified as it may be, this framework is the backbone on which the clinical governance and modernisation activities are based. There are three key aspects to it: *setting quality standards*, *delivering quality standards* and *monitoring quality standards*. In each aspect, the activities start with having *clear national standards of service* from the National Institute for Clinical Excellence (NICE) and the National Service Frameworks (NSFs). The standards are expected and are being implemented with a focus on *patient and public involvement* in the care process in an environment of professional self-regulation, clinical governance, and lifelong learning, with the deliberate intention that the service will lead to *dependable local delivery*. The former Commission for Health Improvement (CHI), now CHAI (the Commission for Health Audit and Inspection), the National Performance Framework (NPF) and the National Patient and User Survey are to ensure that the services delivered are based on *monitored standards*.

The model allows the clinical care practitioner and the student of leadership and management to negotiate the journey through the 'permanent white waters' (Vaills 1990) of the health and social care environment. As a 'form of sage on the stage' the CLINLAP model encourages the practitioner to have an overview of the clinical functions and activities. Practitioners are assisted in seeing the extent to which they are fully utilising the capabilities within their clinical enterprise. The model focuses on:

- how practitioners could apply theory to practice
- how to become effective team leaders, through strategic learning

by ensuring in their practice that

- their clinical goals are *agreed* and *specific*
- that clinical roles are made *explicit* to avoid role ambiguity, role strain, role confusion, role underload and overload (Handy 1999)
- that clinical processes to deliver the role are *clear*; and above all
- that all these clinical activities take place within an environment that promotes *open relationships*.

Specific clinical goals – stages 1 and 2 of the model

The activities of a surgical Ward Sister are used to illustrate stages 1–4 of this seven-stage model (see Fig. 6.1). Within the CLINLAP model, stages 1 and 2 have been configured to assist the aspiring clinical leader to:

- align nursing care goals with stakeholder expectations and
- plan for quality and agreed nursing actions.

In relation to this project the Ward Sister identified all the disciplines involved as key stakeholders. The nursing staff had a lot to gain from this new development because of the usefulness of an appropriate multifunctional room for teaching, meetings, having 'breaks' and also staff appraisals. The Ward Sister also recognised that the surgical medical staff also saw this as an excellent opportunity for using the room for their morning teaching and patient 'clerking'. As team leader, she felt that both nursing and medical staff goals were compatible in their expectations as the key stakeholders.

If this had not been the case, the change process would have been delayed or may never have happened at all. Work conflicts would have arisen if the key stakeholders had different goals. Other stakeholders identified included the people actually carrying out the work, namely the Estates Department within the NHS Trust. The CLINLAP model advocates the use of a stakeholder mapping exercise to identify stakeholder expectations and stakeholder power as well as assisting the Ward Sister to decide on political priorities. This allowed her to make informed decisions on the level of interest and power of each stakeholder to meet their own expectations.

Explicit clinical roles

Within the CLINLAP model, stages 3 and 4 (see Fig. 6.1) have been configured so as to assist the aspiring clinical leader to: (1) use tools to promote common language, clinical learning and actions, and (2) match nursing actions with stakeholder needs.

Success at stages 3 and 4 of the CLINLAP model was less problematic for the Ward Sister and her team since the first two stages were managed effectively. The overall goal here was for the Ward Sister to begin the process of solution formulation to the specific goals she and her team had set. In essence, what she did with her team was to show an awareness of the impact of forces in the external environment on the ward's activities: for example, the Government's White Papers, the NHS Trust's strategy on Recruitment and Retention, the activities within the other directorates, the impact of the behaviour of the Surgical Consultant, the influence of the Estates and Facilities Department (E&FD) as well as the other surgical wards in the hospital.

Internally, the Ward Sister and her team became sensitive to and acted according to the effect on and of internal politics (within the ward, the Surgical Directorate and the NHS Trust), due to changes within the healthcare industry, and the new NHS. In an attempt to make an exemplary use of the value chain, the Ward Sister and her team identified the resources and capabilities needed for the team's viability and for the success of this project. The identification of the resources and capabilities was made using SWOT analysis. Table 6.1 shows the surgical ward's strengths and the opportunities facing it. They reached the conclusion from the SWOT analysis after using the seven Ss framework (7Ss – *strategy; structure; systems; staff; skills; style;* and *shared values*) (Peters & Waterman 1982) and Lewin's Force Field Analysis (Grundy 1993).

Operationalising the model through the five strategic questions

Key questions about the practitioner's enterprise, department or unit, such as 'What parts connect to one another?' 'How should processes and people come together?' 'Whose ideas have to flow where?', are made easier to answer because of the flexibility and realism built into the CLINLAP model (see Fig. 6.1). The seven stages of the CLINLAP model allow and assist the practitioners to find some answers to these five strategic questions (SQs):

(1) What do we need to do within our clinical practice and why? (WANT)
(2) Where are we now and why? (CAN)
(3) How do we get there and why? (MIGHT)
(4) Which direction might we take and why? (MIGHT)
(5) Who and what do we need to sustain our achievements and why? (SHOULD)

Table 6.1 SWOT analysis of the surgical ward showing its strengths and opportunities mapped against its resources.

Resources (THEIMM, Jumaa 1997)	Strengths	Opportunities
Time (reputation/culture)	New Ward Sister	No continuing professional development (CPD) facility on the ward. The Surgical Consultant supported the idea of a ward-based CPD facility
Human	Motivated, collaborative and skilled staff	The Surgical Consultant pledged to invite the nursing staff to the multi-disciplinary team (MDT) meetings
Equipment/estates	Available space to be 'used'. 'Street-smart' Ward Sister; knowledge of the building trade	Flexible Estates and Facilities Department provides itemised estimates to assist cost-efficiency
Information	Networking skills of the 'new' Ward Sister and her ambition to develop her staff and retain them	The University College, London (UCL) Hospitals NHS Trust's focus on recruitment and retention strategic issues
Material	The 'new' Ward Sister as a graduate nurse has many relevant books	The Surgical Consultant donated some of the books he had authored and pharmaceutical firms provided other professional articles for the ward's CPD initiatives, including pens, paper, etc.
Money	Effective management of the value chain, and application of risk benefit analysis and cost-effective use of the 'under-spent' ward's budget	The purchase of a large fish tank from the 'savings', which became a source of satisfaction, conversation and relaxation for the patients on the ward

These questions could also be modified to read 'I'. The tools, concepts, techniques and frameworks suggested for use during any application of the model were always offered, not as a prescription, but as a structure to assist the participants to become more effective in their practice. Practitioners are always encouraged to use any other concepts if they help to explain the processes and reasons for their activities. Stages 1–4 of the seven-stage model (see Fig. 6.1) have been presented in more detail above with reference to how the Ward Sister applied the model. The Sister, within a surgical ward, set SMART objectives agreed by most of the surgical team members (see Box 6.2), and also created a SWOT analysis of the surgical ward showing its strengths and opportunities mapped against its resources (see Table 6.1).

Despite strong resistance from other key stakeholders on the ward who were also interested in converting the 'derelict' space into a continuing professional development (CPD) facility, the Ward Sister agreed the SMART objectives shown in Box 6.2 with the surgical team.

The CLINLAP model has been shown to produce effective leadership and a process that encourages *learning how to learn* (Jumaa & Alleyne 2002). The research and development process that led to the formation of the CLINLAP model is presented in Ashburner (2001, pp. 256–278). It is important to note that this is an iterative model, and the diagram (see Fig. 6.1) ideally should be represented as a spiral form. The project activity was ordered through the processes of aspiring to achieve on this surgical ward:

- specific clinical goals
- explicit clinical roles
- clear clinical processes
- open clinical relationships relating to facility development on a surgical ward

Box 6.2 Five rules of setting goals and objectives (SMART) (Kennedy 2000) applied to the surgical team by the Ward Sister.

	Surgical team's objectives
Specific	Establish a designated area on the ward for continuing professional development (CPD) and multidisciplinary team (MDT) interactions
Measurable	Show a visible structural change within 6 months of coming in as a new Ward Sister
Achievable/ambitious	Exploit the considerable 'under-spent' ward budget, the nursing staff and the MDT's needs for ward-based CPD facility
Realistic	Convert an existing 'derelict' space on the ward to a CPD facility within 6 months
Timely	Implement change within 6 months as a new Ward Sister to the ward

The Ward Sister and her surgical team's activities led to the successful implementation of a CPD facility in a surgical ward at University College, London (UCL) Hospitals NHS Trust. These activities are presented in Box 6.3.

This process was part of an in-depth case study approach for a doctorate in Strategic Leadership and Strategic Learning in Nursing and Healthcare (Jumaa 2001). It was written up as a management report (Kennedy 2000) and as a research paper presented by the Ward Sister at an international conference on *Strategic Issues in Health Care Management* (Kennedy & Jumaa 2002).

Box 6.3   Specific strategic leadership and strategic learning activities contributing to the successful implementation of the creation of a CPD facility in a surgical ward at UCL Hospitals NHS Trust, London (Kennedy 2000).

Specific goals for the surgical ward project via	• Stating the purpose of the conversion of the 'derelict' space to a CPD facility. The purpose was based on an • Understanding of stakeholder issues, analysis and management, leading to • Deciding and agreeing on SMART goals and objectives for this project for this ward
Explicit roles for the surgical ward project via	• Awareness of the impact of forces in the external environment on the ward's activities • The effect on and of internal politics (within the ward, the Surgical Directorate and the NHS Trust), due to changes within the healthcare industry, and the new NHS • Identification of the required resources and capabilities for the team's viability and success • Recognising internal competition for securing the title of a progressive ward.
Clear processes for the surgical ward project via	• SWOT analysis to determine the ward team's relative strengths and opportunities

Continued

Box 6.3 *Continued*

	• Knowing the team's key success factors • Knowing the directorate's and the NHS Trust's key success factors • Identifying the difference between *needs* and *wants* and the cost implications for patient care and services • A working knowledge of the new NHS clinical governance quality framework, and a detailed understanding of the NHS Trust's policies, procedures and processes for innovative nursing projects • Ability to analyse cause and effect of 'open' and 'hidden' staff activities (nursing, MDT and support staff) • Understanding and articulating power issues, and effects on what gets done, by whom, where, when, why, to whom and how
Open relationships for the surgical ward project via	• Management of resistance to lead proposed change on the ward • Having the capacity to manage constant change • Demonstrating the ability to work with/change the dominant cultural paradigm • Challenging and 'dismantling' the 'unprogressive' dominant cultural paradigm • Making explicit the 'pay-offs' for all stakeholders involved in the change process

Finding answers to the five strategic questions

Sub-strategic questions have to be asked and explored in order to find appropriate responses for the projects in hand so as to achieve efficient management

91

Box 6.4   Exploring how to align stakeholders' expectations.

Sub-strategic questions for stage 1 of the CLINLAP model

- Who are the stakeholders for this particular activity or group of activities?
- Who are the *key* stakeholders and why?
- Are the goals of the key stakeholders compatible with the nursing/ clinical goal?
- Why should nursing goals be compatible with those of the key stake-holders?
- If goals are not compatible, how could we make them so?
- Do you have an accurate and realistic understanding of what you are trying to do?
- Do you need a broad domain and direction planning for this activity?
- Do you have to be precise, and have a goal-directed plan?
- Are you clear of the immediate, short- and long-term aspects of this activity?

and effective leadership. It is the case that smart managers do not always know everything. Their strengths lie in the fact that they ask many 'SMART' questions, as shown in Box 6.4, in order to explore how to *align stakeholders' expectations*.

These and any other relevant questions are encouraged for exploration and discussion to ensure that prior to the start of a particular clinical project, or a care process, there is a significant level of support. The model is, therefore, actively assisting and allowing the practitioner to enlist the necessary resources prior to the commencement of a work project. Resources are configured in this model to mean *time, human, equipment, information, material* and *money* (THEIMM) (Jumaa 1997). Some of the relevant management and leadership tools and approaches to assist the practitioner to answer these and other questions from an evidence-based perspective are shown in Chapter 2.

The final stage of the model – implementing high quality service/care

Grundy (1993) explained why implementing and leading strategic change does not always work. This was because the style and allocated time of managing and leading change were not appropriate. About 80% of available time is spent on implementing the project, while the diagnosis and planning stages receive less than 15%. An effective leader and efficient manager of change would spend about 40% of available time on the diagnosis and planning stages and about 40% on implementing the project. Reflect on those changes you have implemented, successfully, and you will see the sense in this approach.

This view is upheld within the CLINLAP model's various applications. This is because the configuration of this model expects such an approach for success and continuity. It is not enough to simply *desire* effective and efficient clinical practice – change will not just take place. What is required is a *disciplined* approach of the kind explored in many parts of this book which leads to *doing* what is feasible for the success of the project (Jumaa 2001). With this approach practitioners are more likely to produce and sustain key and vital clinical changes.

What are the findings and lessons learnt from these activities?

These activities relate to Senge's 'Dance of Change' (Senge 1990). Some of the management and leadership tools and approaches that will assist the practitioner to answer these and other relevant questions from an evidence-based perspective are shown in Table 2.2 and Table 7.1. The overall lessons learnt, however, can be seen from the activities of the Ward Sister and her team (Box 6.3). Efficiently and effectively implementing some or all of the above or similar approaches will help the practitioner find answers to the five strategic questions. Successfully implementing the seven stages of the CLINLAP model will be an indication that the practitioner has made a significant contribution to evidence-based nursing management and leadership, and also be in a position to deliver nursing and care services without having to be defensive about the rationale for the actions taken. Professional behaviour of this nature clearly places the practitioner in the position of one of the creators of new professional nursing and interprofessional knowledge (see Box 6.3).

Creating and establishing a new nursing managerial strategic problem-solving process is not easy, nor would it ever be easy, although it is possible if it is desirable, if it is disciplined, i.e. a 'structure' is used, and if the doing is based on the necessary strategic architecture (Jumaa 2001). It is always difficult despite the *desire*, *discipline* and *doing* – the cornerstones of effective holistic leadership. This is because, according to Niccolo Machiavelli:

> There is nothing more difficult to plan, more doubtful of success nor more dangerous to manage than the creation of a new order of things. . . . Whenever his enemies have occasion to attack the innovator they do so with the passion of partisans, while the others defend him sluggishly so that the innovator and his party alike are vulnerable. (Martin 1998, p. 20)

Why the CLINLAP model approach?

> In an economy where the only certainty is uncertainty, the one sure source of lasting competitive advantage is knowledge. When markets shift, technologies proliferate,

competitors multiply, and products become obsolete almost overnight, successful companies are those that consistently create new knowledge, disseminate it widely throughout the organisation, and quickly embody it in new technologies and products. These activities define the 'knowledge-creating' company, whose sole business is continuous innovation. (Nonaka 1991, p. 96)

The context that Nonaka has described also represents the turbulent environment of the UK's NHS and all other healthcare contexts. However, the NHS, like all other organisations, is part of today's context, described by Vaills (1990) as 'permanent white waters' (unremitting turbulence). It is for these reasons that the creative iterative processes embedded within the CLINLAP model were used.

Strategic healthcare leadership is defined in this chapter and within the model as:

An open process of creative decision-making, which seeks to persuade and influence the client, the service user, the customer, and work colleagues to agree to the chosen direction in relation to social and health services provision. This process is premised on a reflection on the internal, the external and the psychological factors impacting on the social and health services. (Jumaa & Alleyne 2002, p. 118)

In the present global knowledge economy, therefore, learning assumes an important strategic dimension. 'Strategic' in CLINLAP has been adopted from Grundy's (1994) definition of strategy:

the deliberate or emergent pattern of decisions which shape an organisation's future and its fit within its environment. These 'decisions' may involve changing the future scope and shape of activities or major areas of internal change aimed at protecting or enhancing capability. (Grundy 1994, p. 28)

It is within this context that strategic learning is used in the CLINLAP model. The model is about resolving messy issues, issues that are usually complex, uncertain and full of dilemmas, the likes of which are an every-day occurrence in the care arena.

Advantages of the CLINLAP model

Effective implementation of the CLINLAP model brings to health and social care organisations, teams and individuals working in the care environment many advantages (Jumaa 2001) that were never realised under inflexible, rigid and obsolete approaches. The most significant include:

- developing and sustaining continuous high quality healthcare performance
- capability development and enhancement of the practitioner, clinician, manager, leader and carer to link theory with practice
- assisting healthcare managers, leaders and carers to facilitate the care and clinical leadership processes

- the ability to challenge the 'givens'
- providing a practical tool for reflective practice
- promotion of the capacity to reflect critically on learning opportunities in the clinical environment
- a flexible style of management
- developing different ways of perceiving
- promoting originality of thought
- amplification of the practitioner's competence in demonstrating innovative approaches to the challenges posed by clinical professional practice, and other professional colleagues
- making sense of patterns from the past and plans for the future.

There are, however, some disadvantages.

Disadvantages of the CLINLAP model

Initially, a facilitator may be required to assist in the implementation of the model. However, the goal of facilitation would be to lead the clinical group to self- and peer determination, autonomous development and action inquiry in their groups through self- and peer group supervision (Jumaa 2001). A more serious problem is when the user of the model chooses an inappropriate approach within the process. Paradoxically, this itself could be rectified because of the spiral and iterative nature of the model. Specific problems may arise as a result of inherent problems in the particular tools, framework, concepts or techniques chosen for action or problem solving. According to Alleyne (2002), in her study, application of the CLINLAP model as a structured approach for focused management and leadership interventions was facilitated through a group clinical supervision approach. This application enabled her to provide a coherent critique of the CLINLAP model, summarised as follows:

- It has a potential lack of accessibility.
- It requires a substantial body of management knowledge and leadership know-how.
- It cannot be viewed as a 'quick fix' for organisational change or performance improvement.
- Users of this model require continuing support and investment for workplace learning to be sustained.
- It is a necessary model for CPD and life-long learning.

Further exploration of this case study is presented in Chapter 8.

Sustainable healthcare performance

The CLINLAP model acknowledges organisational focus on adaptive competence and the importance of congruence or 'fit' between managerial knowledge and job demands. The model, however, goes further, from adaptive learning to sustainable clinical nursing learning. Sustaining quality healthcare performance requires superior clinical nursing resources, which depends upon healthcare organisational and nursing managerial capability (Jumaa & Alleyne 2001). The CLINLAP model, used effectively, helps to achieve clinical learning and nursing innovation, which according to Johnson & Scholes (2002) is dependent on the *'dominant paradigm'* of a healthcare organisation. The term *'dominant paradigm'* is used to describe relationships, both formal and informal, amongst staff, with clients, customers and inter-organisational collaborative arrangements. That these relationships exist is not a revelation; unfortunately, though, they are 'often taken for granted' (Johnson & Scholes 2002). What the CLINLAP model does is make them and their importance much more explicit (Alleyne 2002, Jumaa 2001).

Facilitating the clinical leadership process

The successful and effective use of the CLINLAP model enables clinical practitioners to improve their skills of facilitating care and leading change in their work contexts. Amongst other uses, the model can assist the nurse, midwife and other healthcare practitioners to:

- sustain the flow of clinical activities
- stop when clinically appropriate
- refrain from wasting time and 'muddling' through
- choose the relevant evidence-based clinical method
- consider organisational politics, and use it effectively (Jumaa 2001)

The environment for CLINLAP

Maximising the full benefits to be gained from using the CLINLAP model requires that the four core conditions needed for its application are observed These are as follows:

- Health and social care staff need to believe in strategic (whole-picture) workplace learning for continuous quality improvement.
- The achievement of the satisfaction of all stakeholders and practitioners involved in the processes of care, recipients and providers is paramount.
- Satisfaction is only possible through collaborative working amongst all health and social care practitioners, including patients, clients and users (Jumaa 2001).

- Rebalancing the power relationships within the workplace is necessary for the development of clinical, managerial and leadership competencies and capabilities (Alleyne 2002).

Summary and conclusions

It is clear from the contents of this chapter that the CLINLAP model was developed specifically to meet and address continuous changes within the work environment. This chapter has provided a picture of the CLINLAP/LEADLAP model and its stages and phases. An important emphasis throughout was the need for sensitivity towards the range of needs of the stakeholders involved in the delivery and consumption of nursing, midwifery and healthcare interventions. Furthermore, I share the view that the individual, therapeutic focus of professional nursing needs to be extended to encompass responsibility for assuring overall quality by facilitating and delegating as well as delivering hands-on-care. Nurses who took part in projects where the model was tested and applied (Alleyne 2002, Jumaa 2001) used the opportunities for management and leadership development in order to take a central role in the organisation of the nursing service in their organisations and worked towards making 'good nursing' and 'good management' synonymous (Mintzberg 1994). It would be naïve to assume that high quality services can be provided effectively without an effective management and leadership role being performed well. The CLINLAP model provides a framework for such role developments to be achieved. The CLINLAP/LEADLAP model has successfully found one harmonious home in which transactional management and transformational leadership can co-exist. Sustained successful performance in nursing and healthcare need efficient management and effective leadership.

References

Alleyne, J. (2002) *Making a Case for Group Clinical Supervision Through Management and Leadership Concepts.* Unpublished Research Project Report, part of a Doctor of Professional Studies (DProf), through work-based learning in clinical nursing leadership, Middlesex University, London.

Alleyne, J. & Zack-Williams, D. (2001) Managing the pain associated with sickle cell disease; learning and leading from evidence-based management practice. In: *Managing Diversity and Inequality in Healthcare* (ed. C. Baxter). Baillière Tindall in association with the Royal College of Nursing, London.

Ashburner, L. (ed.) (2001) *Organisation Behaviour and Organisation Studies in Health Care: Reflections on the Future.* Palgrave (Macmillan), Basingstoke.

Department of Health (1998) *A First Class Service: Quality in the New NHS.* The Stationery Office, London.

Department of Health (1999) *Making a Difference: Strengthening the Nursing, Midwifery and Health Visiting Contribution to Health and Healthcare*. The Stationery Office, London.

Department of Health (2000a) *The NHS Plan*. The Stationery Office, London.

Department of Health (2000b) *Quality and Performance in the NHS. Performance Indicators*. The Stationery Office, London.

Department of Health (2001) *Building a Safer NHS for Patients. Implementing an Organisation with a Memory*. The Stationery Office, London.

Ferlie, E., Gabbay, J., Fitzgerald, L., Locock, L. & Dopson, S. (2001) Evidence-based medicine and organisational change: an overview of some recent qualitative research. In: *Organisation Behaviour and Organisation Studies in Healthcare: Reflections on the Future* (ed. L. Ashburner). Palgrave (Macmillan), Basingstoke.

Goffee, R. & Jones, G. (2000) Why should anyone be led by you? *Harvard Business Review*, **78** (5), 62–69.

Grundy, T. (1993) *Implementing Strategic Change*. Kogan Page, London.

Grundy, T. (1994) *Strategic Learning in Action: How to Accelerate and Sustain Business Change*. McGraw-Hill, London.

Handy, C. (1999) *Understanding Organisations*. Penguin Books, London.

Johnson, G. & Scholes, K. (2002) *Exploring Corporate Strategy; Text and Cases*, 6th edn. Prentice Hall, Hemel Hempstead.

Jumaa, M.O. (1997) *Strategic Clinical Team Learning Through Leadership*. Unpublished Research Project Report, part of an MA-WBLS (Strategic Nursing Leadership and Management), Middlesex University, London.

Jumaa, M.O. (2001) *Enhancing Individual Learning and Organisational Capability Through Learning Projects and Developmental Interventions*. Unpublished Research Project Report, part of a Doctor of Professional Studies (DProf), through work-based learning in strategic leadership and strategic learning in nursing and healthcare, Middlesex University, London.

Jumaa, M.O. & Alleyne, J. (2000) New money, new nursing, new management, and new solutions. *Nursing Management*, **7** (4), 6–7.

Jumaa, M.O. & Alleyne, J. (2001) Learning, unlearning and relearning: facilitation in community nursing for delivering the new primary care agenda. In: *Organisation Behaviour and Organisation Studies in Healthcare: Reflections on the Future* (ed. L. Ashburner). Palgrave (Macmillan), Basingstoke.

Jumaa, M.O. & Alleyne, J. (2002) Strategic leadership in health care, in challenging times. In: *Strategic Issues in Health Care Management: Efficiency, Quality and Access in Health Care* (eds. M. Tavakoli, *et al.*). University of St. Andrews Press, Fife.

Kennedy, N. (2000) Money alone is not the answer: an evidence-based approach to improving patient care, through facilities development. A Management Report on the outcome of the interventions of a co-researcher on a doctorate programme. Cited in: *Enhancing Individual Learning and Organisational Capability Through Learning Projects and Developmental Interventions* (M.O. Jumaa, 2001). Middlesex University, London.

Kennedy, N. & Jumaa, M.O. (2002) *Money alone is not the solution to continuous quality service delivery: an evidence based approach to quality service through facilities management*. Paper presented at the 5th International Conference on Strategic Issues in Health Care Management, Policy, Finance and Performance in Health Care, 11–13 April, St Andrew's University, Fife.

Martin, J. (1998) *B882 Creative Management, Block 2 Techniques*. The Open University Business School, Milton Keynes.

Mintzberg, H. (1994) Managing as blended care. *Journal of Nursing Administration*, **24** (9), 29–36.

Moxon, P. (1993) *Building a Better Team*. Gower, Aldershot.

Nonaka, I. (1991) The knowledge-creating company. *Harvard Business Review*, **69** (6), 96–104.

Peters, T.J. & Waterman, R.H. (1982) *In Search of Excellence*. Harper and Row, New York.

Schon, D. (1983) *The Reflective Practitioner: How Professionals Think in Action*. Basic Books, New York.

Senge, P. (1990) *The Fifth Discipline: The Art and Practice of the Learning Organisation*. Century Business, New York.

Vaills, P. (1990) *Managing as a Performing Art*. Jossey Bass, San Francisco.

Further reading

Department of Health (1997) *The New NHS: Modern and Dependable*. The Stationery Office, London.

Department of Health (1998a) *Partnership in Action; New Opportunities for Joint Working Between Health and Social Services*. The Stationery Office, London.

Department of Health (1998b) *Our Healthier Nation*. Government Green Paper. The Stationery Office, London.

Department of Health (1999) *The Health Act*. The Stationery Office, London.

Jumaa, M.O., Smith, A. & Bailey, J. (2000a) The NHS Plan. *Nursing Management*, **7** (6), 36–37.

Jumaa, M.O., Talib, Y. & Shuldham, C. (2000b) The 5 Ps of nursing management. *Nursing Management*, **7** (3), 6–7.

Lewis, D. (1995) *10-Minute Time and Stress Management: How to Gain an 'Extra' 10 Hours a Week*. BCA, London.

Mintzberg, H. (1973) *The Nature of Managerial Work*. Harper and Row, New York.

NHS Modernisation Agency (2002) *Managing the Human Dimensions of Change*. Ancient House Printing Group, Ipswich.

7 Implementing the CLINLAP Model – A Case Study of Policy Change in Managing Deliberate Self-Harm

Janice Phillips, Helen Julu, Gülnur Salih and Chris Gbolo

Introduction

In the modern and rapidly changing National Health Service (NHS), imaginative, dynamic and intelligent leadership at all levels is essential in creating a more flexible and modern workforce, responsive to the needs of patients (Allen 2000, Cook 1999, 2001, DH 1999, Faugier & Woolnough 2002). It necessitates a proactive, innovative, inspirational and sustained approach which seeks to motivate others to pursue high standards of care and attain long-term service goals, through the articulation of a shared vision and a harmonious 'people-centred' culture. Two-way communication concerning organisational objectives is essential for reducing uncertainty among staff teams, promoting trust and fostering loyalty and compliance with the continual change processes that pervade the NHS (Joshua-Amadi 2003). It necessitates high emotional intelligence in being aware of how to regulate one's own emotions, monitor the emotions of others and use this information to guide thinking and actions (Goleman 2000).

While the authors of this chapter work in different parts of the NHS, they encounter common problems in their different services. The overall problems in all four situations related to information management and managing change for effective and continuous quality healthcare delivery. Focus in this chapter will be on the activities carried out within the four phases and seven stages of the strategic nursing management performance implementation model, the CLINLAP model. This chapter serves as a detailed case study application of the CLINLAP model within a policy change clinical context (see Chapter 6 for a detailed discussion of the model).

Table 7.1 Application of the CLINLAP model using management and leadership concepts.

Four phases and seven stages of the CLINLAP model	Concepts, principles, tools, techniques and frameworks (used for improvement of services)
Phase 1 – Analysing the service problem Stage 1: Aligning stakeholder expectation Stage 2: Plan for quality action	Stakeholder mapping Power and Interest Matrix Ashridge Mission model SMART objectives
Phase 2 – Formulating service solutions Stage 3: Use tools to promote common language actions Stage 4: Match actions with stakeholder needs	Key success factors SWOT analysis PEST'O' The 7Ss THEIMM for resources
Phase 3 – Challenging rigid and obsolete assumptions Stage 5: Re-assess stakeholders' needs and rectify identified gaps Stage 6: Establish a fit with stakeholders' needs	'Fish bone' analysis (Ishikawa diagram; see Fig. 3.2) PJQIM Johnson & Scholes test
Phase 4 – Implementing a quality service Stage 7: Provide quality service	The Cultural Web The OPEN approach The 7Es – economic, efficiency, effectiveness, equity, ethics, environment, empowerment

The learning disability–forensic care context illustrates how management and leadership concepts, principles, tools, techniques and frameworks (see Table 7.1) were used to improve care and directly link learning at work with specific improvement in the processes of care delivery. Throughout the rest of this chapter the model will be referred to as the CLINLAP model (Jumaa & Alleyne 2001).

Background

Osprey Ward is a mixed sex, acute admissions ward for learning-disabled offenders. Like other medium secure services, admissions derive from the courts, prisons, special hospitals and private hospitals. Osprey Ward only accepts patients with an IQ score of below 80. Frequency of admissions, transfers, discharges and duration of stay vary dramatically, depending upon the section imposed and/or the person's responsiveness to treatment. Patients ideally move through the ward within 6–12 months, either being transferred to a rehabilitation ward, another service provision, back to prison, or in some cases on to special hospitals such as Rampton High Security Hospital. The ward has an establishment of 22 staff – qualified Registered Nurses making up just over 50%. Each staff member has a clearly defined role on each shift, with all communications directed towards the nurse in charge, who in turn reports to the shift co-ordinator responsible for ensuring and monitoring human resource management across the entire 76-bedded in-patient service.

The ward operates in parallel with the other 15-bedded acute forensic admission ward, with the exception that it has fewer beds, a higher staff to patient ratio and a more structured environment. Mentally ill patients who have an additional cognitive impairment require this because patients with impaired cognitive functioning (or learning disability) often have communication problems and a lack of understanding about their situation, their illness, their offending behaviour and the risks they pose to others. As a result self-harm occurs frequently and acts of violence occur daily because frustration is often expressed by a patient's behaviour.

The increased structure and need for consistency is pertinent in reinforcing boundary setting in order to minimise the day-to-day risk of impulsive, violent and self-harming behaviour. Many patients use self-harm as a form of communication due to impaired cognitive functioning, but also in reaction to constraints of the secure environment (Phillips 2001). Indeed, in the first author's first year of being in post there were three suicide attempts, only unsuccessful because of early and rapid intervention.

Policies direct care intervention, compensating for skills deficits by ensuring standardised practice across the organisation as a whole. However, they discourage the use of specialised interventions specific to patients' needs. Often valuable information is ignored, as the policy overrides patients' needs by restricting the interventions permitted. Policies also devalue the specialist skills of learning disability nurses in avoiding behavioural reinforcement, promoting dignity and respect and also in placing the patient at the heart of care delivery. A marked increase in incidents of self-harm and violence on the ward was resulting from invasive intervention when the act of self-harm was occurring. It became apparent that addressing this problem through open relationships with all involved parties would facilitate the process of change. The only question was where to begin.

At the start of this initiative, staff had already been exposed to a number of service and management changes within a very short period of time and they were distrustful and fearful of the ingrained 'blame culture'. The ever-increasing number of incidents of violence, deliberate self-harm (DSH) and suicide attempts made this more apparent. With a general lack of leadership most care interventions had become reactive and the effectiveness of service delivery was severely compromised by high sickness levels, a fragile staffing structure and a number of workplace injuries. The first 3 months were spent talking to the staff and developing some degree of understanding about their future vision of the service, and why they generally felt dissatisfied with their jobs, their roles and the general standard of care provision. Staff felt strongly that they were forced to work within a restrictive and suppressed nursing culture and most showed a general commitment to wanting to make changes for the good, being keen to adopt and develop any strategy that attempted to improve the current situation. With the turbulent nature of the clinical environment, the adoption and implementation of a strategic approach was essential if radical change was to be effected. The CLINLAP model proved to be an effective model because, with the use of appropriate management and leadership concepts, tools, techniques and frameworks, it assisted with meeting the challenge of improving the quality of service delivery on a continual basis amidst a climate of uncertainty and dwindling resources.

Application of the CLINLAP model in effective care processes

Analysing the service problem (phase 1 of the model)

In terms of analysing the service problem (phase 1 and stages 1 and 2 of the CLINLAP model) we had to align stakeholder expectations and then plan quality action. Through spontaneous brainstorming we began stakeholder mapping which enabled the identification of all internal and external stakeholders who influence how we work (see Table 7.2). Whilst this phase's effectiveness is only as good as one's own knowledge of the internal and external parties involved and the task to be carried out, we found it to be of particular value in that it encouraged lateral and vertical thinking beyond the narrow-mindedness of the internal environment. Being new to the service and with little knowledge of the key people in different departments, we were able to understand the importance of identifying key people, whereas, before, we may simply have been inclined to run the ideas past those we had contact with and knew. One danger was that we may not have analysed, anticipated or managed the legitimate interests of the various stakeholders appropriately and consequently they may have sought to jeopardise or sabotage the proposal later on, resulting in wastage of time, human, money, material and information resources. The CLINLAP model suggests the use of the power/interest matrix (see Johnson & Scholes 2002, pp. 206–209), which was of particular value in being easy to use as it provided guidance on the degree of involvement or consultation that each stakeholder needed in gaining support and acceptance of the proposed vision, and in avoiding conflict. However, the use of this tool is reliant upon subjective diagnosis. Baker *et al.* (1999) imply that such subjective diagnosis could lead to misdiagnosis, and where this occurs inappropriate managerial strategy may

Table 7.2 Stakeholder analysis.

		LEVEL OF INTEREST	
		LOW	**HIGH**
LEVEL OF POWER	**LOW**	(Minimum effort) Patients and public MIND (National Association for Mental Health)/advocates Primary Care Groups (PCGs) Finance	(Keep informed) RCN/Unison Legal representatives NHS Litigation Authority
	HIGH	(Keep satisfied) Home Office Commission for Health Improvement (CHI) Strategic Health Authorities Trust Board	(Key players) Multidisciplinary team (MDT) Head of Nursing Nursing team

result. A further criticism of this tool (the power/interest matrix) is that because money buys power and choice within public services the patient does not appear at the heart of strategy formulation, being neither informed nor involved, in service changes. Cortis (1999), Hannigan (1998) and James (1995) all support the fact that where the receiver of services is not the person with the power and the money, then the receiver of the actual services provided is not central to strategy formulation. This seems to contradict the very goal that government legislation has been trying to achieve, that of keeping the patient at the centre and heart of care delivery.

Having identified the key players, we then had to have a clear understanding of the organisation's mission, so that proposals for change were commensurate with the views and interests of the various stakeholders' interests, as well as recognising the resource implications. With the absence of a formal written mission statement, we used the Ashridge Mission model, which assisted us to make sense of our mission through considering four key elements for the survival of the ward – our purpose, values, strategy and behaviour standards (Campbell & Yeung 1990). Conflict between organisational and employee values was apparent when applying the model. This had arisen because although the (learning disability) service operates within a strong behavioural culture we were forced to operate within the wider forensic value system. This required us to conform to behavioural standards we did not agree with or that actually contravened the specialist behaviour shaping skills that learning disability nurses possess.

This was most apparent with the constant application of one-to-one intervention that reinforced DSH because it was often the desired response sought by the patient. However, it was difficult to analyse which values were the right values; a weakness also identified by Campbell & Yeung (1990).

We concluded that values that increase patients' satisfaction and make them more comfortable must be the 'right' values. This raised awareness of the relationships we needed to foster and guided the formulation of objectives. We needed to ensure that proposals were appropriate in trying to bridge the gap between organisational and employee values (Campbell & Yeung 1990). Four specific, measurable, achievable, reliable and time-bound (SMART) core objectives were proposed within 6 months, which we set out to achieve, as shown in Box 7.1.

Box 7.1   Objectives set for achievement using the SMART acronym.

(1)   To redefine the mission within the forensic learning disability service
This was essential for ensuring accurate perceptions and interpretations of the purpose of the service, and in seeking to motivate individual staff and align their expectations of what the quality of current care provision should entail (demonstrated using the *Ashridge Mission model*).

(2)   To establish the extent of deliberate self-harm (DSH) within the learning disability service
Given the needs of this patient group, a large proportion of behavioural interventions are used due to the limited communication and cognitive ability. Therefore, a review of incidents over the previous 12 months was essential for two reasons: it would provide information on the existing management of DSH and provide a baseline against which any perceived change could be measured.

(3)   To review existing policies and guidelines
A review of all existing policies relating to DSH was essential in ensuring that the Trust's strategy, clinical governance and the needs of patients on Osprey Ward were reflected in order to learn from previous serious incidents, devolve responsibility for proactive risk assessment and management to individual practitioners and ensure that policies relating to DSH are based on best possible practice, integrating research, clinical audit and user empowerment.

(4)   To create training and development opportunities
Devolving responsibility, in terms of proactive risk assessment and management, can only be done effectively if clinical staff are equipped to take on the responsibility. The training needs of staff would be highlighted from interviews and from the information gained through reviewing incidents, upon which a needs-led training package could be formulated.

SMART captured all aspects necessary to guide our strategy at an operational level whilst enabling a continuous assessment of whether the actions had been achieved within the defined time period, providing an opportunity to update and replace objectives. The tool was easy to use, valid as it can be applied to objectives in any given situation, and reliable as it can be applied time and time again, with success still being measurable against it.

Formulating service solutions (phase 2 of the model)

The next phase of the CLINLAP model sought to formulate service solutions through analysis of current service provision. It was essential to understand the key success factors (KSFs) as these are the product and service features particularly valued by customers and where the organisation must excel to outperform competition (Grant 1995, Johnson & Scholes 2002). Therefore we tried to identify what the mutual KSFs would be for both the 'customers' (i.e. purchasing authorities) and the patients (i.e. non-paying receivers of care). We decided that safe care, followed by degree of patient involvement and gaining an understanding of presenting problems and behaviours would be our priorities. Organisational values included the avoidance of litigation, patient involvement and cost efficiency.

We then needed to match the activities of the organisation to the environment it operates in to ensure strategic fit (Richardson 2002). This necessitated identifying opportunities existing within the environment and tailoring our future strategy in order to capitalise upon them. A SWOT analysis identified the organisation's capabilities and the opportunities and threats that may impact upon strategy development. This was pertinent to ensuring an 'open relationship' as all stakeholders needed to be fully informed. The use of PEST'O' and the 7Ss (Peters & Waterman 1982) was important as they guided the exercise in looking at specific aspects and key influences of the internal and external environments and how they impact collectively. They also helped to avoid overlooking any aspects of the service provision that could impact upon strategy implementation.

The 'O' factor in PEST'O' (Jumaa 2001) enabled consideration to be given to any other aspect not covered by Martin & Henderson's (2001) acronym PEST. These tools generated open thinking beyond the here and now and encouraged anticipation of future events. This is critical in terms of minimising the impact of likely pitfalls and in developing the ability to sense change in the environment, as any change would signal a need for a change in strategy (Richardson 2002). With an increasing need to make services cost-effective, balance must be achieved between the likelihood of risk occurring and the resources used in preventing it (Martin 2001b). THEIMM (Jumaa 2001) was useful in terms of analysing resource utilisation and requirements because it encourages creative thinking and an understanding of how different types of resources contribute to the safety of the service collectively. Resources are often considered independent of one another (Grant 1995); however,

THEIMM raises awareness of the existing resource utilisation from a wider, more open-minded perspective. This helped to generate more creative cost-efficient planning when putting forward new strategies or proposals.

Challenging rigid and obsolete assumptions (phase 3 of the model)

By making sense of these different issues a full understanding enabled us to see why change was necessary, providing guidance on what needs to be and can be done in order to deal with the problem. The most evident barrier to implementing a policy that permits DSH was the fear of litigation. A policy of non-intervention by staff in self-harming behaviour contradicts a professional's 'duty of care' and infers neglect. However, it also raised additional fears including:

- taking on the responsibility of wound care
- when to make the decision to utilise emergency services
- feelings of not being in control of the patients' actions.

To overcome these barriers specific policy guidance was essential. Ward-based intervention in DSH events, and those that require attendance at the Accident and Emergency department, needed to be specified to provide protection against litigation. Likewise, emphasising multidisciplinary team (MDT)-based decision-making promoted collective accountability. Environmental security also needed improvement, with additional investment in mirrored domes to remove existing blind spots where self-harm generally occurs. Having finalised our proposals, it was pertinent at this stage to both check the strategic position and analyse the value of investing time and energy into such an information system.

The Phillips and Jumaa Quality of Information Matrix (PJQIM)

We were aware that the effectiveness of formulating and implementing a separate DSH policy would be dependent upon the value and use of other current information systems on Osprey Ward. With information being a complex and vital, yet an underestimated, misunderstood and undervalued resource, it would be easy to implement a new policy without giving consideration to the wider context of whether the existing information management system will support its implementation in practice. Therefore, in terms of reviewing the current information management systems on Osprey Ward, we used the Phillips and Jumaa Quality of Information Matrix (PJQIM) (Table 7.3). This is the first public presentation of this matrix synthesised by Phillips and Jumaa in 2003, at Middlesex University, London. Dr. Jumaa presented, in his lectures, how to evaluate any given information through: the *content*; the *sources*; the *types of communication*; the *analysis of its quality* through PARTNER (i.e. whether precise, adequate, reliable, timed, needed, economic and readable) (The Open College 1992); and the *purpose* of the information. Ms Phillips, a former student on the programme, then configured these into the matrix called

Table 7.3 The Phillips and Jumaa Quality of Information Matrix applied to information on Osprey Ward. PARTNER (The Open College 1992) stands for precise, adequate, reliable, timed, needed, economic and readable analysis of quality of information.

Information	Source		Types of communication				Analysis of quality of information using the acronym PARTNER	Purpose
	Internal	External	Voice	Image	Text	Data		**Seeking information** **Informing**
Referrals, Pre-Admission, Assess and Risk Assessments and Care Plans	✓		✓ Phone, informal meetings, formal meetings, face to face		✓ Typed document	✓ All plans are held on computer, with paper copies filed in notes	**P** – Data are specific to index offences and health-care needs and all have a Care Plan **A** – Form structure ensures adequacy, all needs discussed in reviews **R** – Data are factual and cross-referenced with other sources of data. Back-up plans identified **T** – All data are obtained before deadline date, based on standards **N** – Data are sought from preformulated questions. Plans only address needs within constraints of policies **E** – Documented data are photocopied, collation can be time-consuming as external data are often unreliable, also duplicate filing system. Sometimes cannot locate computer-held info, as no synchronised filing system **R** – All data are typed in easy to read, standardised, format	

Continued

Table 7.3 *Continued*

Information	Source		Types of communication				Analysis of quality of information using the acronym PARTNER	Purpose
	Internal	External	Voice	Image	Text	Data		
Government circulars, NICE Guidelines, CHI monitoring	✓	✓				✓ Circulated via email	**P** – Provides guidelines for clinical practice **A** – Sets standards of working practice **R** – Data are produced by legitimate source **T** – Specifies identified achievement time frames, although computer systems are not reliable **N** – Identifies and rationalises need for change/standard **E** – Is not always accessible, can be time-consuming to locate **R** – Is typed, but not always easy to convert into context of working practice	**Instructing Motivating**

Continued

Table 7.3 *Continued*

Information	Source		Types of communication				Purpose
	Internal	External	Voice	Image	Text	Data	
Budget statements	✓					✓ Computer-generated budget sheets	**Informing Motivating**

Analysis of quality of information using the acronym PARTNER

P – Financial codes are not reflective of ward needs, or expenditure
A – Financial reports do not highlight or reflect staffing activity, or increase in DSH care costs (i.e. one-to-one)
R – Data are consistent with expenditure
T – Infrequent reports, unable to keep check of expenditure
N – Bear little purpose to constant overspends on staffing, due to one-to-one
E – Often have to calculate own figures, or check data
R – Clear and understandable typed data printouts

Continued

Table 7.3 *Continued*

Information	Source		Types of communication				Analysis of quality of information using the acronym PARTNER	Purpose
	Internal	External	Voice	Image	Text	Data		
Suicide/DSH policy	✓				✓ Files located on each ward	✓ Policies held on on email folder	**P** – Seeks to intervene and control or prevent DSH. Disallows freedom of expression. Induces violent behaviour, contravenes staff values **A** – Guidance is comprehensive, standardises practice **R** – Is used as the basis for all DSH intervention **T** – Is easily available and reviewed annually **N** – Does not meet the specific needs of DSH patients, is more designed to meet needs of suicidal patients and avoidance of litigation **E** – Easily accessible on each ward, and on computer **R** – Is typed in standardised format	**Instructing**

Continued

Table 7.3 *Continued*

Information	Source		Types of communication				Analysis of quality of information using the acronym PARTNER	Purpose
	Internal	External	Voice	Image	Text	Data		Informing Motivating
Patient records	✓	✓		✓ ID sheets	✓ All paper copies of files held in central office file	✓ ID sheets and photographs held on central folder of computer	**P** – All information relating to patient is held. Some info is irrelevant for care interventions or day-to-day use **A** – Is a central point for access to records, but bulky and standardised filing system **R** – All patients have same format, but contents will be filed differently, making location difficult at a later date **T** – File instigated on initial contact and goes with patients in the service. Policy identifies specified time delay for written entries **N** – All multidisciplinary team work, interventions and documentation are combined in one central folder. There is too much unnecessary information for day-to-day use. Folders are bulky, making needed info much harder to find **E** – All info centralised in one place, but becomes tatty or lost with overload and constant use **R** – Some typed information and nursing written entries conform to professional standards, other professionals do not conform to same standards. Some entries are illegible, some entries use abbreviations	

the PJQIM. When completed by nurses and healthcare workers, this matrix provides a graphic illustration of the information in any given situation. Over 50 management and leadership students have used the PJQIM for information management in their workplaces with significant positive effects.

When completed in a transparent manner this provides a graphic illustration of the information in any given unit:

- the *content* (column one)
- the *sources*, whether internal or external (columns two and three)
- the *types of communication*, whether voice, image, text and/or data (columns four to seven)
- the *analysis of its quality*, i.e. whether precise, adequate, reliable, timed, needed, economic and readable (column eight)
- the *purpose of the information*, i.e. whether for seeking information, informing, instructing and/or motivating (column nine).

We applied it to various types of information essential to the care provision of a patient with DSH in order to identify what additional resources may be required to support the implementation of a new DSH policy. Whilst staff have a thorough understanding of local policies and excellent risk assessment and risk management skills, they are unable to be creative in implementing individual care packages because the policies dictated reactive interventions. All assessments and patient needs were clearly recorded, but this valuable information was often wasted as the policy overrides patient need by restricting permitted interventions. With added complications due to lost information as a result of poor and bulky filing systems, duplicated assessments, extended assessment periods and the implementation of inappropriate interventions, patient progress was delayed or inhibited. The problematic filing and storage of information was also difficult to analyse, especially when attempting to make correlations concerning incident frequency and antecedents to specific behaviours. With the lack of guidance governing inter-agency disclosure of information, the process of information gathering was time-consuming, lengthy and frustrating. This could be financially costly, in terms of both the workforce hours it took to carry out such procedures and litigation following failure to obtain a full and comprehensive history of the patient that may place the public at unnecessary risk (Davies 1999). Identified problems relating to current information management may have resulted in the new policy being unworkable unless additional resources were secured. In this respect the development of a new policy also necessitated the following resources:

- the production of a working agreement between the police, prison services and child protection teams for cross-agency disclosure
- the appointment of a unit-based file co-ordinator to implement a standardised filing system, enabling easier access to risk information and freeing up valuable nursing time for patient care
- the production of a standardised filing system for patient information which includes a separate section for withheld information.

In terms of reviewing the strategic position, the Johnson & Scholes test (2002) was particularly useful in acting as a checklist. By considering accept-ability, suitability and feasibility, an opportunity was created to review the situation, ensure that the proposal had not 'drifted' from the strategic focus and, if it had, modify it to match stakeholder satisfaction. We found this particularly useful, as normally we might have been inclined to 'plod on' with current strategy until it was completed before reassessing the situation. Had we failed to ensure a match between stakeholder satisfaction and the proposals at this stage, it could have resulted in some stakeholders exerting negative power over the project and placing it in jeopardy, or else we might have wasted time and energy moving in the wrong direction. In applying the Johnson & Scholes test (2002) we found that the proposals did 'fit' the needs of patients. They were feasible, because by introducing a new policy that 'permitted' self-harm in a controlled environment, the reactive costs and current overspend of providing one-to-one intervention could be re-employed to support the creation of a file co-ordinator post, secure training for staff and support the purchase of two mirrored domes to remove the existing blind spots on the ward. The proposals were:

- suitable, as they sought to improve the quality and efficiency of care intervention for patients by generating greater patient empowerment
- feasible, in that the proposals sought only to recycle time, human and monetary resources
- acceptable to all stakeholders, as they sought to improve the quality, efficiency and value of patient care.

Implementing a quality service (phase 4 of the model)

The final phase of the CLINLAP model was concerned with the actual implementation of the given strategy. This required a structure to ensure the organisation could deal with the demands of the environment and a culture that enhances effectiveness. The Cultural Web, as a tool, seeks to assess and make sense of the culture within an organisation. The culture of Osprey Ward is represented in Fig. 7.1.

This is important because unstated values, behaviours and paradigms can result in strategic drift and affect the ability to implement change due to resistance (Curtis & White 2002, Johnson & Scholes 2002, Martin & Hender-son 2001). An awareness of cultural type is important as it will impact on strategy selection (Handy 1993, Johnson & Scholes 2002, Richardson 2002). However, a disadvantage of the tool was its apparent prescriptive nature in terms of the strategy to be adopted within any given organisational culture, rather than seeking to change, adapt or assist the culture to accommodate alternative strategies. As can be seen in Fig. 7.1, Osprey Ward had a rigid, defensive and medically dominated culture affecting the ability to effect change and implement the proposed strategy. An OPEN relationship (Jumaa 2001; see below) can reduce resistance to change. This primarily

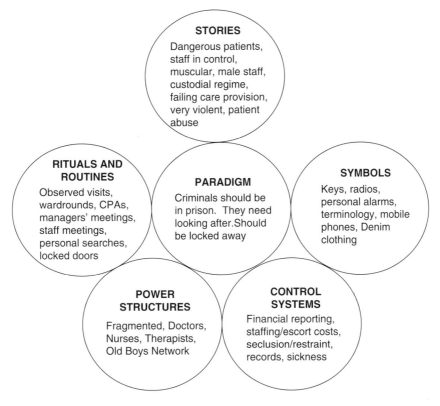

Fig 7.1 The taken-for-granted aspects of Osprey Ward, using the Cultural Web.

involved the dissemination of information, open and honest communication, education and facilitation, and support.

- Open thinking: expects all to approach management problems in a fresh way; to rethink negative traditional approaches; to challenge and modify the way things are currently done if they are counterproductive. Open thinking promotes bottom-up participation.
- Professional and personal impact: expects all to influence each other through respectful and professional behaviour; by setting personal example and recognising each individual's needs and aspirations.
- Empowering all levels of staff: expects all to be assisted to improve their skills and capabilities and build commitment through clear job roles and objectives; by clarifying and respecting individuals' contributions.
- Networking to increase personal satisfaction and improve services offered: expects all, especially those who have access to more information, to share this information in order to aid the achievement of the service objectives, as well as to celebrate success.

This was especially important, as it is not the change itself that individuals resist but the perceived losses that the change will bring. Accepting that change had to occur, and should not be viewed as a threat, it was important to be aware of the reasons for change, the resistance to it, and to adopt strategies that sought to reduce or prevent the occurrence of that resistance (Curtis & White 2002). We used the 7 Es framework (Jumaa 2001), as shown in Box 7.2, to assist in identifying the benefits of implementing such a change for all potential stakeholders.

The mnemonic 7 Es was a useful tool for assessing the quality and performance of the policy and service change as we were able to ascertain exactly which aspects of service provision had been improved. Most improvements were considered purely in terms of cost-cutting exercises; indeed, this would have been the most beneficial aspect of implementing a new DSH policy. However, by applying the 7 Es we were able to look in greater depth at other improvements. Whilst there may be debate over the 'ethics' of such a proposal, one could certainly argue that it sought to empower patients fully. In addition the environment has been improved in terms of safety and care is more effective and efficient because of the proactive interventions.

Furthermore, the implementation of a separate DSH policy embraced the following aspects of new NHS performance measurement areas (DH 2000):

- Health improvement – the reduction of adverse fatal incidents.
- Effective delivery of appropriate healthcare – more therapeutic, less invasive intervention in management of DSH and easier access to information, ensuring all risk areas are identified.
- Efficiency – reduced expenditure on one-to-one reactive interventions, less wastage of time and human resources and easier flow of information.

Box 7.2   Reviewing service provision using the 7 Es framework.

Economic	The strategy seeks to reduce the existing expenditure, on one-to-one interventions.
Efficiency	There are opportunities to develop a specialist service, which could generate more income, due to the lack of existing resources.
Effectiveness	The strategy seeks to promote more therapeutic interventions.
Equity	The strategy will be used for all patients with identified histories of DSH.
Ethics	It seeks to empower patients, and care is based on collective decision-making by all MDT members.
Environment	Improvements to the environment reduce the risk of fatality.
Empowerment	Patients have greater autonomy to express themselves, in a safe fashion.

- Patient/carer experience – greater autonomy, empowerment and insight into the need to self-harm, and appropriate care intervention from the point of admission.
- Health outcomes of NHS care – increased quality of services, reduced expenditure and seeking to be responsive to patients' needs all meet the needs identified by clinical governance, NHS frameworks and standards set by external regulators, such as the National Institute for Clinical Excellence (NICE) and Commission for Health Audit and Improvement (CHAI) (now the Healthcare Commission).

The application of the entire process was considerably time-consuming. In the context of day-to-day management it would be unrealistic and impractical to apply all of the theoretical aspects to any given project systematically. However, from a practical stance certain tools could be used or aspects of the model adopted intrinsically to enable strategic, focused thinking within the ward's turbulent environment.

Conclusions

Clinical governance emphasises the need for NHS organisations to be accountable for improving the quality of their services continuously and safeguarding high standards of care (DH 1997, 1998, 2001). With the focus for improvement in partnerships, performance, professions, patient care and prevention – the 5 Ps (Jumaa *et al.* 2000, Martin 2001a), care systems rely upon effective interprofessional co-operation and partnership. Whilst these interventions gave rise to ethical debate, it should be emphasised that the implementation of this policy sought to reduce the number of fatal incidents and violence directly attributable to patients engaging in DSH. The emphasis on patient and staff empowerment sought to capitalise on the behavioural philosophy adopted within the learning disability environment and to utilise existing resources in a more proactive, efficient and effective manner. The application of the evidence-based CLINLAP model ensured that this was done in a structured, deliverable and achievable fashion, providing a clear focus for the forensic learning disability service and other services who use this approach.

These true, tried and tested management and leadership concepts, tools, techniques and theories, presented through the overarching organising framework of the CLINLAP model, have helped us in a significant way as nurse managers and healthcare practitioners. With the emphasis upon power sharing, they seek to apply theory to practice systematically, in a workable and user-friendly way, amid the turbulent and ever-changing political environment. Current managers are expected to implement strategy, influence change and meet stakeholder expectations; the CLINLAP model assisted strategic thinking without neglecting clinical practice. This is contrary to beliefs that the creation of such a 'toolbox' can imply that management is just a series of 'tricks' that anyone can perform (McSweeney 1997). With education and experience, these tools provided a framework that assisted strategy formulation and implementation. After all, what matters is how such tools were owned, co-ordinated and put to good use in improving and sustaining continuous quality service to patients.

References

Allen, D. (2000) The NHS is in need of strong leadership. *Nursing Standard*, **14** (25), 25.

Baker, C., Ogden, S., Prapaipanich, W., Keith, C., Beattie, L. & Nickleson, L. (1999) Hospital consolidation: applying stakeholder analysis to merger life-cycle. *Journal of Nursing Administration*, **29** (3), 11–20.

Campbell, A. & Yeung, S. (1990) *Do You Need a Mission Statement (Ashridge Mission Model)*. Special Report no. 1208. The Economist Publications Management Guides, London.

Cook, M.J. (1999) Improving care requires leadership in nursing. *Nurse Education Today*, **19** (4), 306–312.

Cook, M.J. (2001) The attributes of effective clinical nurse leaders. *Nursing Standard*, **15** (35), 33–36.

Cortis, J. (1999) Patients first? *Nursing Management*, **5** (10), 15–18.

Curtis, E. & White, P. (2002) Resistance to change: causes and solutions. *Nursing Management*, **8** (10), 15–20.

Davies, M. (1999) A simple approach to the management of risk in a local mental health service. *Psychiatric Bulletin*, **23**, 649–651.

Department of Health (1997) *The New NHS: Modern and Dependable: A National Framework for Assessing Performance*. The Stationery Office, London.

Department of Health (1998) *A First Class Service: Quality in the NHS*. The Stationery Office, London.

Department of Health (1999) *The NHS Costing Manual*. The Stationery Office, London.

Department of Health (2000) *Quality and Performance in the NHS. Performance Indicators*. The Stationery Office, London.

Department of Health (2001) *Building a Safer NHS for Patients. Implementing an Organisation with a Memory*. The Stationery Office, London.

Faugier, J. & Woolnough, H. (2002) National Nursing Leadership Programme. *Learning Disability Practice*, **5** (10), 32–37.

Goleman, D. (2000) Leadership that gets results. *Harvard Business Review*, March–April, 78–90.

Grant, R.M. (1995) *Contemporary Strategy Analysis: Concepts, Techniques, Applications*. Blackwell Business, Oxford.

Handy, C. (1993) Trust and the virtual organisation. *Harvard Business Review*, May–June, 40–50.

Hannigan, B. (1998) Assessing the new public management: the case of the National Health Service. *Journal of Nursing Management*, **6** (5), 307–312.

James, V. (1995) Health care provision: the six key players. *Nursing Standard*, **9** (39), 30–32.

Johnson, G. & Scholes, K. (2002) *Exploring Corporate Strategy; Text and Cases*, 6th edn. Prentice Hall, Hemel Hempstead.

Joshua-Amadi, M. (2003) A study in motivation. *Nursing Management*, **9** (9), 14–19.

Jumaa, M.O. (2001) *Enhancing Individual Learning and Organisational Capability Through Learning Projects and Developmental Interventions.* Unpublished Research Project Report, part of a Doctor of Professional Studies (DProf), through work-based learning in strategic leadership and strategic learning in nursing and healthcare, Middlesex University, London.

Jumaa, M.O. & Alleyne, J. (2001) Learning, unlearning and relearning: facilitation in community nursing for delivering the new primary care agenda. In: *Organisation Behaviour and Organisation Studies in Healthcare: Reflections on the Future* (ed L. Ashburner). Palgrave (Macmillan), Basingstoke.

Jumaa, M.O., Talib, Y. & Shuldham, C. (2000) The 5 Ps of nursing management. *Nursing Management*, **7** (3), 6–7.

Martin, V. (2001a) Service planning and governance. *Nursing Management*, **8** (2), 32–36.

Martin, V. (2001b) Service planning and governance: part two: managing accountability and risk. *Nursing Management*, **8** (3), 33–37.

Martin, V. & Henderson, E. (2001) *Managing in Health and Social Care.* Routledge, London.

McSweeney, P. (1997) People come before plans. *Nursing Management*, **3** (8), 16–17.

The Open College (1992) *The PARTNER Approach. Managing Information* (Workbook 1). The Open College, Didsbury.

Peters, T. & Waterman, R.H. (1982) *In Search of Excellence.* Harper and Row, New York.

Phillips, J. (2001) Risky business. *Learning Disability Practice*, **4** (3), 18–24.

Richardson, A. (2002) Competitive advantage: implementing strategy in the NHS. *Nursing Management*, **9** (4), 14–17.

Further reading

Jumaa, M.O. & Alleyne, J. (2002) Strategic leadership in health care in challenging times. In: *Organisation Development in Health Care, Strategic Issues in Healthcare Management* (eds R.K. Rushmer, H.T.O. Davies, M. Tavakoli & M. Malek). Ashgate Press, Slough.

Martin, V. (2000) Effective team leadership. *Nursing Management*, **10** (5), 26–27.

NHS Modernisation Agency (2002) *Managing the Human Dimensions of Change.* Ancient House Printing Group, Ipswich.

Porter, M.E. (1985) *Competitive Advantage: Creating and Sustaining Superior Performance.* The Free Press, New York.

8 Leadership Through Group Clinical Supervision

Jo Alleyne and Mansour Jumaa

Introduction

The context of district nursing practice is very different to hospital-based nursing as district nurses are involved with multiple stakeholders, both within and outside the National Health Service (NHS). This includes clients' homes, General Practitioners' surgeries, social services residential care homes, health centres and clinics. In addition to providing nursing care, district nurses need to develop specialist skills such as the application of new technologies in chronic disease management. The location of the district nurse's workplace is variable, and there is an expectation that district nurses are accessible and available to meet the multiple stakeholder requirements. The current emphasis on 'shared-care' involves working with a multidisciplinary network of teams and practitioners. Thus the 'workplace' is a highly complex organisation in which health and social care objectives can only be met through effective collaborative relationships.

This project was concerned with learning together and working together, using co-operative inquiry in the development of district nursing sisters' management and leadership competencies, through group clinical supervision sessions. The co-researchers in this study were attempting to respond to the pressures for change within a complex NHS environment. Meeting the needs of multiple stakeholders with conflicting objectives and priorities amidst considerable constraints heightened the anxieties of this group of experienced practitioners, yet they had received little preparation or induction for these new ways of working. This study demonstrated that a structured approach to leadership and management development prepared the district nurses for new ways of working. This was achieved through focused management and leadership developmental activities within a supportive environment of group clinical supervision. Throughout this chapter we discuss the concept of clinical supervision, its structure and function, and provide a rationale for the group format adopted for this study, concluding with what in our view is the value added of this approach.

What is clinical supervision?

This study sought to evaluate the application of the CLINLAP model as the major intervention for the facilitation of group clinical supervision, initially because of the perceived cost-effectiveness of this approach. The research literature offers definitions of the term clinical supervision as well as personal opinion on its structures and functions, evidence of its benefits and theoretical perspectives on the interpersonal processes between supervisor and supervisee.

Clinical supervision has variously been defined as:

- a formal process of professional support and learning which enables practitioners to develop knowledge and competence, assume responsibility for their own practice and enhance consumer protection and safety of care in complex situations (DH 1993, p. 3)
- an exchange between practising professionals to assist the development of professional skills (Butterworth & Faugier 1993, p. 12)
- the process whereby a practitioner reviews with another person his or her ongoing clinical work and relevant aspects of his/her own reaction to that work (Minot & Adamski 1989, p. 23)
- a practice-focused professional relationship involving a practitioner reflecting on practice, guided by a skilled supervisor (UKCC 1996, p. 4)
- a dynamic, interpersonally focused experience, which promotes the development of therapeutic proficiency (CPNA 1985)
- an interpersonal process where a skilled practitioner helps a less skilled or experienced practitioner to achieve professional abilities appropriate to his or her role and at the same time offers counsel and support (Barber & Norman 1987)

As can be seen from these definitions the expectations of clinical supervision are far-reaching and include therapeutic proficiency, professional development opportunities, acquisition of new knowledge and the provision of supportive networks. The emphasis in each of these definitions is on individual development through the dynamic nature of the interpersonal process. At a basic level, clinical supervision is:

- an interpersonal process involving at least two people, a supervisor and a supervisee
- focused on learning from work experiences
- mutually agreed between the participants in terms of its purpose, process and expectations
- confidential to those involved
- aimed at personal development
- concerned with safe professional practice
- driven through reflection on practice and analysis of practice situations
- intended to be an element of all practitioners' practice.

There is much debate within the literature regarding the nature of clinical supervision, especially in regard to the role reflection plays within it. Fowler & Chevannes (1998), for instance, suggest that reflection may be inappropriate for some practitioners, especially those that are inexperienced, whereas Binnie & Titchen (1995) consider that the functions and tasks of clinical supervision are inexplicably linked to the development of critical reflection, suggesting that clinical supervision provides the formalised setting within which reflection can take place (Rolfe *et al.* 2001).

However, clinical supervision is often perceived as a form of 'therapy' and this, whilst potentially helpful, is vague and limited. We can also see from this discussion that none of these descriptions suggests models that could guide reflection – perhaps there is an assumption that the practitioners have the reflective skills required? There is also an imbalance of the power relationship between supervisor and supervisee suggested within these definitions, and there is no suggestion that management or leadership models and frameworks could be useful in framing and providing boundaries for the sessions. Nor do any of these descriptions mention the importance of managing the emotions that supervision sessions might stimulate. Whilst acknowledging that this approach might be relevant for some, it is not comprehensive enough to include the environment of care.

Many models and frameworks for clinical supervision have been proposed, and these can be used in both individual and group supervision settings. They fall into several types:

- The humanistic model, e.g. Rogers (1981)
- The cognitive-behavioural model, e.g. Beck (1976)
- The systemic model, e.g. Holloway (1995)
- Structural frameworks, e.g. the cyclical model of Page & Woskett (1994)
- Developmental frameworks, e.g. Hawkins & Shohet (1989)
- Goal-orientated frameworks, e.g. Proctor (1986)

Within each of these are a number of variables, the combination of which provides a multitude of styles and modes through which clinical supervision may occur. Success of supervision is dependent upon a clear contract being drawn up at the start of a supervisory relationship detailing such issues as the nature and purpose of supervision, the conditions under which it operates, the values and beliefs underpinning the relationship, and the focus that supervision will take. The result of these will direct the nature of the relationship itself, and the style of supervision that occurs.

Group clinical supervision

Rolfe et al. (2001, p. 121) summarise the features of group clinical supervision (Box 8.1) and offer several models that can be used, together with exploration of the roles of group members and that of the group facilitator.

However, caution is offered concerning the possibility of group dynamics dominating the proceedings at the expense of supervision, game playing as

Box 8.1 Summary of the features of group clinical supervision. (Adapted from Rolfe *et al.* 2001, pp. 84, 100–103.)

- The group is formed for a specific common purpose.
- Case material can be used in such a way that it provides a learning opportunity for the whole group.
- It is crucial to the function of the group to establish ground rules and to discuss equal access to supervision.
- There is potential for the group to be used as a resource for feedback processes and the creation of a variety of perspectives.
- The size of the group can affect the success of the supervision.
- It is more economic than individual supervision.
- Peer support and peer feedback can be facilitated.
- There is access to a wide variety of experiences within the group.
- Functions range between intrapersonal group supervision, interpersonal group supervision and transpersonal group supervision.

part of the dynamics, and that individuals receive less specific attention to their own issues (Hawkins & Shohet 1989, Rolfe *et al.* 2001).

Overall though, the literature lacks focus on the context in which various nursing activities take place. There is little reference made to the external and internal environmental factors, which may impact or even impede the delivery of high quality nursing activities. Yet what is evident from the literature is the view that organisational factors have impeded the implementation of group clinical supervision. If we consider the number of policy drivers for quality implementation and monitoring, life-long learning and self-regulation for example, these factors alone have presented healthcare organisations with a challenge to transform the way in which they operate. Such drivers also provided the impetus for this study to adopt a renewed interest in clinical supervision. Management and leadership development were seen as crucial factors to be explored.

Why was this project needed?

We have argued in the section above that generally the approaches taken towards the implementation of clinical supervision largely ignore the issue that nursing does not take place solely as a personal practice. Nursing is located within a community, within complex organisations, including other disciplines and teams working together within organisational cultures which are notoriously 'messy'. Approaches to clinical supervision have not considered the importance of the dominant cultural paradigm of the organisation (Johnson & Scholes 2002) and how this paradigm impacts on the development of individuals' capabilities and their performance within these organisations.

Enhancing the learning of individual nurses can only be accomplished within an appropriately supportive environment. Such support must acknowledge and take into account the power differentials within such contexts. Any approach that focuses on training and development of inter-personal relations at the expense of exploring the structural, technological and organisational power systems is doomed to failure (Bloor 1999). It is our view that a pluralist approach is needed which takes account of the effective management of the cultural web (Johnson & Scholes 2002). This has the potential to create an environment for strategic learning to occur in, but without strategic thinking it will not occur. Strategic learning for the purpose of this study was seen to have been achieved when the co-researchers began to make things happen within their organisation. Such a pluralist approach is not reflected in any of the structures currently used within the processes of clinical supervision. This may well be one of the significant factors for its ad hoc implementation, even when it is part of an organisational strategy.

What are leadership and management?

This study was premised on the view that leadership is a 'special' form of management, a view consistent with that of Rajan (2000), who contends that there is confusion about management and leadership. Management within the frame of this study is about today, rational processes and process man-agement, whereas leadership is about tomorrow, emotional horizons and change management. These views provided further rationale for the theoret-ical frameworks used throughout the inquiry and provided us with the opportunity to consider the context, content and processes which further informed the scope of the inquiry.

A critical review of the relevant literature relating to the concept of group clinical supervision demonstrated a gap in professional implementation of group clinical supervision for district nurses and provided the theoretical basis for the inquiry. Relevant theoretical perspectives were considered, with a particular focus on the role of evidence-based management and leadership frameworks, inherent within the CLINLAP model.

How can group clinical supervision facilitate leadership/management development?

We adopted the view that group clinical supervision, when effectively imple-mented via Heron's (1983, 1989, 1990) approach, together with the relevant management and leadership concepts via the CLINLAP model, represented an effective process of clinical leadership; that is, when the district nurses effectively facilitated sessions, focusing specifically on interpersonal skills, group skills, affective skills, and appropriate management and leadership developmental activities, they were demonstrating effective clinical leadership. This perspective informed the operational definition of clinical supervision designed specifically for the study as:

> a purposive formal activity, which facilitates the solution of interpersonal and group problems, by focusing on workplace problems and conflicts, with the primary purpose of improving healthcare services through managerial clinical decision making. (Alleyne 2002)

Towards a new definition of group clinical supervision

This new definition was developed because it builds on elements of previous definitions and makes explicit the tensions, complexities and conflicts that existed in the context of district nursing at the time of the study; a context in which clinical and managerial responsibilities were a feature of the district nurses' work, and yet they were attempting to 'juggle' competing demands – from their line managers, GPs, clients and team colleagues. This context of uncertainty, change and ambiguity provided a rationale for the selection of the CLINLAP model for the inquiry because it views strategic nursing leadership and learning as essential prerequisites for the development of nursing practice within the complex social and organisational milieu of health and social care situations. As Ashburner (2001) noted, the CLINLAP model focuses on actionable knowledge through an exploration of issues of effective leadership development.

Why the CLINLAP way?

The assumptions of the CLINLAP model needed to be understood and accepted if they were to be compatible with the aims of the inquiry, and it has been acknowledged that in this inquiry that was the case. The assumptions are as follows:

- Clinical staff need to believe in strategic workplace learning for continuous quality improvement.
- The achievement of multiconstituent satisfaction of all practitioners involved in the processes of care, recipients and providers is paramount.
- Satisfaction is only possible through collaborative working amongst all health and social care practitioners, including patients, clients and users.

Whilst in our view these assumptions were compatible with the aims of the inquiry, they did not appear to address directly the major cultural change which is a central feature of the NHS Modernisation Agenda generally and clinical leadership development specifically. Therefore, for the purpose of the inquiry within the context of district nursing, we added the assumption that:

- Rebalancing the power relationships within the district nursing work-place is necessary for the development of clinical, managerial and leadership competencies.

Research aim and questions

The overall aim of this research was to *identify, create and evaluate effective processes for collaborative working so that the nurses' capacity for clinical/managerial decision-making could be improved*. The inquiry was conducted over two and a half years and sought to answer the following questions:

- How have expertly facilitated group clinical supervision sessions assisted district nurses to improve their clinical leadership/managerial competencies?
- What has been the impact of focused interventions of management and leadership developmental activities on the practice of district nurse team leaders?
- What needs to happen in a collaborative way for district nurses to exploit the workplace as a source of learning?
- What contribution has the CLINLAP model made to the balance of power relations within the world of district nurses?

Methodology

A case study approach for the focused group clinical supervision sessions was used, involving six district nurses and two doctoral candidates. The district nurses had previously attended a two–day management development workshop and were subsequently required as part of the NHS Trust clinical governance framework to receive clinical supervision. We were asked by the Chair of the district nurses forum to provide them with clinical supervision and it was agreed that the authors of this chapter would co-facilitate the supervision sessions using the small group approach. One of us is an accredited facilitator of personal, group and organisational development. Working with him had provided the others with opportunities for enhancing their own facilitation skills. The supervision group, having requested two facilitators, clearly found that the approach met their developmental needs. The lead author became the main facilitator for the group after one year, and by then we had agreed that the inquiry group should be established for the purpose of this research project. The collaborative relationship between us continued, providing significant peer consultancy and supervision throughout the remainder of this inquiry. This approach ensured that throughout the life of the inquiry the co-researchers were able to achieve a sufficient degree of inter-dependent collaborative reflection and management, thereby ensuring that this work was genuinely 'with the participants and not just about them or on them' (Heron & Reason 1997, p. l85).

When can research and development become an empowerment process?

The co-operative inquiry approach was utilised for the exploration and illumination of the lives of the district nurses and ourselves as co-researchers and facilitators of the focused group clinical supervision sessions. We had three closely interdependent and fundamental issues relating to the empowerment of others to consider:

- the initiation of group members into the methodology of the inquiry, in this case the CLINLAP model and Heron's politics of learning (Cognitive and Methodological Empowerment)
- the emergence of participative decision-making and authentic collaboration so that the inquiry became truly co-operative (Political Empowerment)
- the development of emotional competence and political maturity, essential for clinical and managerial development (Interpersonal Empowerment)

A further influence on the method of inquiry was feminist research perspectives. Feminist research seeks to reject the discourses and practices that ignore, marginalise and objectify women's experiences. Feminist perspectives, which specifically emphasise the value of diversities and antidiscriminatory practices, are essential features of emancipatory research and provide ways of challenging masculine power structures – in this case the biomedical model and hierarchical structures of district nursing.

A feminist perspective offers an opportunity to 'reconceptualise' research methodology, through its strong critique of the traditional positivist view of science, and these views are well articulated within the literature. It is our view that feminist research is also appropriate as a critical form of inquiry when seeking to question previous assumptions, patterns of behaviour and power relations, which have previously been taken for granted. This inquiry has also indicated how management theories, tools and techniques, which have been accused of a 'gender-blind' bias, when carefully and sensitively crafted and applied, can provide useful frameworks, which would enable the co-researchers to manage their district nursing work effectively.

Rowan (1981) articulated a 'formalised' approach to cooperative inquiry through a dynamic model of six stages or processes. The co-operative inquiry approach adopted for this study was an example of the dialectical process, in which the co-researchers determined the purpose of the inquiry as being of significance to the way in which they worked as district nurses. More importantly, the research method focused on ways of creating knowledge that involved learning from investigation and applying what was learned to problems they encountered in their workplace. In order to extend the concept

Box 8.2 Diagrammatic representation of the Rowan (1981) research cycle, CLINLAP, Heron's (1989) interventions.

R & D domain*		
BEING	**PHASE ONE** **GCS issue analysis** *Where are we going?* **Stage 1–Align**	**Specific goals** *Supportive and informative interventions; valuing and meaning dimensions; awareness*
THINKING	**PHASE ONE** *Where are we going?* **Stage 2–Plan**	**Specific goals** *Prescriptive intervention; planning dimension; ownership*
PROJECT	**PHASE TWO** **GCS issue solution formulation** *Where are we now?* **Stage 3–Use tools** **Stage 4–Match**	**Explicit roles** *Catalytic (×2) intervention; structuring dimension (×2); identification discrimination*
ENCOUNTER	**PHASE THREE** **Challenging rigidities via GCS** *How are we going to get there?* **Stage 5–Reassess**	**Clear processes** *Confronting intervention; confronting dimension; acceptance*
MAKING SENSE	**PHASE THREE** **Challenging rigidities via GCS** *Which route should we take?* **Stage 6–Fit**	*Cathartic intervention; feeling dimension; choice*
COMMUNICATION	**PHASE FOUR** **Implement quality service via GCS** *How do we ensure we arrive as agreed and also check our journey?* **Stage 7–Act**	**Open relationships** *Supportive intervention; valuing dimension; transmutation; expression; control; catharsis*

*Rowan's Research Cycle (1981)

of collaborative inquiry this study utilised management and leadership knowledge and frameworks with the sole aim of developing the district nurses' ability to analyse their problems, develop their own solutions and take actions to facilitate change.

The CLINLAP model as an iterative process provided the methods and strategy for the district nurses to engage in effective problem-solving through achieving a consensus on their goals and priorities, as well as determining ways and means to implement these in order to work collaboratively within their teams. The diagrammatic representation of the research cycle, the CLINLAP model and Heron's (1989) interventions are shown in Box 8.2.

Project activities

The participants in this project were largely driven by anxiety about their performance as district nurse team leaders within the same organisation. There was a question mark over organisational structures and staffing, so the future of some of the co-researchers was in doubt. We recognised the need to address anxiety as a powerful block to learning and practice development. By mutual agreement the group clinical supervision sessions focused on the practical issues relating to the participants' roles, rather than focusing on issues that were outside of their control. It was also agreed that we would use frameworks and theories to ensure that the participants were acting legitimately and with responsibility and accountability. Our role as facilitators meant that we convened the group sessions, facilitated the discussions and acted as 'devil's advocate' when appropriate.

What follows is a brief analysis of the group clinical supervision stories in the first phase of the research cycle when we introduced the Cultural Web (Johnson & Scholes 2002) to tease out the district nurses' perceptions of their internal workplace environment.

Power structures

The district nurses were aware of their own form of 'expert power' in relation to their patients because of the importance of their direct clinical actions on patients' wellbeing. However, their power was dependent on their ability to satisfy other major stakeholders, such as the patients' families. Power was also perceived to be located with the GPs, who were also viewed as key stakeholders. The district nurses held the view that the development of nursing leadership, described in various policy documents such as *Making a Difference* (DH 1999), would be resisted by GPs. The clinical service managers were also attributed as holding positional power within the nursing hierarchy. The balance of power relations was seen to be shared unequally between doctors and managers, with the district nurses perceiving themselves to hold less formal power or authority than the GPs and their line managers.

Organisational structures

The complex world of the district nurses has been described in the earlier sections of this chapter. The formal organisation of a large NHS Trust remained very hierarchical, with few informal networks available for the district nurses in this study. The lack of team-working between health centres and clinics across the four quadrants of the Trust appeared to encourage a sense of competitiveness rather than collaboration between district nursing teams.

Control systems

The district nurses' performance had previously been monitored directly by their line managers; however, an organisational restructuring of clinical service managers had resulted in a reduction in the number of these posts. Centralisation of the line managers' locations meant that they were not in the same health centre as their teams. This had resulted in the delegation of team management responsibilities to the district nurses. The method of monitoring performance appeared to be that of an over-reliance on disciplinary procedures.

Stories and myths, rituals, routines and symbols

The district nurses' stories were consistent in the way in which they perceived themselves as having an overwhelming workload including patient caseloads. Such clinical activities prevented them from managing effectively. They provided examples of clinical routines and rituals that were not always substantiated by research evidence and provided accounts of how they 'infantilised' the processes of patient care by 'putting patients in their place'. The district nurses perceived themselves as having 'lost' previous status symbols such as designated offices and car parking permits. In relation to other primary care nurses, the nurses perceived themselves as the 'poor relation'. The consensus view at this stage of the inquiry was that they perceived the workplace environment as unsupportive of their leadership and management developmental needs.

The context of the district nurse's world prior to group clinical supervision

The cultural web analysis provides a snapshot of the district nurses' perceptions of their expressions of powerlessness within an organisation they viewed as 'hostile'. The cultural change required, for example for the implementation of clinical governance requirements, was viewed with skepticism. The district nurses anticipated resistance to change, primarily from the GPs.

The organisational climate at this time did not appear to the district nurses to be supportive in terms of their continuing professional development needs. The concept of clinical supervision being introduced by the organisation was also viewed with suspicion as a way of 'management is controlling' or 'policing' their practice.

This analysis of the internal environment of the district nurses' world has provided the backdrop against which this inquiry was made. The negative view of the organisation provided a challenge for the inquiry group, who were taking the power relationships for granted. Some of the district nurses sought to ignore the hierarchical relations of instrumental power, which they viewed as inevitable, choosing to focus on developing interpersonal relationships within their teams as a form of 'defence mechanism'. However, these attempts were interpreted by their line managers as examples of 'disruptive' interventions and failure to manage effectively.

Having described the organisational context of the district nurses' work, we now consider the content and processes we engaged in through the group clinical supervision sessions facilitated using focused leadership and management interventions.

Content and processes of group clinical supervision

The following sections of this chapter provide an account of some of the project activities, focusing on the strategic questions and the sub-questions used to inform the process of the group clinical supervision interventions. We also include a description and discussion of some of the management and leadership tools and techniques that were introduced at each stage. Extracts from the transcribed audiotaped interviews of the sessions are presented to illustrate the processes of the inquiry and the themes that emerged from the analysis of the narratives. These themes indicate areas of concern for the district nurses which appeared to be having a negative impact on their roles as clinical leaders/managers.

Problems with goals

The first strategic clinical question relates to alignment and planning, which involves the processes of aligning stakeholder expectations and setting specific goals. In this case the stakeholders needing to be satisfied were GPs, clinical nurse managers, district nursing staff, clients and families. An exploration of aligning district nurses' goals with those of the multiple stakeholders enabled problems to be surfaced and the planning dimension to be considered. This was achieved through the hierarchical (authoritative) mode of facilitation (Heron 1989), which was initially facilitator-centered interventions. The hierarchical mode was used in the early stages of the inquiry, the co-operative mode was used mid-way and the autonomous mode towards the later stages.

The group deliberations focused on how we could arrive at a set of object-ives that would satisfy the needs of multiple stakeholders. This was an important stage of the project as the district nurses reported that they were often unsure who the stakeholders were, and who the key stakeholders were.

This lack of clarity often meant that the district nurses were unclear as to the objectives they were attempting to achieve, and were unsure how to align clinical goals with stakeholder expectations. Furthermore, they were not sure how to plan and agree quality actions. Such concerns are related to the themes of 'not feeling valued' and 'fear of becoming stale'. These themes are illustrated by the following comments:

> Well, it's like I feel unsure at times just what I am supposed to do, and who I should be listening to. I'm covering three areas now, all with different GPs and they like things done their way, and with all that has been going on, I mean people have been disciplined and you feel for how they have been treated and wonder, because no-one says . . . what it is they've done. So I check the policy and even then . . . like when the specialist practitioner and I meet she's got her own view and that is looking at the same policy. . . . Different interpretations and like doctor . . . he likes things done his way and he's used to it and here am I new to his practice and he expects that things will be done that way. (District Nurse 1)

This district nurse's concerns about her own clinical competence were shared by others. She was also relating how she perceived a lack of confidence in existing clinical policies. In addition, she was having to respond to the de-mands of the doctor on the one hand and the interpretation of her manager of existing policies for care management on the other. This occurred within a climate where disciplinary action was being used in an aggressive manner, which had an 'unsettling' effect on her clinical performance. Focusing on goal setting, which is identifying who she had to satisfy, enabled us to determine an accurate and realistic understanding of what she was attempting to achieve. Concepts such as stakeholder mapping clarified who the key stakeholders were in this situation. The imbalance of power between the district nurses, the GPs and the line managers was also mediated through this approach, as the setting of *specific goals* was agreed to be a collaborative issue and not one that had to be viewed as contradictory or conflictual. This reduced some of the emotional 'labouring' that the district nurses were exhibiting.

Initially the district nurses demonstrated a lack of awareness of the stra-tegic goals and objectives of the NHS Trust, and, in most cases, the oper-ational objectives of their managers and the GPs. This inevitably led to conflict situations between district nurses, their managers and the GPs within and across the district nursing teams. The emotional impact of this situation is clearly demonstrated in the example given above. Simple rules for setting goals and objectives were introduced (such as SMART: Specific, Measurable, Achievable Realistic, Time-bound; Lewis 1995). This encouraged the district nurses to experiment with setting objectives for themselves and their district nursing teams. These techniques also reduced the anxieties which were frequently expressed during the sessions.

Power relations

Discussions about power relations were also addressed because of the relationship between power structures and goal setting. The key role played by GPs in determining the prescription of medical care was discussed. This provided an opportunity to reaffirm the contribution of the district nurses to care planning processes, with a general agreement that their work involved more than delivery of the medical aspects of patient care. They frequently described themselves as being 'torn' between the expectations of the clinical service manager and the GPs, resulting in them feeling pressurised and unable to plan or prioritise the caseload. All activities were viewed as important, with the district nurses unable to manage these competing demands.

The aims of the group clinical supervision sessions were to influence and direct the behaviours of the district nurses explicitly. They had agreed that they needed supportive interventions combined with information and the opportunities for experiential testing of frameworks, techniques and tools. They were keen to understand and apply the 4Ds (see below). The use of this matrix focused the group discussion on setting clinical practice priorities and at the same time reduced perceptions of conflict between themselves, their managers and the GPs. The district nurses were keen to use tools to improve their goal setting abilities and improve clinical decisions in relation to which tasks were:

- urgent and important – therefore it is a *do it* task
- important but less urgent – therefore it is a *delegate it* task
- less important to short-term needs and less urgent – therefore it is a *delay it* task
- low urgency and low importance – therefore it is a *drop it for now* task

Problems with roles

The district nurses were not always clear who should be involved in the delivery of care packages to clients or what information had been used to determine which care package should be received. These decisions were made by the clinical service manager responsible for determining the type of care – nursing or social care – based on the cost of each care package, including the time it would take to deliver the care to each client. It appeared that rather 'crude' measurements were being applied; this system was also causing concern for the district nurses:

> Why she decided it should be nurses doing personal care I don't know ... it should be social services. I don't understand, does it have to be a nurse? To me he doesn't need a nurse, he needs medicine but nothing else, he doesn't need feeding or bathing, but we don't do that any more ... the package of care would be better from one person. ... (District Nurse 4)

The district nurses frequently expressed feelings of frustration about their roles and it became clear that this related to a great deal of role ambiguity. They were introduced to Mintzberg's managerial roles (1973), which suggest that managers have 'formal' authority and status in their jobs and from this position come interpersonal roles which should inform informational and decisional roles. The district nurses were unsure which of the management roles they were expected to perform, as much of their usual work involved 'doing' everything themselves. The district nurses were introduced to a matrix which is a synthesis of Mintzberg's ten managerial roles on the vertical axis plotted against Reed's (1976) organisational roles analysis on the horizontal axis (Mansour's Matrix). This was completed as an inventory by each of the district nurses in order to identify their usual or preferred management role. This activity revealed that the majority of them were engaged in 'fire fighting', 'disturbance handling' and 'crisis management' which involved 'borrowing' staff from other teams or making a case for the employment of agency nurses to cover vacant posts. The district nurses had not received any management development and perceived that there was little support from their line managers:

> I know my role is management and leadership, I've not been prepared for that in anyway...it's very hard when you finish the district nursing course...not much management on that course, but you're put into a team leader's role. (District Nurse 3)

whilst another comment suggested that:

> A good manager should give you space, set objectives...be realistic and fair...is the main thing for me, being there for you, not being threatened or insecure...feeling undermined, many other things they should do...not let things slide for weeks, months, years in some cases, yes years, that is what has happened in some cases'. (District Nurse 4)

The district nurses' role analysis highlighted the need to develop other aspects of their management roles, such as communicating, seeking and receiving information and sharing information with their staff. Throughout these sessions we also focused on simple activities to assess the district nurses' emotional intelligence. Goleman (1999) describes the chief characteristics of someone with high emotional intelligence as being aware of emotions and being able to regulate them – this is termed 'personal competence' – whilst 'social competence' involves awareness and recognition of others' emotions.

Most of the narratives referred to 'teams'. The district nurses shared concerns about the size of the team, usually understaffed, team members not performing, identification of tensions within or across teams, or times when team members were not 'caring' towards each other, for example:

> Two people are not a team, we work well but it's a lot of pressure, she's doing the 998 course and that's added pressure, and I worry about...when I have a day off.

The other team ... there is one district nurse who when you're on the phone or when we try to have a meeting she's constantly butting in ... telling you how to run your caseload and she will only have heard half of the story ... and she's constantly stressed ... she stresses me out, when she's there it's chaotic ... is it her role to question what we do? (District Nurse 2)

Problems with processes

This is the fifth and sixth stage and third phase of CLINLAP, which emphasises the clear processes that are required for effective and efficient delivery of clinical services. At this stage the focus of the group clinical supervision was the reassessment of the organisation's needs, challenging rigidities and obsolete assumptions in the process. The key emotional requirement was acceptance. The targets for this part of the 'journey' are premised on a clear and comprehensive understanding of the developments in their enterprise's far and near external environment, as well as the internal capabilities of their enterprise. Then and only then will the district nurses be in a vantage position to know the most appropriate strategic decisions to achieve the enterprise's goals. The key questions addressed at this stage were:

- how nursing care is currently carried out
- why it is carried out this way
- how else it could be carried out
- what general strategic directions should be followed, given the identified present situation

Issues of caseloads

To provide a context for how these questions were used to guide the group interventions, we discuss one issue identified by the district nurses associated with a lack of clarity about resource allocation processes for the management of caseloads between different health centres. This is illustrated by the following comment:

we're always in crisis ... bailing out other services and the resources come from us ... always taking on more work despite a diminishing team ... joint working ... there's still resistance and it seems like the money comes from us.

In order to understand the perceived 'unfairness' of resource allocation the THEIMM tool (shown in Box 8.3) was introduced and provided a clearer process through which resource requirements could be established.

Engaging in this level of resource analysis enabled the district nurses to make effective decisions informed by a thorough understanding of the budget statement, resource allocation and resource management. Consequently, they made a case to their managers about the distribution of caseloads across the Trust.

Box 8.3 The THEIMM tool (Jumaa 2001).

Some examples

Time:	What are the requirements in terms of carrying out clinical actions?
Human:	What staff are required to carry out certain tasks? Does it always have to be a qualified nurse or someone else within the team?
Equipment:	Did staff have the appropriate technology for the task?
Information:	Did staff members have the appropriate evidence on which to base their practice?
Materials:	Which disposable products were required? Did nursing staff have access to them or did they have to travel for supplies?
Money:	Has a case been made for the necessary funds for this project?

Problems with relationships

The seventh stage and the fourth phase of CLINLAP focus on the implementation of a clinical leadership and management strategy for the achievement of high quality care. The following strategic questions were the focus of group sessions at this stage, which aimed to ensure the successful implementation of change:

- What are the main action stages and are they specific enough?
- What and where are the resources and do we have the agreed amount?
- Who is involved in the implementation process, how have they been informed, have they been informed clearly of their accountabilities, and how explicit are their roles?
- How open are the relationships, so as to expect support of other people?

The focus for effective district nursing service provision took into account the dominant cultural paradigm discussed earlier in this chapter. By this final stage of the project, after 18 months of group clinical supervision, the district nurses' views of the cultural paradigm had begun to change and they no longer viewed their service managers in such a negative manner.

Project outcomes

By the end of this inquiry the district nurses demonstrated how they were making sense of patterns from the past and planning for the future and facilitating the clinical leadership process. Examples of such developments included:

- the adoption of a project management approach to various initiatives such as leading a working party that produced a caseload-weighting model
- working together to devise a flexible staff rostering system within and across health centres
- questioning the dominance of GPs by initiating and leading case conferences with the multidisciplinary teams
- one participant facilitated group clinical supervision for other district nursing teams

They have all continued to apply the management and leadership frameworks, tools and techniques acquired through the group clinical supervision sessions.

Management and leadership skills for supervisors of group clinical supervision

The group sessions provided a fertile and supportive environment for creative thinking and for challenging commonly held assumptions and rigid approaches to the delivery of district nursing services. This inquiry clearly identified a strong and necessary component to group clinical supervision that is essentially managerial and leadership in nature, thus requiring skills and capabilities similar to those of nurse managers and executives. It would be difficult to accept the information in this chapter without recognising that the issues faced by the co-researchers in this study had to be managed appropriately within the clinical supervisory relationship. Therefore the challenge for practitioners wishing to apply the group clinical supervision approach will be achieved when 'good nursing' is accepted as being synonymous with 'good management'. However, high quality services can only be provided effectively when an effective management and leadership role is being performed well, and the CLINLAP model operationalised through group clinical supervision provided a framework for such developments to be achieved.

References

Alleyne, J. (2002) *Making a Case for Group Clinical Supervision Through Management and Leadership Concepts*. Unpublished Research Project Report, part of a Doctor of Professional Studies (DProf), through work-based learning in clinical nursing leadership, Middlesex University, London.

Ashburner, L. (ed.) (2001) *Organisational Behaviour and Organisational Studies in Health Care: Reflections on the Future*. Palgrave (Macmillan), Basingstoke.

Barber, P. & Norman, I.J. (1987) Skills in supervision. *Nursing Times*, **83** (2), 56–57.

Beck, A.T. (1976) *Cognitive Therapy and the Emotional Disorders*. International Universities Press, New York.

Binnie, A. & Titchen, A. (1995) The art of clinical supervision. *British Journal of Nursing*, **4**, 327–334.

Bloor, G. (1999) Organisational culture, organisational learning and total quality management; a literature review and synthesis. *Australian Health Review*, **12** (3), 152–179.

Butterworth, T. & Faugier, J. (eds) (1993) *Clinical Supervision and Mentorship in Nursing*. Stanley Thornes, Cheltenham.

Community Psychiatric Nurses Association (CPNA) (1985) *The Clinical Nursing Responsibilities of the CPN*. CPNA, Bristol.

Department of Health (1993) *A Vision for the Future: The Nursing, Midwifery and Health Visiting Contribution to Health and Health Care*. The Stationery Office, London.

Department of Health (1999) *Making a Difference*. The Stationery Office, London.

Fowler, J. & Chevannes, M. (1998) Evaluating the efficacy of reflective practice within the context of clinical supervision. *Journal of Advanced Nursing*, **27**, 471–478.

Goleman, D. (1999) *Working with Emotional Intelligence*. Bloomsbury, London.

Hawkins, P. & Shohet, R. (1989) *Supervision in the Helping Professions*. Open University Press, Buckingham.

Heron, J. (1983) *Education of the Affect*. University of Surrey, Guildford.

Heron, J. (1989) *The Facilitator's Handbook*. Kogan Page, London.

Heron, J. (1990) *Helping the Client. A Creative Practical Guide*. Sage, London.

Heron, J. & Reason, P. (1997) A participatory inquiry paradigm. *Qualitative Inquiry*, **3**, 274–294.

Holloway, E. (1995) *Clinical Supervision: A Systems Approach*. Sage, London.

Johnson, G. & Scholes, K. (2002) *Exploring Corporate Strategy; Text and Cases*, 6th edn. Prentice Hall, Hemel Hempstead.

Jumaa, M.O. (2001) *Enhancing Individual Learning and Organisational Capability Through Learning Projects and Developmental Interventions*. Unpublished Research Project Report, part of a Doctor of Professional Studies (DProf), through work-based learning in strategic leadership and strategic learning in nursing and healthcare, Middlesex University, London.

Lewis, D. (1995) *10-Minute Time and Stress Management: How to Gain an 'Extra' 10 Hours a Week*. BCA, London.

Minot, S.P. & Adamski, T.J. (1989) Elements of effective clinical supervision. *Perspectives of Psychiatric Care*, **25**, 22–26.

Mintzberg, H. (1973) *Nature of Managerial Work*. Harper and Row, New York.

Page, S. & Woskett, V. (1994) *Supervising the Counsellor*. Routledge, London.

Proctor, B. (1986) Supervision: a co-operative exercise in accountability. In: *Enabling and Ensuring* (eds M. Marken & M. Payne). National Youth Bureau and Council for Education and Training in Youth and Community Work, Leicester.

Rajan, A. (2000) Leadership in the knowledge age. *RSA Journal*, **2/4**, 60–63.

Reed, B. (1976) Organisational role analysis. In: *Developing Social Skills in Managers: Advances in Group Training* (ed. C.L. Cooper). Macmillan, London.

Rogers, C. (1981) *Client Centred Therapy*. Constable, London.

Rolfe, G., Freshwater, D. & Jasper, M. (2001) *Critical Reflection for Nursing and the Helping Professions: A User's Guide*. Palgrave, Basingstoke.

Rowan, J. (1981) A dialectical paradigm for research. In: *Human Inquiry* (eds P. Reason and P. Rowan). Wiley, London.

United Kingdom Central Council for Nursing, Midwifery and Health Visiting (UKCC) (1996) *Position Statement on Clinical Supervision for Nursing and Health Visiting*. UKCC, London.

9 Leadership for Evidence-Based Practice

Mansour Jumaa, Ilkka Kunnamo and Melanie Jasper

Introduction

Evidence-based medicine was introduced as a way of informing healthcare at the end of the 1980s and defined by Sackett *et al*. (1996) as combining the best possible evidence with clinical judgement. Since then the concept has been broadened to 'evidence-based practice' (EBP) as the basis for healthcare within all disciplines. The challenge, therefore, for leaders in healthcare is how this fundamental shift in the way we expect practitioners to inform their practice is implemented as a change strategy.

This chapter presents the results of a post-doctoral study[1] which explored the leadership successes of the '*Finnish way*' to EBP by general practitioners (GPs). It illustrates, using the LEADLAP model for analysis, how the problem of tackling healthcare delivery to a diverse, both geographically and culturally, population was implemented successfully. This provides a real-life example of how effective leadership strategies can be adopted for large-scale changes in the fundamental ways that healthcare practitioners use information to inform their practice.

The context of the study – the Finnish healthcare system

Since 1989 primary care physicians in Finland have consistently been using evidence-based medicine (EBM) guidelines for quality practice (Makela & Kunnamo 2001). In 2002 almost 100% of GPs and a growing number of nurses used these guidelines. This study set out to explore the management and leadership processes of the success of the 'Finnish way', and how it could be modified for nurses in the UK and elsewhere. To understand the Finnish way

[1] This post-doctoral travel study was possible through a Florence Nightingale Foundation Scholarship, awarded to Dr. Jumaa sponsored by the St Mary's Hospital League of Nurses, London.

139

we need to have some knowledge and understanding of the Finnish healthcare system[2].

The Finnish healthcare system is attracting international attention as a result of the special features it has compared to healthcare systems in other parts of the world (www.observatory.dk). When compared internationally, these features are as follows:

- The main responsibility for organising and financing healthcare has been devolved to the 448 municipalities.
- It has exceptionally small population bases.
- Parallel financing and delivery systems exist alongside the municipal service system.
- The number of nurses per head of population is one of the highest in Europe.
- Nurses have an extended role particularly in primary care and in the delivery of preventive services.

The Finnish healthcare system survived the severe economic crisis of the 1990s despite marked cuts in public sector budgets, including healthcare. The quantity and quality of healthcare services were largely maintained by improved evidence-based management and resource allocation.

The terms of reference of the study and the research questions

The overall aims of this project were:

- *in the short term*, to advance the study of evidence-based nursing practice through the use of management and leadership concepts. The *specific short-term aim* was to explore the 'leadership' success of the Finnish way, in terms of EBP by Finnish GPs (primary care physicians) and how it could be modified for use by nurses and others in the UK and elsewhere to promote their professional, management, leadership and personal development in relation to the implementation of EBP.
- *in the long term*
  - to promote excellence in nursing practice through the use of management and leadership concepts
  - to extend nursing knowledge and skills to meet changing needs in the UK NHS.

The project was required to:

- identify the key **attitudes**, **skills** and **knowledge** required to use and apply evidence (acceptable best practice) consistently during the process of care

---

[2] Readers who are interested in more details could access the website of the Finnish Ministry of Social Affairs and Health. Additionally, analytical and comparative information about the Finnish healthcare system is available from the European Observatory on Health Care Systems (www.observatory.dk). The Observatory has launched reports examining this health system alongside that of other European countries.

- recognise the role and influence of the dominant cultural paradigm (for example: rituals and routines; stories and myths; symbols; and organisational structures) in the consistent use and application of evidence in the process of care
- analyse the contribution of effective facilitation skills in the workplace in order to deliver EBP consistently.

The overall research and development questions were as follows:

- How would a focus on feelings and political skills, using systematic available evidence, assist with effective workplace EBP?
- What is the role of 'management learning projects' (LP) (Poell 1996) and 'leadership development interventions' (LDI) (Jumaa 2001) in a constantly changing workplace environment?
- How would a strategic leadership role address multiple stakeholder needs in the workplace in order to improve the quality of service delivery to patients based on acceptable evidence?

A focused literature review

Fundamental to this study were three key concepts, deemed to be interrelated to the notion of exploring the psychology and implementation of a change to the ways that nurses practice. These concepts are evidence-based nursing practice, emotions in healthcare and organisational culture.

Evidence-based nursing practice

Mulhall (1998, p. 5) suggests:

> Evidence-based care concerns the incorporation of evidence from research, clinical expertise and patient preferences into decisions about the health care of individual patients.

It thereby identifies the multiplicity of sources that evidence for practice can be drawn from. Hewitt-Taylor (2002, p. 48) goes on to say:

> The type of information used to generate an evidence-base for practice should be decided according to how appropriate each form of evidence is for the issue in question, and the availability of evidence.

This supports the rather obvious notion that evidence for practice is wide ranging. This is often confused with *research-based practice*, with only research findings perceived as evidence. If we accept this perception, it narrows the types of evidence available for practitioners to only that generated from research. McKenna *et al.* (2002) suggest that some types of evidence are regarded as better than others, and, indeed, this has led to what has been called a 'hierarchy of evidence', as shown in Box 9.1.

Box 9.1 The hierarchy of evidence (Ellis 2000).

1. The NHS Centre for Research and Dissemination or Cochrane database review
2. Large scale well-designed primary studies, RCTs and other controlled studies
3. Large scale primary studies using other methodologies
4a. Descriptive studies and reports (including national and local standards, guidelines, customer surveys, support groups)
4b. The opinions and experiences of respected authorities based on clinical experience and professional consensus

Not only are some types of evidence considered 'better', but also using a hierarchy suggests they are considered as more valuable and reliable than others. This can be seen as the source of the confusion that many practitioners have about EBP. Recently, the Grading of Recommendations, Assessment, Development and Evaluation (GRADE) group tried to develop a common, sensible approach to grading quality of evidence and strength of recommendations (the GRADE Working Group 2004).

However, if we return to the roots of evidence-based medicine, as proposed by Sackett *et al.* in the mid-1990s, we will see that the narrow definition of 'evidence' as research based was not intended. Sackett *et al.* (1996, p. 311) define evidence-based medicine as:

> the conscientious, explicit and judicious use of current best evidence in making decisions about the care of individual patients. The practice of evidence based medicine means integrating individual clinical expertise with the best available external clinical evidence from systematic research. By individual expertise we mean the proficiency and judgment that individual clinicians acquire through clinical experience and clinical practice.

This gives equal weighting to the clinical expertise and experience of the practitioner by suggesting that evidence alone is insufficient for decision-making – it is the *combination* of best evidence with clinical expertise that leads to EBP. As will be seen in the case study presented later in this chapter, it is this wider definition of EBP that is used within the Finnish primary care practitioners' everyday practice, as they combine the available objective evidence with their own professional judgment.

Achieving effective EBP in nursing specifically and health and social care generally and sustaining it requires nurses and others to engage in strategic management processes which would help to develop strategic thinking and strategic learning in their practice. Unfortunately, many nurse managers and leaders we know do not seek and utilise an evidence and knowledge base for sound decisions for their policy and practice (Hunt 1984, 1997). Nursing's track record in relation to research utilisation is not good. Constant criticisms and concerns about the lack of nurses' utilisation of research to ensure EBP is a perennial problem within the nursing profession (Hunt 1984, 1997, McGuire 1990).

Given this situation, success in the implementation of EBP in nursing requires emotional competence and capability, as described by Goleman (1999). EBP as a concept for the delivery of care by nurses and other healthcare professionals is relatively new, stemming as it does from the work of Sackett *et al*. Its widespread acceptance, initially by medicine, then latterly by the British government, is directing healthcare practitioners to change the way they have traditionally delivered care to their clients. It is clear that a wholesale change in practice in this way needs to engage the practitioners themselves in evaluating their foundational beliefs and values. This in turn is threatening, as it challenges the ways in which practitioners practice, and asking people to change in this way runs the risk of highly charged emotional responses. Thus, the implementation of EBP is a change that needs to embrace an holistic approach of the 'hearts, minds, hands and feet' of practitioners if it is to succeed; there is little in the literature to suggest that this has been addressed in combination.

Emotions in healthcare

Nursing is not alone in its apparent neglect of theories and empirical knowledge about feelings and how these relate to behaviour and decisions – these are also absent in the field of organisational behaviour. The most sophisticated knowledge about this subject appears to be in British and US television soap dramas. Those of us who help healthcare personnel learn emotional competence at work have few healthcare research studies to draw on. Few definitions of organisational behaviour research refer to feelings, yet feelings profoundly affect management decisions and practice (Ovretveit 2001). Feelings influence clinical practice and are important in patients' experience and behaviour, yet there is little scientific nursing research into or theories about the subject[3].

Enabling nurses, midwives, doctors and managers to understand their own and others' feelings in different situations could facilitate the implementation of EBP in nursing and healthcare. Nurse researchers can develop models and theories about feelings from empirical research into different healthcare situations, as demonstrated by Jumaa (2001), Alleyne (2002), Kennedy & Jumaa (2002) and McDaid (2002). In particular, it is important to find out more about emotional reactions to the imposition of change and how this impacts on individual and group behaviour. This could then be used to plan strategies for change that engage practitioners at both an emotional and an operational level.

However, change rarely affects just one person, nor does it operate in a cultural vacuum – in whatever environment we work we need to be aware of the organisational culture that underpins service delivery.

---

[3] One notable exception is Pam Smith's seminal study of '*The Emotional Labour of Nursing*' (Smith 1992).

Organisational culture

Bloor (1999) referenced key issues relating to organisational culture using Hatch's (1993) work identifying four major elements of culture – assumptions, values, artefacts and symbols – and the processes that link them which allow for both cultural change and stability.

Assumptions

The underlying assumptions that people have as general expectations of what is, or ought to be, organisational reality are proactively manifested as values. Changes in assumptions may, therefore, result in new values, as shown by a series of works by Jumaa & Alleyne (Alleyne 2002, Jumaa 1997, 2001, Jumaa & Alleyne 2001, 2002). New values, however, may reinforce assumptions or realign them through retroactive manifestation.

Values and artefacts

Processes of realisation link values and artefacts. For example, a rule that patient consent must be obtained before any procedure may realise a value of respecting patients' rights, but the action itself reinforces the value. Conversely, introducing new procedures has the potential to alter values retroactively. A concern for patients may lead to a need to collect information about them in order to fund new services, but the introduction of a data collection form may result in a new value of concern for comprehensive data collection that supplants the former one.

Symbols

Artefacts have the potential to take on a symbolic meaning through prospective symbolisation. For instance, spacious offices and large desks may symbolise status within an organisation rather than simply being tools. Retrospective symbolisation can result in actions consistent with symbols.

What Hatch (1993) identified is similar to the writings of Schein (1980) and Johnson (1988). All reinforce the fact that the dominant cultural paradigm in the workplace is central to all change management efforts, particularly in this case of the implementation of EBP. Successful and sustained implementation of EBP must pay special attention to the management and leadership of the dominant cultural paradigm.

What emerges from the literature is the interconnectedness, interdependence and interreliance of the emotional and cultural aspects of change when attempting to introduce new working practices into a healthcare environment. This study, in exploring the factors underpinning the success of the introduction of EBP into Finnish general practice, attempted to identify just how these had been approached in one culture, with the intention of generalising their findings.

Project activity including methods and processes

Table 9.1 summarises the features of the research design, which adopted an action research approach of collaborative enquiry[4].

Rationale for collaborative inquiry

Action research traces its origins back to the experiments of Kurt Lewin in the l940s, through socio-technical experiments which began at the Tavistock Institute, in London, and in particular their application to practices of social democracy and organisational change (Greenwood & Levin 1998). It is important to note that the idea of action research as a collaborative inquiry is simple: this is because, fundamentally, a collaborative inquiry as a research process means that people work together as co-researchers in exploring and changing their world. Research is carried out *with* them and not *on* them. Action research in this context is located within a *'new paradigm'* of thinking (Jumaa 2001). Reason & Bradbury (2001) proposed five broadly shared features which characterise action research. They are that action research:

- is about working towards practical outcomes
- aims to create new forms of understanding
- is a participative research process, and all participative research must be action research
- is emancipatory
- produces practical knowledge that is useful to people in the everyday conduct of their lives (Jumaa 2004, p. 60)

These represent the fundamental basis of this inquiry.

This inquiry was unique in the sense that it used participants' everyday reality as the focus of the study – no existing studies reporting this being used to study the implementation of EBP from a management and leadership perspective were found. In addition the assumptions that underpin the LEADLAP (Leadership Learning and Action Process) model made it explicit that skills for effective management and leadership within public sector organisations require managers who possess interpersonal, group and emotional competence skills (Jumaa 2001). Despite the dearth of hard evidence concerning this particular approach, drawing upon the knowledge of group dynamics, affective and emotional intelligence, political skill, management and leadership concepts and principles helped to provide support for the choice of this approach.

---

[4] Readers who are interested in more detailed discussions on the methodology and project activities similar to those adopted for this project would find Jumaa & Alleyne (2001, 2002) of interest.

Table 9.1 Summary of the project methodology.

Study design	Approach	Purpose
Method	Semi-structured interviews One-to-one sessions Workshops Discussions Document analysis	Identification of significant indicators, and assessment of evidence-based practice (EBP) qualities
Data sources	The inquiry group consisted of primary care physicians, nurses, managers, language interpreters within a medical professional organisation, senior officials from the national professional nursing organisation, academic staff from polytechnics and university nursing departments, multidisciplinary staff of a health centre in central Finland and volunteered members of the public in two large cities of Finland – Helsinki and Turku	Making sense of quality EBP and contextual influences
Investigator	One main researcher and co-researchers as detailed above	Collaborative inquiry combines theoretical and methodological expertise, promoting new ways of thinking, learning and doing. Does 'research' *with* others and not *on* them
Unit of analysis	Individuals; professional groups; relevant organisations; and significant events	An holistic, affective and political understanding of the context of and implementation of EBP
Theory	Review; application; development	Understanding, analysis and evaluation of EBP activities

Box 9.2 Using the LEADLAP model to elicit feedback about the 'Finnish way' (Jumaa 2003). EBP - Evidence-based practice.

Where do we need to be in relation to EBP? (SQ 1)
- Who are the stakeholders affected by the introduction of EBP?
- Are the goals of the key stakeholder compatible with the concept of EBP?
- What do you really, really want to do?
- Why must it be done at this time?
- Do you have an accurate and realistic understanding of what you are trying to do?

Where are we now in our EBP? (SQ2)
- Who does what? Why that person(s)? Who else could do it? Who should do it?
- What issues and problems must be resolved before you can achieve your goals?
- What are the key capabilities of your organization/unit/department?
- How are you going to establish a match between what you could, might, want and can do?

How are we going to get to our EBP goal? (SQ3)
- How is our service carried out currently?
- How else could it be carried out?
- How should it be carried out within the needs of the organisation?
- What are the key success factors (KSFs) for EBP within the organisation?
- What is the relationship of our strengths and weaknesses in relation to the identified KSFs?

Which route must we take to get to our EBP goal? (SQ4)
- What general strategic directions should we follow, given the identified present situation?
- What are the main strategic clinical options to meet our objectives for EBP?
- How do we intend to seek and maintain EBP as significant to the organisation's goals?
- What, if anything, is going to change in our professional actions?
- Which clinical strategy would suit EBP best?
- How well does the EBP strategy fit with our SWOT analysis?
- How well does the EBP strategy fit with organisation goals?
- Do we have the resources to deliver the agreed strategy on EBP?
- Will the staff and key stakeholders support the EBP strategy?

Continued

Box 9.2 *Continued*

How should we plan the 'exploration', as well as check our progress, in order to ensure we arrive at our EBP goal? (SQ5)

- How are we going to implement our EBP strategy?
- When must each step be completed?
- What are the main stages involved in putting the strategy into action?
- What is the logical sequence of the stages?
- How long do we expect each stage to take?
- What specific resources are required, and when must they be available?
- Which are the main tasks associated with the implementation of this strategy?
- What sort of clinical performance can we expect to see in certain key areas of this project to confirm that the EBP strategy is going according to plan?
- What specific factors might affect the success of this clinical strategy?
- What factors could the leader measure in order to monitor the success of this strategy?
- Which area of performance, what nature of data source and which type of data source are to be included in the EBP audit?
- What corrective actions would be suggested if the strategy is not implemented as planned?
- On reflection how was information put to strategic use in this EBP clinical strategy process?

The format was based on the five strategic questions (SQ1–5)[5] of the LEADLAP model (Jumaa 1997, 2001) presented in Box 9.2. The LEADLAP model is a

> strategic management and leadership performance implementation learning process that positions strategic learning as a driving force within health and social care organisations, on a day to day basis, in the management of goals; roles; processes; and relationships. (Jumaa 1997, 2001)

The participants were interviewed using the five strategic questions as the framework. Particular emphasis was placed on the role of the development of emotional intelligence, political maturity and leadership styles during the implementation of the EBP process.

---

[5] Most of this information refers to the in-depth, one-to-one sessions with the Editor-in-Chief of the Evidence-Based Medicine (EBM) Guidelines, Dr. Ilkka Kunnamo. Relevant information from the other sources of data collection are included as appropriate.

A small case study – the hallmark of the 'Finnish way'

Makela & Kunnamo (2001) describe the continuing success of EBP using a presentation of the typical features and benefits of the use of electronic guidelines in Finnish primary healthcare practice. The following description (Case study 9.1) presents an example of typical feedback from different stakeholders. The members of the public interviewed reported and confirmed

---

Case study 9.1   Diagnosing a skin condition using EBP

The patient was a 5-year-old boy brought in by his mother. The presenting symptoms did not relate to any of the boy's past medical history or any similar symptoms in the family. He now presented with a history of tiredness and irritability for 2 days. On that day he had woken up with an itching maculopapular exanthema all over his body and a pain in his left foot. The doctor admitted she had not seen anything like this in her 4 years at the health centre and felt she needed to consult the more experienced colleague next door. Prior to speaking to her colleague, she consulted the EBM Guidelines on her computer. The doctor, the patient and his mother all looked at the computer screen together for 'joint' diagnosis of the boy's skin condition. 'This is a little unusual. Let's see what the guidelines tell us', the doctor said to the patient and his mother as she opened the EBM Guidelines program and typed in search words in Finnish. 'Joint' gave 354 hits, 'exanthema' 211 and both words appear in 21 articles. The highlighted main eight headings include fever and exanthema in children, urticarial arthritis, Pogosta disease and Lyme disease.

The doctor quickly scanned the articles and the high-quality pictures of skin eruptions linked to them and brought up a picture of an exanthema almost identical to the one the boy had. All three of them looked and agreed that Pogosta disease, caused by Sindbis virus and occurring in epidemics in late summer, looked very similar to the boy's problem. The guideline text stated that this arbovirus is spread by mosquito bites, typically causing a monoarthritis that debuts simultaneously with the skin eruption. Both should heal spontaneously, the exanthema in a few days. NSAIDs can be given to ameliorate symptoms. Serology can be used to confirm the diagnosis.

The GP's main aim, in this instance, was to recognise the disease and avoid unnecessary investigations and inconvenience to both the boy and his mother. According to the EBM Guidelines article, if the boy had had fever, the main aim of GP work in 'Fever and exanthema in children' would have been to recognise severe infections requiring hospitalisation,

Continued

Case study 9.1 *Continued*

such as a meningococcal infection or Kawasaki disease. The guidelines warn against diagnosing drug allergy too eagerly and prompts that viral exanthemas are common. As a form of triangulation approach, the doctor sought to confirm her uncommon diagnosis by consulting with her more experienced colleague. After listening to the doctor's story, the senior colleague looked at the boy and the guidelines and agreed with the diagnosis. The boy and his mother left the health centre feeling reassured about the diagnosis – and very happy and relieved about the fact that the boy can go back to day care as soon as he feels fit to do so. Another doctor in the health centre saw an adult patient with a similar skin eruption 2 days after this visit and the patient was asked to return the following week. They decided to take serology from this adult patient and to discuss this with the microbiologist at the central hospital, who can inform physicians in the area about a potential epidemic.

the comprehensiveness and holistic approach of the primary care physicians with their patients and their carers.

This approach is a distinctive but everyday procedure at Finnish health centres and helps to explain why Finnish GPs are world leaders in this area of EBP. Unlike most nurses, the Finnish GP can and does make a 'free choice'. Furthermore, the Finnish way has overcome most, if not all, the barriers to evidence-based medicine in that:

- the existence of evidence does not guarantee its application by individual physicians; they have to need to do it – they have to feel that applying evidence makes their work easier and of better quality
- it means that consultation with colleagues is complemented by the guidelines
- it means strict and professional self-regulation regarding ethical adherence to the use of EBM guidelines

From the year 2002 electronic guidelines for nurses made by nurses have been available in Finland in the same format as EBM Guidelines. Partly stemming from an initiative from Karstula Health Centre, one of the sites of the study, a new distribution of clinical tasks between doctors and nurses is under way in more than ten pilot areas located all over Finland. This involves the use of the following as the tools for implementing change:

- guidelines and protocols
- multiprofessional, practice-oriented quality management teams
- adoption of new technology (e.g. tympanometers, maxillary sinus ultrasound, on-site laboratory tests performed by nurses)
- empowerment of patients by sharing of information and decision-making (see www.resourcefulpatient.org, Muir Gray 2002)

The clinical autonomy of nurses in the management of both chronic diseases and acute conditions, including all common respiratory tract infections, has increased since the implementation of this approach.

Key findings of the inquiry

The analysis and evaluation revealed a profile appropriate for effective implementation of EBP. This is the same profile appropriate for the effective development and implementation of strategic leadership and strategic learning in the workplace (Jumaa 2001).

Emerging themes from this study (Jumaa 2003) confirmed that during periods of uncertainty, as is currently the case in the UK's NHS:

- leadership without emotional intelligence will not improve services based on evidence
- whole-picture (strategic) thinking and learning is essential for evidence-based continuous effective quality care provision
- motivated and inspired staff will make a difference to patient outcomes and patient costs through EBP
- embedded people processes, such as the LEADLAP model, enhance the conditions for holistic care and learning, and provide a framework to locate the 'politics' and 'emotional' aspects of implementing EBP

The study concluded that the interplay of the following factors was responsible for sustaining EBP amongst the Finnish primary care physicians:

- a felt need for change, and also understanding that change through exploring *specific goals*
- the nature of the environment for healthcare practice and the practitioner's role in it through *explicit roles*
- the strategic issues of power in the workplace observed through *clear processes*
- the ability and the capability to convert tacit knowledge into explicit knowledge through *clear processes*
- the roles of stories, symbols and routines in the workplace negotiated through *open relationships*

The need to accommodate the reader's pre-existing knowledge is recognised. Hence, in order to reduce the likelihood of misinterpretation, this inquiry has used many methods and procedures (see Table 9.1) to collect the data. Whilst acknowledging that it is impossible to repeat perfectly the observations and interpretations relating to this inquiry, a process of using multiple perceptions (see Fig. 9.1) has been adopted. This, it is hoped, will clarify meanings through identifying different ways in which the phenomenon of implementing EBP is being seen.

Researchers using action research are aware of the crucial importance of conceptual knowledge, but also consciously engage in extended forms of

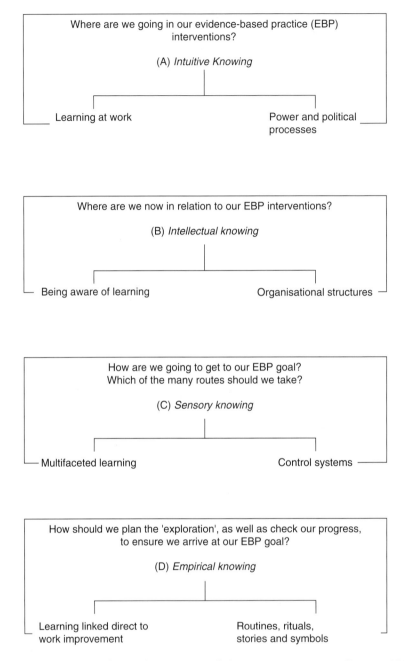

Fig 9.1 Framework for making sense of the project activities (Jumaa 2001).

epistemologies. This inquiry is no exception. In our analysis and evaluation of this case study we have shown how different ways of knowing (Torbert 1991) (see Fig. 9.1 and Table 9.2), in addition to more theoretical, conceptual ways of knowing, have been drawn on, and how they have informed the ways in which this work is represented.

Table 9.2 Synthesis of the outcomes of the study (Jumaa 2001).

Learning projects	Cultural web	Ways of knowing
Learning together	Power structures	Intuitive level of knowing
Being aware of learning	Organisational structures	Intellectual level of knowing
Multifaceted learning	Control systems	Sensory level of knowing
Learning linked to work improvement	Ritual and routines, symbols, stories and myths	Empirical level of knowing

The following sections of this chapter will now discuss and present the evidence, both theoretical and via the case study, of one of the 'new' seven roles of the strategic leader and strategic learner (Jumaa 2001), roles that are essential for the effective implementation of EBP.

The new nurse leader as stakeholder manager and strategic planner for EBP – a felt need for change and acting on that change

Stakeholders are those individuals and groups within and outside the nurse leader's organisation who depend on the organisation to fulfil their own goals and on whom, in turn, the organisation depends (Johnson & Scholes 2001). One of the potential dangers a nurse leader implementing EBP could fall foul of when identifying stakeholders for this type of project is to depend heavily on formal structure as a basis for this process. It is always advisable to unearth the 'informal network' of stakeholder groups and assess their importance. This was precisely what the small group of Finnish primary care physicians did at the beginning of their 'crusade' to add value to their medical practice through the use of guidelines in daily practice.

While this remains a difficult task to accomplish, it appears that the best structure for the management of the relationships and contracts between stakeholders is to be realistic about the balance of power between them. Morgan (1986) identified twelve sources of power that might affect a stakeholder analysis intended to assist the strategic nurse leader and strategic nurse learner to determine the objectives of their unit and/or organisation, particularly as they relate to implementing EBP. We outline below seven of these sources of power. They are:

- formal authority
- control of scarce resources
- organisational structures and procedures

- control of decision processes
- control of knowledge and information
- boundary management
- the ability to manage uncertainty

Nurses desiring to implement EBP have to be able to influence significantly, as the Finnish primary care physicians did, many if not all of these power bases. One of the implications of this requires the nurse to have a conceptual, as well as a practical, working knowledge of the nature of stakeholder relationships.

The Finnish primary care physicians' EBP represents a vivid and successful example of managing strategic change. The role played by the key change agents – now the Editorial Team of EBMG (Evidence-Based Medicine Guidelines) – clearly demonstrates the role of the leaders in managing meaning. When their activities were examined in detail, they reflected many of the ideas and precepts of leadership espoused by Senge (1990). They played the role of:

- designers, thus ensuring that EBM Guidelines (www.ebm-guidelines.com) written mainly by Finnish specialists were thoroughly edited to suit primary care use
- teachers, thus providing academic and professional supervision to other GPs implementing and investigating the clinical use of computerised primary care guidelines (e.g. Jousimaa 2001)
- stewards, by recognising and defusing defensive routines, focusing on areas of high leverage, and providing sympathetic explanations of negative management practices, as and when they occurred

These are some of the essential capabilities that nurses must display for an effective and sustained implementation of EBP.

A high quality R&D activity – could this approach be applied elsewhere?

The contributions from this study are well positioned to address current and key observed societal changes and developments. These include:

- the changing nature of knowing in the workplace
- the changing nature of work
- the effects of the global knowledge economy
- the urgent need to have a structure for nurses in the workplace to convert *tacit knowledge* into *explicit knowledge*
- the complexity and discontinuous change in health and social care which need a different type of leadership and learning

These could be applied elsewhere with the assistance of the strategies presented in this chapter, including Table 9.3.

This is the changing nature of knowing in the workplace. Survival in the workplace of the future demands that the nurse, midwife, health visitor and all

Table 9.3 Effective leadership for implementing EBP through the LEADLAP model (Jumaa 2003).

PHASE ONE (Stages 1 and 2) Specific *goals* via	• stating the purpose of the EBP team, based on an • understanding of stakeholder issues, analysis and management, leading to • deciding and agreeing on SMART[1] goals and objectives for EBP • recognising the role of ASTREAM[2] in planning for EBP
PHASE TWO (Stages 3 and 4) Explicit *roles* via	• an awareness of the impact of forces in the external environment that will affect implementation of EBP • the effect on health and social care due to changes within the healthcare industry and the NHS • identification of the required resources and clinical capabilities for the EBP team's viability and success
PHASE THREE (Stages 5 and 6) Clear *processes* via	• SWOT[3] analysis to determine the EBP team's relative strengths and opportunities • knowing the team's key success factors (KSFs) in care services • identifying the difference between needs and wants and the cost implications of EBP • a working knowledge of the new NHS clinical governance quality framework, and the modernisation agenda for the human resources performance framework. Ability to analyse cause and effect of clinical, managerial and/or leadership activities • understanding power issues and effect on what gets done. Recognising resistance in health and social services
PHASE FOUR (Stage 7) *Open relationships* via	• management of resistance against EBP • having the capacity to manage constant change in '*challenging*' contexts • ability to work with and/or change the dominant cultural paradigm in health and social care

[1]SMART – specific; measurable; achievable; realistic/relevant; time-bound/timely; [2]ASTREAM – agreed; specific; time-bound/timely; realistic/relevant; empowerment; achievable; measurable; [3]SWOT – strengths; weaknesses; opportunities; threats

other healthcare practitioners become capable of converting their many years of *tacit* knowledge into *explicit* knowledge for the benefit of their organisations, professions and themselves. This was the main strength behind the success of the Finnish way. Unfortunately, this is an area that needs significant improvement by nurses and nursing. The conversion of tacit knowledge into explicit knowledge through the processes of internalisation, socialisation, articulation and combination (Nonaka 1991) is built into the LEADLAP model. This capacity was one of the key success factors of the Finnish way and has enriched our understanding of the following (after Ferlie *et al.* 2001):

- a method of data collection which allowed for the empirical data to have strong internal validity – that is, 'it told it as it really was' (*validity*)
- the extent to which this inquiry went beyond pure empiricism to enable us to see relationships with a body of generic organisational theory (*authenticity*)
- different contexts allowed for the inquiry to demonstrate relevance to practice as well as to theory (*currency*)
- an opportunity to provide an explicit treatment of work-based learning methodology and research design (*transparency*)
- the inquiry moved beyond purely local studies to uncover underlying patterns and tendencies across sites by linking our findings to published works (*sufficiency*).

Conclusions and recommendations

The study set out to identify the success of the 'Finnish way' and how it could be modified for nurses in the UK and elsewhere. A number of management and leadership concepts, principles, tools and frameworks, located within the LEADLAP model, were used to reflect on and make sense of how EBP has been implemented and sustained by the Finnish primary care physicians and, increasingly, by nurses. They are now put forward, for your use, in the form of a template (Table 9.3) for your practice, as 'tried and tested' practical ways of grappling with the continuous changes taking place within the 'new' NHS. They are not presented as a panacea for all known health and social care ills. These tools, frameworks and methods need to be worked on with practice and persistence in order to yield the type of continuous high quality service and results demanded by patients, the government, the public and the nursing profession.

References

Alleyne, J. (2002) *Making a Case for Group Clinical Supervision Through Management and Leadership Concepts*. Unpublished Research Project Report, part of a Doctor of Professional Studies (DProf), through work-based learning in clinical nursing leadership, Middlesex University, London.

Bloor, G. (1999) Organisational culture, organisational learning and total quality management; a literature review and synthesis. *Australian Health Review*, **12** (3), 162–179.

Ellis, J. (2000) Sharing the evidence: clinical practice benchmarking to improve continuously the quality of care. *Journal of Advanced Nursing*, **32** (1), 215–225.

Ferlie, E., Gabbay, J., Fitzgerald, L., Locock, L. & Dopson, S. (2001) Evidence-based medicine and organisational change: an overview of some recent qualitative research. In: *Organisation Behaviour and Organisation Studies in Healthcare: Reflections on the Future* (ed. L. Ashburner). Palgrave (Macmillan), Basingstoke.

Goleman, D. (1999) *Working with Emotional Intelligence*. Bloomsbury, London.

The GRADE Working Group (2004) Grading quality of evidence and strength of recommendations. *British Medical Journal*, **328**, 1490–1494.

Greenwood, D.J. & Levin, M. (1998) *Introduction to Action Research: Social Research for Social Change*. Sage, Thousand Oaks, California.

Hatch, M.J. (1993) The dynamics of organisational culture. *Academy of Management Review*, **18** (4), 657–693

Hewitt-Taylor, J. (2002) Evidence-based practice. *Nursing Standard*, **17**, 14–15, 47–52.

Hunt, J. (1984) Why don't we use these findings? *Nursing Mirror*, **158** (8), 29.

Hunt, J. (1997) Towards evidence based practice. *Nursing Management*, **4** (2), 14–17.

Johnson, G. (1988) Rethinking incrementalism. *Strategic Management Journal*, **9**, 75–91.

Johnson, G. & Scholes, K. (2001) *Exploring Corporate Strategy*, 6th edn. Prentice Hall, London.

Jousimaa, J. (2001) *The Clinical Use of Computerised Primary Care Guidelines*. Doctoral dissertation, D. Medical Sciences 250, Kuopio University Publications.

Jumaa, M.O. (1997) *Strategic Clinical Team Learning Through Leadership*. Unpublished Research Project Report, part of an MA-WBLS (Strategic Nursing Leadership and Management), Middlesex University, London.

Jumaa, M.O. (2001) *Enhancing Individual Learning and Organisational Capability Through Learning Projects and Developmental Interventions*. Unpublished Research Project Report, part of a Doctor of Professional Studies (DProf), through work-based learning in strategic leadership and strategic learning in nursing and healthcare, Middlesex University, London.

Jumaa, M.O. (2003) *You 2 Can Make a Difference: Developing Evidence Based Practice in Nursing and Healthcare, Lessons from Finland*. Travel Scholarship Project Report, Florence Nightingale Foundation, London.

Jumaa, M.O. (2004) Creativity, innovation and change: the major challenges facing nurses and midwives in West Africa. *West African Journal of Nursing*, **15** (1), 59–64.

Jumaa, M.O. & Alleyne, J. (2001) Learning, unlearning and relearning: facilitation in community nursing for delivering the new primary care agenda. In: *Organisation Behaviour and Organisation Studies in Healthcare: Reflections on the Future* (ed. L. Ashburner). Palgrave (Macmillan), Basingstoke.

Jumaa, M.O. & Alleyne, J. (2002) Strategic leadership in health care, in challenging times. In: *Strategic Issues in Health Care Management: Efficiency, Quality and Access in Health Care* (eds M. Tavakoli *et al.*). University of St. Andrews Press, Fife.

Kennedy, N. & Jumaa, M.O. (2002) *Money Alone Is Not the Solution to Continuous Quality Service Delivery: An Evidence Based Approach to Quality Service Through Facilities Management*. Paper presented at the 5th International Conference on Strategic Issues in Health Care Management, Policy, Finance and Performance in Health Care, 11–13 April, St Andrew's University.

Makela, M. & Kunnamo, I. (2001) Implementing evidence in Finnish primary care. Use of electronic guidelines in daily practice. *Scandinavian Journal of Primary Health Care,* **19** (4), 214–217.

McDaid, M. (2002) *Personal Reflection on the Application of the CLINLAP Model as a Means of Achieving Multi-professional Team Working in Primary Care.* Unpublished Final Dissertation, part of a BSc (Hons) in Professional Practice Nursing, Middlesex University, London.

McGuire, J. (1990) Putting nursing research findings into practice: research utilization as an aspect of management of change. *Journal of Advanced Nursing,* **15**, 614–620.

McKenna, H., Cutliffe, J. & McKenna, P.(2000) Evidence-based practice – demolishing some myths. *Nursing Standard,* **14** (16), 39–42.

Muir Gray, J.A. (2002) *The Resourceful Patient.* Rosetta Press, Oxford.

Mulhall, A. (1998) Nursing research and the evidence. *Evidence-Based Nursing,* **1** (1), 4–6.

Nonaka, I. (1991) The knowledge-creating company. *Harvard Business Review,* Nov–Dec, 96–104.

Ovretveit, J. (2001) Organisational behaviour research in healthcare: an overview. In: *Organisation Behaviour and Organisation Studies in Healthcare: Reflections on the Future* (ed. L. Ashburner). Palgrave (Macmillan), Basingstoke.

Poell, R.F. (1996) Learning projects in organisations. Paper presented at the EGRIS Conference, Lifelong Learning in Europe, 28–30 November, Dresden, Germany. Cited in Poell R. et al. (1997) Can Learning Projects Help to Develop a Learning Organisation? *Lifelong Learning in Europe,* **2** (2), 67–75.

Reason, P. & Bradbury, H. (2001) (eds) *Handbook of Action Research: Participative Inquiry and Practice.* Sage, London.

Sackett, D.L., Rosenberg, W.M.C., Muir Gray, J.A., Haynes, R.B. & Richardson, W.S. (1996) Evidence-based medicine: what it is and what it isn't. *British Medical Journal,* **312**, 71–72.

Schein, E. (1980) *Organizational Psychology,* 3rd edn. Prentice-Hall, Englewood Cliffs, New Jersey.

Senge, P. (1990) *The Fifth Discipline: The Art and Practice of the Learning Organisation.* Century Business, New York.

Smith, P. (1992) *The Emotional Labour of Nursing: How Nurses Care.* Macmillan, Basingstoke.

Torbert, W.R. (1991) *The Power of Balance: Transforming Self, Society, and Scientific Inquiry.* Sage, Newbury Park, California.

Useful websites

www.ebm-guidelines.com
www.observatory.dk
www.resourcefulpatient.org
www.vn.fi/stm/english/index.htm

10 Leadership for Emotional Intelligence

Mansour Jumaa

Introduction

This chapter is about leadership for emotional intelligence (EI) resources and capabilities. It is based on some of the processes that took place during a research and development doctorate in strategic leadership and strategic learning in nursing and healthcare. It explores one of the study's research questions, 'How would a focus on *feelings* and political skills, using systematic available evidence, assist with effective workplace strategic leadership and learning development in nursing and in healthcare?' Four collaborative inquiry case study groups participated in this study:

- Managing Services (Nursing Education) Inquiry Group (in-depth case study)
- Managing Services (Acute Nursing) Inquiry Group (in-depth case study)
- Managing Services (Primary Care Nursing) Inquiry Group (in-depth case study), and
- Managing Services (Management Students) Inquiry Group

This chapter will focus on the *'feelings development'* (EI) aspects of the Managing Services (Nursing Education) Inquiry Group.

In this brief presentation, the chapter will: explore what is meant by resources and capabilities for leadership in emotional intelligence; consider some of the 'theories' of emotional intelligence in order to understand what is emotional intelligence; explore why we need to develop emotional intelligence competencies and capabilities in nursing and healthcare; and use some of the activities in the doctorate studies to illustrate the leadership necessary for the development and sustaining of necessary competencies and capabilities. To assist with this process the chapter uses Dr Jumaa's Strategic Recipe for Emotional Leadership (EL) for Developing Practical EI for Continuous Quality Service Through Teams (see Box 10.3).

What is meant by resources and capabilities for leadership in emotional intelligence?

Grant (1991) describes resources as inputs into the production (transformation/conversion) process, the basic units of analysis of any given activity. He went on to further state that if resources are left on their own, only few would be productive. Only few would produce lasting results and have an impact in the workplace. What is required, he argued, is that productive activity within organisations requires the *co-operation* and *co-ordination* of teams of resources. These processes of *co-operation* and *co-ordination* (these transformation processes) of teams of resources is what he refers to as the *capability* of that organisation, the team or the individuals within it. A capability is the *capacity* for a team of resources to perform some task or activity. While resources are the *sources* of an organisation's or the team's or the individual's capabilities, capabilities are the main sources of their excellence, what Grant (1991) terms as the competitive advantage. Expressed as an equation it could be considered as follows:

Resources × Capacity = Capability (Jumaa & Alleyne 2002).

Making a case for evidence-based management and leadership at a glance, Jumaa & Alleyne (2002) showed and confirmed that their collaborative inquiry research studies supported Grant's assertions provided certain conditions are fulfilled. They suggest that when management and leadership resources interact with capacity effectively and efficiently, the outcome would be the desired outcome of management and leadership capability, which in this chapter is *'capability for leadership in emotional intelligence'*. Resources are represented as THEIMM (time, human, equipment/estates, information, materials and money), and capacity is presented as consisting of: process, values and climate. The climate necessary for effective leadership results has been eloquently argued by Goleman (2000) as comprising of: flexibility, responsibility, standards, rewards, clarity and commitment. Box 8.3 in Chapter 8 provides an illustration of the use of THEIMM in the workplace.

These statements further confirmed the importance of the need to have a thorough grasp of the real meaning and applications of resources and capabilities if we want effective leadership for emotional intelligence in nursing and in healthcare. This need becomes acute when research has confirmed that leadership styles affect the six drivers of climate (flexibility; responsibility, standards, rewards, clarity and commitment) (Goleman 2000, Jumaa & Alleyne 2002). This is the view that is taken when the terms resources and capability are used in this chapter. This section has argued the case for a thorough understanding of the need for resources and capabilities if we want effective leadership for emotional intelligence in nursing and in healthcare.

Next, we consider some of the 'theories' of emotional intelligence in order to understand what emotional intelligence is.

What is emotional intelligence?

We are all familiar with the concept of 'intelligence quotient' (IQ). These cognitive ability tests were designed at the beginning of the twentieth century with the purpose of measuring cognitive ability and intellect. Do many still believe today that this is the most reliable way to appraise intelligence? How many nursing and healthcare establishments are you aware of that use emotional intelligence tests to predict and appraise performance? Both you and I know that IQ does not tell us enough about our capabilities to get on with each other at work, rest or play. The change in attitude was made, initially, an academic focus by Howard Gardner in 1983 when he challenged the status quo in his book *Frames of Mind*, in which he sets out his research on 'multiple intelligences'. According to him, we have many types of intelligence, including spatial, musical, bodily/kinaesthetic, intrapersonal (self-knowledge) and interpersonal (dealing with other people), as well as the logical-mathematical and linguistic capabilities traditionally thought of as intelligence. It soon became obvious why IQ on its own was not a reliable predictor of success in most areas of life.

Reuven Bar-On, a clinical psychologist at Tel Aviv University, developed psychological tests to measure a person's 'emotional quotient' or 'EQ' (Reuven, Bar-On 1992). He describes emotional intelligence as, 'an array of personal, emotional, and social abilities that influence one's ability to succeed in coping with environmental demands and pressures' (cited in Goleman 1998, p. 371). Meanwhile, a comprehensive theory of emotional intelligence was proposed in 1990 by psychologists John Mayer and Peter Salovey (Salovey and Mayer 1990). They claimed that the concept of 'emotional intelligence' is made up of five 'competencies' or skills:

- self-knowledge (knowing your own emotions)
- self-management (managing your own emotions)
- motivation
- empathy (recognising emotions in others)
- understanding and handling relationships

Daniel Goleman popularised these categories in the best-selling books *Emotional Intelligence* (Goleman 1996) and *Working with Emotional Intelligence* (Goleman 1998). He argues that the competencies of emotional intelligence are at least as important as traditional IQ in determining success in work and life. This theme has been further developed in one of Goleman's recent books (Goleman *et al.* 2002). The most widely known and easiest to understand of the competing models is the five-competency model of emotional intelligence. Goleman has adapted these five basic emotional and social competencies and describes them as: self-awareness; self-regulation; motivation; empathy; and social skills (Goleman 1998). He perceives them as follows:

- Self-awareness: 'the ability to know what we are feeling in the moment and using those preferences to guide our decision making; having a realistic assessment of our own abilities and a well-grounded sense of self-confidence'.
- Self-regulation: 'handling our emotions so that they facilitate rather than interfere with the task at hand; being conscientious and delaying gratification to pursue goals; recovering well from emotional distress'.
- Motivation: 'using our deepest preferences to move and guide us towards our goals, to help us take initiative and strive to improve and to persevere in the face of setbacks and frustrations'. Kelly Holmes, the first female Briton to win double Gold Medals at the same Olympic Games – in 800 m and 1500 m races and the Gold Medal Great Britain Sprint quartet relay team – at the Athens 2004 Olympics, is a recent good example of this emotional competency.
- Empathy: 'sensing what people are feeling, being able to take their perspective, and cultivating rapport and attunement with a broad diversity of people'.
- Social skills: 'handling emotions in relationships well and accurately reading social situations and networks, interacting smoothly; using these skills to persuade and lead, negotiate and settle differences for cooperation and teamwork'. (Goleman 1998, p. 318)

Prior to Daniel Goleman coming along and making EI a popular topic for everyday discussions, there are those humanistic psychology practitioners, like myself, who have been working on and applying the concept of emotional competence in an educational capacity and as a vehicle for personal development. My first exposure to the theory and practical application of emotional competence was at the University of Surrey, England, in 1984. I was later prepared and accredited as a facilitator of organisational, group and personal development at the longest serving centre for humanistic psychology in Europe, the Human Potential Resource Group (HPRG) at the University of Surrey. My final accreditation process by the Institute for the Development of Human Potential (IDHP) was through a 5-day residential intensive peer assessment process (PAP) which was rigorous and emotionally challenging. My teachers included 'giants' in the field of humanistic psychology – practitioners such as Meg Bond, John Heron, John Mulligan, James Kilty, Petruska Clarkson, Kate Hopkins and Jean Anderson, to name but a few. On reflection, one fundamental 'drawback' of our approach then, I perceive, was the 'lack of rigorous theory' and the almost 'total' dominance of the practical aspects and application of emotional competence without a detailed conceptual basis.

This background information is necessary and important because current focus on EI, while suggesting the theoretical and scientific basis of EI and providing guidance on its application to everyday activities (Goleman 1998, Goleman *et al.* 2002), is weak on the practical development of emotional competence and capabilities when compared with texts such as Dixon (1981) and Mulligan (1988); Heron (1990) on interpersonal relations; and Heron (1989) on dimensions of group activities and emotional competence. The definition of emotional competence by John Heron (1983) was as useful then as it would be today. Heron regards emotional competence as one of the primary aspects of the characteristics needed for effective helping: 'Emotional competence. For helpers, this means that their own anxiety and distress, accumulated from past traumatic experience, does not drive and distort their attempts to help' (Heron 1990, p. 12). I have taken these observations into account in my doctorate studies, particularly Heron's work on emotional competence (Heron 1990). One of the outcomes is reflected in what I have described as 'Dr Jumaa's Strategic Recipe for Emotional Leadership (EL) for Developing Practical EI for Continuous Quality Service Through Teams' (see Box 10.3). Goleman's five basic emotional and social competencies are shown in Box 10.1. My emotional and social competencies approach was based on the actor's (be it an organisation's, a team's or an individual's) specific goals, explicit roles, clear processes and open relationships activities (Jumaa 2001). This approach perceives 'motivation' as a necessary driver for all the emotional and social competencies.

My emotional leadership approach (Jumaa 2001) gives credence to both theory and practice. The emotional concepts in the left-hand column of Box 10.1 (after Heron 1990) have been tested and proven to apply and work in practice, reflecting the type of emotional capabilities needed for specific goals, explicit roles, clear processes and open relationships (Jumaa 2001). It concentrates on the relevance of local (tacit) knowledge and how that knowledge could be made available to others through conversion to explicit knowledge which is publicly shared. This is one of the significant advantages of a doctorate study adopting a research and development perspective.

Box 10.1 Jumaa's emotional and social competencies approach (Jumaa 2001). 'Motivation' is a necessary driver for all the emotional and social competencies.

Emotional intelligence required for effective living (Jumaa 2001)	Goleman's five basic emotional and social competencies (Goleman 1998)
Awareness; Ownership Identification; Discrimination Acceptance; Choice Transmutation; Expression; Control; Catharsis	Motivation; Self-awareness Self-regulation Empathy Social skills

This section has presented a brief insight into the main competing models of emotional intelligence. The texts cited are adequate for interested readers who would like to develop or improve or, at the least, have a greater understanding of this very essential transformation process – emotional intelligence.

Why develop emotional intelligence competencies and capabilities in nursing and healthcare?

There is very little empirical evidence of studies on emotions or feelings available either in organisation behaviour research (OBR) in healthcare or in the nursing literature. OBR in healthcare could be perceived as the systematic study of the behaviour of individuals, groups and organisations whose aim in healthcare is to contribute to the solution of practical problems and to scientific knowledge concerning people and organisations. My literature review confirmed this perspective. Some of the conclusions in my ground-breaking study (Jumaa 2001) were that during periods of *uncertainties*, as is currently the case in the UK's 'new' National Health Service (NHS):

- leadership without emotional intelligence will not improve service delivery
- whole-picture thinking and learning is essential for continuous effective quality care provision, and
- motivated and inspired staff will make a difference to patient outcomes and patient costs

These outcomes, shown in Box 10.2, are also about 'new ways of seeing', 'new ways of working' and 'new approaches to methodology' (Ashburner 2001). According to Daniel Goleman, research in brain-based learning suggests that emotional health is fundamental to effective learning. A report from the National Center for Clinical Infant Programs (USA) claims that the most critical element in a student's success in school is an understanding of how to learn (Goleman 1996, p. 193). The key ingredients for this understanding are:

- confidence
- curiosity
- intentionality
- self-control
- relatedness
- capacity to communicate
- ability to co-operate

These traits are all aspects of emotional intelligence. Basically, a student who learns to learn is much more apt to succeed. Emotional intelligence has proven a better predictor of future success than traditional methods such as the US grade point average (GPA), IQ and standardised test scores (Goleman 1996).

Box 10.2 Meeting the challenges of the twenty-first century labour market: implications for emotional intelligence. (*A summary of Trends – 1997–1998*. Skills and Enterprise Network, DfEE, http://www.open.gov.uk/dfee/skillnet/ senhome.htm.)

Challenges to Britain's skills

The workforce needs to be highly skilled, flexible and motivated. Therefore, those planning education and training provision need to aim to produce skills that will be wanted by employers immediately, as well as giving a good basis for developing the new skills that will be needed in the future. Providers will need information about the labour market and trends in training and education.

Employment growth and changes in forms of working continue

The workforce has risen since 1993 to 26.4 million in 1996, and is expected to carry on rising to 2006 (nearly 27 million estimated) (source - Business Strategies Ltd.).

   The female share of total employment is expected to rise from 46% in 1996 to 48% in 2006. The number of part-time employees is projected to increase by 11% and self-employment by 24%. If working patterns are becoming more flexible, so must training and education delivery. Also it must meet the needs of small and very small businesses, which are expected to continue to grow in number. *Growth will be concentrated in the service sector.*

Higher level occupations are growing fastest

The shift towards managerial, professional and technical occupations means that an increase in higher level qualifications and skills will be needed.

... but a continuing supply of skills for all types of jobs will be needed also

Although jobs in some sectors are declining, there will still be vacancies needing skilled recruits.

... and a broader range of skills will be demanded in most jobs.

   Building one's emotional intelligence has a lifelong impact. Many parents and educators, alarmed by increasing levels of conflict in young schoolchildren – from low self-esteem, early drug and alcohol use to depression – are very concerned to teach students the skills necessary for emotional intelligence. In corporations, the inclusion of emotional intelligence in training programs has helped employees co-operate better and motivate more, thereby increasing productivity and profits (Goleman 1998). These are some of the significant reasons why we need to develop emotional intelligence resources and capabilities in nursing and healthcare.

Although concentrating on observable behaviour and performance, OBR also investigates perceptions, emotions and cultures which may explain behaviour (Ovretveit 2001). Currently, many in nursing and in healthcare are excited about the 'promise' of transformational leadership. However, this approach often utilises charismatic powers and emotion, which can be dangerous in organisations. It can be temperamental and may become volatile, can be misdirected and is often short-lived. The excitement and emotional power of this form of leadership is inherently unstable, especially when employed irresponsibly or for personal ends.

> If the entrepreneurial heroes hold center stage in this drama, the rest of the vast work force plays a supporting role – supporting and unheralded average workers in this myth are drones – cogs in the Big Machines, so many interchangeable parts, unable to perform without direction from above . . .To the entrepreneurial hero belongs all the inspiration; the drones are governed by the rules and valued for their reliability and pliability . . . There is just one fatal problem with this dominant myth: it is obsolete. (Reich 1987, p. 77)

A very important area that OB and nursing research has neglected is in the theories and empirical knowledge about feelings in healthcare and how feelings relate to behaviour and decisions (Ovretveit 2001). The most sophisticated knowledge about this subject, Ovretveit observes, appears to be in British and US television soap dramas, not in OBR or in nursing journals. Those of us who help healthcare personnel learn emotional competence at work have few healthcare research studies to use as examples to draw on. This situation is changing as evident from the research studies referred to in this chapter and elsewhere in this book. Few definitions of OB refer to feelings, yet feelings profoundly affect management decisions and practice. Feelings influence clinical practice, and are important in patients' experience and behaviour, but there is little scientific research into or theories about the subject.

Management performance could be improved by enabling managers to better understand their own and others feelings in different situations. OB and nursing research could develop models, such as the CLINLAP/LEADLAP model, and theories about feelings from empirical research in different healthcare situations. This would give a relevant research base to complement other educational methods developing emotional competence. The areas cited below, according to Ovretveit (2001), require further attention in the future:

- Feelings are at work in nursing and healthcare (see Alleyne 2002, Jumaa 2001).
- Feelings are facts: you only partially understand a situation if you do not understand your own and others feelings.
- There is little OBR into feelings or unconscious processes in healthcare.
- Empirical and theoretical research on the subject from healthcare settings would improve educational programmes for developing managers' and practitioners' emotional competence at work.

All these affect employee motivation and employees' perceptions of the meaning of work.

How can we possibly justify all the excitement about the work–life balance when issues of bullying, harassment and persistent workplace stress are rife in our places of work (O'Donnell 2003)?

A report by the Chartered Management Institute (2002) *Leading Change in the Public Sector: Making the Difference* claims that the Government's public sector reform agenda is in danger of stalling due to the lack of good quality leadership within the public services. As the public sector attempts to realign itself in order to satisfy rising customer expectations and engage its communities, managers want their leaders to 'ditch a skill set that is ten years out of date'. This a key finding of the Chartered Management Institute's in-depth survey examining current leadership performance based on the views of 1900 public sector managers as they face the daily pressures of the public reform agenda. Managers talk of a 'blame culture', where all too often priorities are blurred and targets are the 'raison d'être'. Leaders need to foster a culture of trust, with increased focus on customers. As one panel member explained: 'we're not going to get better just by getting better at measuring performance'.

The growing case for improvements within the new NHS is supported by both patients who use the service and the staff who provide these services. Healthcare Commission chief executive Anna Walker said:

> More than 200,000 people have told us what it is like to work in the NHS. Many said they were generally satisfied with their jobs, but further analysis of the results show that some groups of staff are more likely to experience violence and bullying, have a poorer work–life balance and report higher levels of work related stress and injury.

A recent Roffey Park Institute's research study, *In Search of Meaning in the Workplace* (Holbeche & McCartney 2004), concludes that

> Leaders need to demonstrate a visible commitment to the organisation that goes beyond the rhetoric of values statements and corporate social responsibility policies.
>
> They need to lead by example and safeguard their credibility by ensuring they act in a manner consistent with their recommendations to others. This aspect of 'walking the talk' is essential if organisations are to build a basis for trust.

The research indicates that perhaps the biggest challenge for organisations in trying to address the issue of meaning is that it requires a paradigm shift by senior managers.

'Much of the problem is trying to get over the jargon', said Linda Holbeche. 'Senior managers can be suspicious or even contemptuous if you try to talk to them about the "spiritual" needs of employees. But part of managing people is about managing their feelings. If senior managers can be convinced of the need to do this, then steps can be taken to help the organisation reap the benefits of a more meaningful work community.' Another key issue as to why we must improve or develop emotional intelligence competencies and capabilities in nursing and healthcare comes from current developments in the areas of health and safety at work. The changing face of workplace health is a very worrying trend. 'With stress overtaking back pain as the number one cause of employee absence', O'Donnell (2003) warns, 'bosses must change the way they think about health' (p. 9).

This section has discussed and explored:

- what is meant by resources and capabilities for leadership in emotional intelligence
- some of the 'theories' of emotional intelligence in order to understand *'what is emotional intelligence?'*
- why we need to develop emotional intelligence competencies and capabilities in nursing and healthcare

The last section will focus on how the leadership necessary for the development and sustaining of necessary emotional intelligence resources and capabilities could be developed. To assist with this process the section uses, as a structure, Dr Jumaa's Strategic Recipe for Emotional Leadership (EL) for Developing Practical EI for Continuous Quality Service Through Teams (see Box 10.3).

The leadership necessary for the development and sustaining of necessary emotional intelligence resources and capabilities

Success was achieved through the use of some of the relevant activities and processes shown in Box 10.3, with particular focus on converting tacit knowledge into explicit knowledge, using the principles of a learning organisation (Senge 1990) and anchoring activities within relevant management and leadership concepts, techniques and frameworks. Table 7.1 in Chapter 7 provides a detailed indication of the types of management and leadership concepts, techniques and frameworks available for use. A detailed treatment ('Specific goals for EL', see Box 10.3) of the leadership necessary for the development and sustaining of necessary emotional intelligence resources and capabilities at this phase will now be discussed.

Most people know more than they can tell. This is particularly true of nursing and nurses. A significant amount of a nurse's personal and professional knowledge is grounded in experience that cannot be expressed in its fullness in a written form. This form of knowledge is described as *tacit knowledge*. I have observed, over the last 30 years of working for and with the NHS and the higher education sector in the UK, that this is one of the major weaknesses of nursing and nurses. This precious asset of nursing knowledge is bound up in the nursing processes, activities and efforts that produced it. It is a procedural knowledge that guides behaviour but is not readily available for introspection. Tacit knowledge is intimately related to action and relevant to the attainment of goals that nurses value. Unfortunately, while tacit knowledge is the primary basis for both effective nursing managerial and leadership actions, paradoxically it is also responsible for the

Box 10.3 Leadership for emotional intelligence. Dr Jumaa's Strategic Recipe for Emotional Leadership (EL) for Developing Practical EI for Continuous Quality Service Through Teams. (Copyright Mansour Jumaa, 2001.)

Leadership, Learning and Action Process (LEADLAP) model (Jumaa 2001)	Tuckman' stages of group development (Tuckman 1965)	Emotional intelligence required (Heron 1990)	Mintzberg's managerial roles (Mintzberg 1973)	Practical competencies and capabilities (Jumaa 2001)
Specific goals for EL (Use SQ 1)	**Forming** Initial awareness, Why are we here?	Awareness; Ownership	Leader Liaison Entrepreneur	Who's who? Team's mission ASTREAM objectives
Explicit roles for EL (Use SQ 2)	**Storming** Self-organisation	Identification; Discrimination	Liaison Resource Allocator Spokesperson Disseminator	Resources and capabilities issues; operating standards; effective communication
Clear processes for EL (Use SQ 3 and SQ 4)	**Norming** Sorting-out process – bidding for control and power	Acceptance; Choice	Liaison Negotiator Monitor	Acceptability; suitability and feasibility
Open relationships for EL (Use SQ 5)	**Performing** Maturity and mutual acceptance	Transmutation; Expression; Control; Catharsis	Liaison Disturbance handler Figurehead Monitor	Resistance management 'Blame-free' context; trust; information sharing; feedback; action

deterioration of nursing managerial and leadership actions. This is because according to Argyris (1993), management and leadership capabilities need both knowledge (tacit and explicit) and skill. The efficacy of nursing's tacit knowledge depends on its being acquired and then being effectively used. To use nursing knowledge effectively demands that it is converted to explicit knowledge through the processes described by Nonaka & Takeuchi (1995), which drives a virtuous cycle of continuous innovation of combination (explicit), internalisation (tacit), socialisation (tacit) through to externalisation.

Organisations and individuals who embrace and practise the concepts of the learning organisation are better positioned, as it was in this study, to achieve the iterative and spiral conversion process of turning tacit knowledge into explicit knowledge. The use of the LEADLAP (Leadership, Learning and Action Process) model accelerated this process and provides a practical and empirical example of leadership for emotional intelligence resources and capabilities. All actions are motivated by feelings. It is our emotions that put us in motion. We can always choose how we respond to an emotion. We can always be in control if we *really* need to be. Feeling in control is empowering. Taking responsibility for our happiness is empowering. A good illustration of the misunderstandings about emotions can be observed in an article in a leading management journal, *Management Today* (Stern 2003). The article appears to convey the message that 'emotional intelligence was the mantra in the touchy-feely '90s' (p. 46). Yet the same article went on to propose 'ten vital *tough* values': self-belief; resilience; focus; drive; control; resolve; nerves of steel; independence; competitiveness; and chillability (pp. 48–51). A perusal of these values concludes that they are, after all, qualities of emotionally intelligent leaders, irrespective of location, sex or age!

> Winners do not play 'helpless,' nor do they play the blaming game. Instead, they assume responsibility for their own lives. They do not give others a false authority over them. Winners are their own bosses and know it. A winner's timing is right. Winners respond appropriately to the situation. Their responses are related to the message sent and preserve the significance, worth, well-being, and dignity of the people involved. Winners know that for everything there is a season and for every activity a time. Winners learn to know their feelings and limitations and to be unafraid of them. Winners are not stopped by their own contradictions and ambivalences. Being authentic, they know when they are angry and can listen when others are angry with them. Winners can give and receive affection. Winners are able to love and be loved. Winners can be spontaneous. They do not have to respond in predetermined, rigid ways, but can change their plans when the situation calls for it. Winners have a zest for life, enjoying work, play, food, other people, sex, and the world of nature. Without guilt they enjoy their own accomplishments. Without envy they enjoy the accomplishments of others. (James & Jongeward 1971, pp 2–3)

Most nurses appear to be uncomfortable with the notion of power and 'winning'. However, which of the messages in this paragraph would be difficult for nurses and healthcare managers to understand? Which ones would nurses and healthcare managers be uncomfortable with?

Words and language are amoral. It is when they are located within cultures and within different contexts that they convey particular meanings. If nurses, healthcare managers and others are uncomfortable with any of these words about winners, in the above quote, what would be preferable? We need to recognise that:

> Although people are born to win, they are also born helpless and totally dependent on their environment. Winners successfully make the transition from total helplessness to independence and then into interdependence. Losers do not. Somewhere along the line, they begin to avoid becoming responsible for their own lives (James & Jongeward 1971, pp 4–5)

According to James & Jongeward (1971), one of the main characteristics of the 'loser' behaviour is to relinquish responsibility for their own actions by blaming others. Losers, evidence suggests, tend not to live in the present, with most statements a catalogue of 'ifs':

- 'If only I had married someone else.'
- 'If only I had a different job.'
- 'If only I had been handsome/beautiful.'
- 'If only I had been born rich.'
- 'If only I had had better education.'
- 'If only I had had better parents.' (James & Jongeward 1971, pp 4–5)

This is extremely unhelpful behaviour. It is futile and unproductive to focus solely on the future or live entirely in the past. It is much more productive, with less anxiety, to reflect on the past, make reasonable plans for the future but live fully for the present.

These last three paragraphs (above) are examples of some of the activities necessary at the onset of a journey to challenge, discover and implement the leadership crucial for the development and sustaining of necessary emotional intelligence resources and capabilities. This was carried out together with structured activities regarding managing stakeholder relationships and setting SMART objectives by the Managing Services (Nursing Education) Inquiry Group. This group consisted of Jo, the practitioner, her line manager and six primary care nurses who took part in Jo's clinical group supervision sessions. As a co-researcher, Jo agreed to produce a management report for her line manager and the main researcher (myself) on the outcomes of her participation in this collaborative research. Box 10.4 shows an abstract and an extract from Jo's management report in which she was responding to *strategic question one* (SQ 1) explored as part of this collaborative research.

Box 10.4 Extracts from the practitioner Jo's management report to her line manager and the main researcher.

To: **Professor Nor Notlimah**

From: **Jo Alleyne** (Mrs), Principal Lecturer, and Co-researcher, on the Collaborative Strategic Leadership Process Inquiry

Reflections on: A Sage on the Stage, to a Guide on the Side

ABSTRACT

In this report I will be discussing the outcomes of a unique action-research study, which has sought to exploit the workplace as a source of learning, through a collaborative form of human inquiry.

This inquiry has involved two work-based learning researchers and six participants, as co-researchers within the study. The main approach adopted for this work has been the facilitation of focussed interventions of management and leadership developmental activities, through a process of clinical supervision sessions for a group of six primary care practitioners.

The focus of these sessions has been the application of the CLINLAP model[1] a *"strategic clinical leadership process that positions strategic learning as a force that drives the health and social care organisations, on a day to day basis, in the management of clinical nursing goals; nursing roles; nursing processes; and nursing relationships"*[2]

The strength of this model is in the way it has integrated knowledge from different disciplines, into a coherent whole, in this case, to enhance the clinical decision making skills and leadership development of the primary care practitioners.

This study signified that this form of co-operative inquiry has been successful in working towards practical nursing outcomes, and has contributed towards the *emancipation* of this group of nurses. It further illustrated the power of this paradigm in developing the human potential, to achieve a level of autonomous management and leadership development, in an environment in which unfamiliar situations are a feature of these practitioners' lives.

The capabilities which the practitioners have developed are as a result of *learning how to learn*, whilst developing the interpersonal, group and emotional skills, which they required in order to act effectively and appropriately in complex, and often stressful healthcare situations.

This study will also contribute towards an understanding of how the effective processes of emotional intelligence, collaborative relationships, and appropriate management knowledge, can identify, create and evaluate the "unsettled" workplace environment so that the individual's capacity and capability in self-direction and decision making can be enhanced. **(end of the Abstract)**

Continued

Box 10.4 *Continued*

Where do we want to go in our nursing practice? (SQ 1)

This was the 1st & 2nd stages and the first phase of CLINLAP. This stage is about aligning stakeholder expectations, setting **specific goals**, and included techniques for goal setting which would align the needs and expectations of multiple stakeholders. In this case, general practitioners, clinical nurse managers, team leaders, district nursing staff, clients and families etc. Thinking about such issues enabled problems to be surfaced, and the planning dimension to be explored, through interventions which were initially facilitator-centred negotiations, to group-centred negotiated. The group deliberations focused at this stage, on how the team could arrive at objectives which would satisfy multiple stakeholders. This was an important stage of the project as the participants reported that they were often unsure **what** objectives they were attempting to achieve, and were unclear as to **how** they were going to align clinical goals with stakeholder expectations. Furthermore, they were unclear as to how they were going to plan and agree quality actions. Through the introduction of examples of management tools and techniques, and the use of acronyms such as **SMART** (Specific, Measurable, Achievable Realistic, Time-bound), to write objectives, the participants were encouraged to experiment with setting objectives, for themselves and their district nursing teams. Concepts such as stakeholder mapping, tools for analysis and discussions about power were also addressed in these early sessions, with participants reflecting on workplace problems, in order to apply some of the information which was given; to enable them to formulate solutions to their workplace issues.

2.2   Emotion in Healthcare

An important feature of this work has been the attention paid to developing emotional literacy, as some of the real life examples from the workplace, re-stimulated feelings associated with a highly stressed workforce; excessive workloads, staff shortages, lack of control over work, and poor management. These experiences are documented in a large body of research.[3] There is also substantial evidence which documents the scale of bullying, harassment and discrimination within the NHS, particularly against ethnic minority and female staff.[4]

With this context in mind, this stage focused on sensitive interventions, aimed to develop the key emotional requirements of *awareness* and *ownership*. This was achieved through effective facilitation using the appropriate dimensions of facilitation, such as feeling, structuring, and valuing.[5] These interventions were facilitated by Mansour, drawing upon his many years of experience, of facilitating 1:1 and 1: group interventions.

Continued

Box 10.4 *Continued*

This approach to developing managers from "the inside" was consistent with such work as Iles (1995), who argues that *"management education must be based on real personal development...the best management schools are recognising that effective management springs not from what you do, but what you are and, crucially from how much you are aware of yourself, your perception, your responses and your impact on others'.*

Simple, focused activities, designed to assess the participant's emotional intelligence were used to establish the participant's level of self-management and ability to manage relationships. This involved rating their own capabilities in self-awareness, self-management, social awareness and social skills.[6] As a consequence of these forms of activities, the participants were enabled to establish *ownership* of the problem/s and were able to move on to the next stage, which involves the *formulation of solutions*, which would be successful because of their development towards "internalisation" (Handy, 1999)[7].

[1] Clinical Nursing Leadership, Learning and Action Process model, Jumaa, M.O. (1997).
[2] Jumaa, M.O. & Alleyne, J. (1998a).
[3] See Improving the Health of the NHS Workforce, Nuffield Trust, 1998.
[4] See for example Nursing in a Multi- Ethnic NHS, Policy Studies Institute, 1995.
[5] Modified from the work of John Heron, 1989.
[6] For more details see Goleman, D. (2000) Leadership that Gets Results, Harvard Business Review, March–April, pp 78–90.
[7] See Charles Handy, Understanding Organisations, 6th edition, St Ives, England.

Conclusions

This chapter has explored and discussed leadership for emotional intelligence resources and capabilities. It is based on some of the processes that took place during a research and development doctorate in strategic leadership and strategic learning in nursing and healthcare, with particular attention on the research and development question, 'How would a focus on *feelings* using systematic available evidence assist with effective workplace strategic leadership and learning development in nursing and in healthcare?' The research activities that explored this question were used for illustration.

It appears that a critical understanding of resources and capabilities for leadership in emotional intelligence is the first mandatory step for effective practice. Although there are various competing models of the theories of emotional intelligence, there appears to be, at the moment, a consensus to adopt the five-competency model of emotional intelligence. Goleman has adapted these five basic emotional and social competencies and described them as *self-awareness, self-regulation, motivation, empathy* and *social skills* (Goleman 1998). The emotional leadership approach by Jumaa (2001) gives credence to both theory and practice. It concentrates on the relevance of local (tacit) knowledge and how that knowledge could be made available to others through conversion to explicit knowledge which is publicly shared. The emotional intelligence required is practical and rooted in everyday activities. It comprises awareness, ownership, identification, discrimination, acceptance, choice, transmutation, expression, control and catharsis.

The case for effective development of resources and capabilities for leadership in emotional intelligence is overwhelming. The chapter ends with an insight into the processes of effective development of resources and capabilities for leadership in emotional intelligence using a presentation of some of the developmental activities that have taken place. An abstract and extract from the doctorate study which contributed to the contents of this chapter was presented. The final words for this chapter come from the management report of the practitioner Jo. She concluded her report with the following words:

> This study was conducted over a two year period and has been informed by a number of theoretical positions and assumptions. Initially, the co-researcher (Doctor Jumaa), led the sessions using facilitation skills and providing appropriate management and leadership frameworks, using the CLINLAP model as a coherent framework to provide structure to the sessions, whilst focussing on the development of emotional intelligence. This process has contributed towards my own professional and personal development, as well as to the development of the six participants. (Alleyne 2002)

References

Alleyne, J. (2002) *Making a Case for Group Clinical Supervision Through Management and Leadership Concepts*. Unpublished Doctorate Research Project Report in Clinical Nursing Leadership, part of a Doctor of Professional Studies (DProf), through work-based learning, Middlesex University, London.

Argyris, C. (1993) *Knowledge for Action*. Jossey-Bass, San Francisco.

Ashburner, L. (2001) Discussion. In: *OB and Organisation Studies in Health Care: Reflections on the Future* (ed. L. Ashburner). Macmillan Palgrave, Basingstoke.

Beishon, S., Virdee, S. & Hagell, A. (1995) *Nursing in a Mult-Ethnic NHS*. Policy Studies Institute, London.

Chartered Management Institute (2002) *Leading Change in the Public Sector: Making the Difference*. CMI, London.

Department for Education and Employment (1999) *Skills and Enterprise Network, a Summary of Trends – 1997–1998*. The Stationery Office, London, (http://www.open.gov.uk/dfee/skillnet/senhome.htm).

Dixon, B. (1981) (ed) *New Approaches to Management Development*. Gower, Aldershot.

Gardner, H. (1983) *Frames of Minds*. Basic Books, New York.

Goleman, D. (1996) *Emotional Intelligence*. Bloomsbury, London.

Goleman, D. (1998) *Working with Emotional Intelligence*. Bloomsbury, London.

Goleman, D. (2000) Leadership that gets results. *Harvard Business Review*, March–April, 78–90.

Goleman, D., Boyatzis, R. & McKee, A. (2002) *The New Leaders: Transforming the Art of Leadership into the Science of Results*. Little, Brown, London.

Grant, R.M. (1991) The resource-based theory of competitive advantage: implications for strategic formulation. *California Management Review*, Spring, 114–135.

Handy, C.B. (1993) *Understanding Organisations*, 6th edn. Penguin, London.

Heron, J. (1983) *Education of the Affect*. University of Surrey, Guildford.

Heron, J. (1989) *The Facilitator's Handbook*. Kogan Page, London.

Heron, J. (1990) *Helping the Client*. Sage, London.

Holbeche, L. & McCartney, C. (2004) *In Search of Meaning in the Workplace*. The Management Agenda 2004. Roffey Park Institute, Horsham. http://www.roffeypark.com/research/managementagenda.html.

Iles, V. (1995) *Really Managing Health Care*. Open University Press, Milton Keynes.

James, M. & Jongeward, D. (1971) *Born to Win: Transactional Analysis with Gestalt Experiments*. Addison-Wesley, Reading, Massachusetts, pp 2–5.

Jumaa, M.O. (1997) *Strategic Clinical Team Learning Through Leadership*. Unpublished Research Project Report, part of an MA-WBLS (Strategic Nursing Leadership and Management), Middlesex University, London.

Jumaa, M.O. (2001) *Enhancing Individual Learning and Organisational Capability Through Learning Projects and Developmental Interventions*. Unpublished Doctorate Research Project Report in Strategic Leadership and Learning in Nursing and Healthcare, part of a Doctor of Professional Studies (DProf), through work-based learning, Middlesex University, London.

Jumaa, M.O. & Alleyne, J. (1998) Clinical Nursing Leadership and Action Process (CLINLAP). Paper presented at the 6th Biennial International Conference on Experiential Learning, 2–5 July, University of Tampere, Finland.

Jumaa, M.O. & Alleyne, J. (2002) Strategic leadership in health care. In: *Challenging Times. Organisation Development in Healthcare* (eds R.K. Rushmer *et al.*). Ashgate Press, Aldershot.

Mintzberg, H. (1973) *The Nature of Managerial Work*. Harper and Row, New York.

Mulligan, J. (1988) *The Personal Management Handbook: How to Make the Most of Your Potential*. Sphere Books, London.

Nonaka, I. & Takeuchi, H. (1995) *The Knowledge-Creating Company: How Japanese Companies Create the Dynamics of Innovation*. Oxford University Press, New York.

Nuffield Trust (1998) *Improving the Health of the NHS Workforce*. Nuffield Trust, London.

O'Donnell, M. (2003) The changing face of workplace health in occupational health. *Financial Protection Extra*, 23 October, 9.

Ovretveit, J. (2001) Organisational behaviour research in healthcare – the future. In: *OB and Organisation Studies in Health Care: Reflections on the Future* (ed. L. Ashburner). Macmillan Palgrave, Basingstoke.

Reich, R. (1987) Entrepreneurship reconsidered: the team as hero. *Harvard Business Review*, May/June, 77.

Reuven, Bar-On (1992) The development of a concept and test of psychological well-being. Unpublished Doctoral Dissertation. Cited in Goleman, D. (1998) *Working with Emotional Intelligence*. Bloomsbury, London, p. 371.

Salovey, P. & Mayer, J.D. (1990) Emotional intelligence. *Imagination, Cognition and Personality*, **9**, 185–211.

Senge, P. (1990) *The Fifth Discipline: The Art and Practice of the Learning Organisation*. Century Business, New York.

Stern, S. (2003) If you think you're HARD enough. *Management Today*, March, 46–51.

Tuckman, B.W. (1965) Development sequence in small groups. *Psychological Bulletin*, **63**, 284–499.

Section Three

Strategies for Making a Difference in Healthcare Leadership

11 Leading Change in Primary and Community Care

Lindsey Hayes

The challenges of the shifting focus of healthcare delivery

The health service is undergoing radical reform, with a shift in focus of healthcare delivery into primary care and community settings and the creation of new structures and organisations. Across the UK, new health and social care organisations have been created to enable the implementation of government modernisation agendas, which have provided opportunities for all healthcare professionals to influence the decision-making process at a strategic level. In order to be proactive and influential within these organisations, healthcare professionals need the skills of influence, negotiation and management of change. They need to be able to switch between policy and practice, ensuring that national imperatives encompass local priorities by identifying and articulating the healthcare needs of local communities and populations. However, the key to the modernisation agenda is the need to change attitudes and the culture within the health service.

This chapter will focus on the leadership skills required to influence the development of primary and community care services strategically, ensuring that the views of all health professionals are clearly articulated and that their voice is heard. A Primary Care Leadership Programme (PCLP), designed specifically for those working in this field, has been developed, delivered and evaluated (Hayes 2002). The underpinning theory, process and outcomes from the programme will be utilised as the basis for this chapter. Through learning from the programme, the roles of nurses and their colleagues will be explored, as the shift in focus towards the development of leadership is recognised as a key element of modernisation for developing individual person and population centred services.

Leadership and the policy framework

All those working within the primary and social care sectors have been charged with the responsibility of developing effective working relationships across all services for the benefit of the client/user group. At the heart of the

179

NHS Plan for England is the focus of improving health and healthcare for individuals and communities (DH 2002). In Scotland, specific policies have been developed to enable greater collaboration between health and social care practitioners by bringing together organisations with the purpose of having single shared assessments, shared budgets and joint management. Whilst joint working may challenge traditional professional boundaries, the contribution each individual brings to this system needs to be recognised and valued (Scottish Executive 2000).

The modernisation of primary health and social care has moved one step further towards challenging the existence of traditional institutional boundaries (DH 2000). Working in partnership builds on existing team working abilities but suggests, in addition, boundaries which are fluid, flexible and allow greater engagement of both professionals and service users in order to meet increasingly complex health needs. This presents a challenge to many professionals who work in a community setting, but it is not a wholly new concept to nurses and their colleagues. However, the Government has clearly stated the importance of collaboration and partnership as a major element of the functions of all Primary Care Trusts (PCTs) in England (DH 2001). PCTs are charged with the following responsibilities:

- to improve the health of the community
- to secure the provision of services
- to integrate health and social care in the local health and social care community

The complexity of healthcare today demands specific skills which enable the creation of sustainable partnerships in order that a whole systems approach is taken to facilitate the sharing of knowledge and to avoid duplication (Howkins & Thornton 2002). It is recognised that the NHS cannot work alone in improving health and tackling health inequalities; there must be a joint approach to increasingly complex health needs within the changing population profile. Whilst nurses and their health professional colleagues are trained according to both a health and social care model, the environment in which they operate must be an enabling one in which innovation and learning flourish. Leaders can create this environment so that risks are taken, mistakes are made and lessons learnt from the point of view of both those providing the service and those using it.

Through the exploration of these issues and within a policy context, nurses and their colleagues can explore similarities and differences in their roles in order for these changes to occur. There is no doubt that multiprofessional leadership training and development will allow this process to flourish, will question traditional approaches to problem solving and facilitate a willingness to work outside conventional boundaries. As one participant on the PCLP stated:

> The Primary Care Leadership Programme was an excellent opportunity to develop my own skills and network with other people in different professions all aiming to do the same thing – improve health and social care. (PCLP participant, 2002)

During primary care leadership training, groups of participants work together to identify gaps in existing services, develop networks across agency boundaries, create partnerships, form alliances and articulate a vision for change which challenges the status quo and ensures that the service user is placed firmly at the centre.

This strategic approach to service development and redesign demands that effective leaders will be required at all levels throughout the organisation (DH 2002, RCN 2001, 2002). In England, healthcare professionals have an additional opportunity to influence these developments, by taking seats on the Professional Executive Committee (PEC) of PCTs, where they act as the voice of their profession and, ultimately, the voice of their user group. One of the challenges for those working at this level is to ensure not only that the voice of the individual and community is represented, but also that the identified health needs of this group are incorporated into organisational strategic development. PCTs have the opportunity to really make a difference in shifting the focus of health to primary care, developing local patient/community focused services that allow for patient choice and professional innovation as well as offering high standards of quality care.

Organisations that harness and recognise creativity and create a culture where change can happen will enable the development of these roles so that both practitioners and senior managerial staff can work collaboratively. In order for this to be successful, roles need to be clearly defined, and the similarities and differences of these roles need to be explored and then acknowledged in an open and inclusive manner. The challenge for many of the clinical practitioners who find themselves operating at a strategic level within their organisation will be to draw on their clinical expertise, incorporate policy and engage their colleagues in the process of reform. This theme will recur throughout this chapter and will be the main focus of a specific section.

Leadership in primary care

The emphasis on leadership in the NHS Plan has been identified as one of the most important priorities for nurses and their health professional colleagues. Leadership throughout organisations and across the whole health economy is viewed as vital for implementing and sustaining change (DH 2002). There is little doubt that effective leadership provides opportunities for those involved to throw off the shackles of traditional practice and embrace change personally, professionally and culturally (Gough 2001).

Within the policy context of primary care, there may be no one style, model or approach that is appropriate for all situations. It is generally recognised (Ewens 2002) that professionals need to work in a flexible and dynamic way, in partnership with service users and others to influence effectively. Moving away from a more traditional transactional model, which involves maintaining a status quo in the organisation, towards a transformational style that encompasses influence, power and networking is necessary in order to facilitate this change. Add the skills necessary to influence policy within and outside of the organisation and there could be an appropriate model! Creativity energises the model and allows for service redesign and the identification of gaps in existing services which will encompass elements of commissioning. This is a more appropriate approach for those who work in a less hierarchical structure in primary care and whose focus is one of collaboration and partnership.

If leadership in primary healthcare is vital to achieving the NHS modernisation agenda it depends on a cultural shift to enable this change in attitudes within the organisation, to facilitate creativity and to support people in making difficult decisions (Howkins & Thornton 2002). Towards this end, practitioners benefit from taking time to think and having the freedom to act. As one participant stated:

> The PCLP has provided me with an opportunity to reflect on my role, and revise and confirm my competencies as a leader. (Occupational therapist, 2002)

Kets de Vries (2001, p. 3) suggests that 'if the leadership dimension isn't properly in place, a company simply can't be successful'. What do we mean by leadership and what are the qualities associated with this activity? Giving nurses the skills and confidence to know they can make a difference at every level within an organisation includes:

- clinical leadership skills (Cunningham & Kitson 2000)
- incorporating some specific skills for engaging in service redesign and commissioning
- incorporating a skills repertoire for shaping and influencing health policy and practice (Antrobus & Kitson 1999)

Table 11.1 outlines the key attributes and themes identified from Royal College of Nursing (RCN) leadership programmes.

Leadership is about both personal development and work-related professional skills and qualities. It encompasses the skills necessary for setting direction, opening possibilities, helping people to achieve, communicating and delivering. It is also about behaviour. The behaviour of leaders is as important as what they say (Crisp 2001). It is for this reason that the context in which the leader both learns and operates is crucial.

Leadership rarely exists in a vacuum and, in this case, the context is health and social care. Within this community arena, structural change has enabled the development of relatively new organisations. Many of these organisations still need to develop a culture that allows professionals to both think and work outside their 'box', to challenge existing structures and assumptions, as well as for leaders to manage uncertainty. One thing that is certain is that change will always be a part of the NHS and learning how to work within this culture to the benefit of the local population will remain a priority.

Table 11.1 Nursing leadership skills and attributes.

Key themes from the RCN Clinical Leadership Programme (Cunningham & Kitson 2000)	Strategic nursing characteristics and attributes	Attributes for influencing and developing practice (Antrobus & Kitson 1999)
• learning to manage self • building, developing and managing team relationships • having a patient focus • networking • political awareness	• visualising the bigger picture • focusing on the future • challenging preconceptions • service development and commissioning • creating alliances and partnerships • influencing others for change • dynamically managing boundaries, both professional and organisational	• a powerful, skilled operator • a strategic thinker • a developer of nursing knowledge • a reflective thinker • a process consultant

Clinicians in strategic leadership roles

Nurses and their colleagues who have a seat on the PEC in PCTs in England view their role as one that brings together their clinical expertise as well as providing clinical and professional leadership for frontline nurses (Hamilton 2003). However, within many organisations, their relationship with the executive nurse director has not been clarified and attending the primary care leadership development programme has offered one group of nurses this opportunity. In a safe environment and away from the workplace they started the process of clarifying their own roles as strategic leaders. It is important to start any person-centred change with the individual before exploring similarities and differences with others and their roles.

These strategic nurses are in a unique position in that they have a clinical role in delivering services and are thus in direct contact with service users. They also have a seat on the PEC as the nursing voice for the PCT. They are in an ideal position to bring to the committee an understanding of the clinical impact of decisions made at a strategic level, but, more importantly, to influence these decisions for the benefit of the health of the local population. In contrast, their senior managerial colleagues are one step removed from clinical practice, and whilst they may have a greater knowledge and understanding of the wider health economy, they need to rely on their clinical colleagues to provide the voice from the 'grassroots'.

In order to achieve this, these clinical strategists must have a broad understanding of the determinants of health and an ability to think in population terms about health and healthcare needs. They could be viewed as specialists in their field and thus be able to use their specialist clinical knowledge as an important source of expertise for commissioning and monitoring clinical standards. However, for many years, nurses have been unable to articulate the skills they bring to healthcare decision-making clearly and may find that their contribution is not recognised by other influential parties (Antrobus 2000). In a survey conducted by the NHS Alliance (2002), leadership was identified as a development issue for this group and one that has been unmet for many. This may be partly due to the imperatives of developing the whole of the executive committee team rather than focusing on the needs of individuals and groups within the team and addressing their more particular development needs.

In 1999, the RCN highlighted the skills and knowledge required for nurses working on the management board of primary care groups and health authorities. Whilst the structures have changed since then, the skills remain appropriate for those on any executive or board level committees as being:

- a strategic thinker
- a political operator
- a practice developer
- an organisational developer
- a manager of self

Box 11.1 Obstacles to engaging colleagues in the commissioning and service redesign process.

- Professional issues including existing boundaries, resistance to change and work pressures.
- Communication, specifically poor communication streams up and down the organisation together with poor IT support.
- Organisational issues such as a dispersed workforce and constant organisational change.
- Interorganisational issues including poorly identified common agendas, shared budgets and lack of ownership.
- Personal issues such as lack of motivation and time.

These principles focused upon strategy formation as well as engaging with grassroots professionals and service users to ensure that existing services and future developments met the needs of the local population. Engaging with grassroots colleagues appeared to be a real issue in the PEC nurse group and had an impact on the motivation of the individuals. It was recognised as crucial to the success of these roles and became the focus of work over one of the development days. The group built upon the work of identifying local health priorities and gaps in existing services and then progressed to identify the barriers and obstacles to engaging their colleagues in the commissioning and service redesign process. The themes shown in Box 11.1 emerged.

The group went on to identify strategies that could be adopted in order to address these issues. The variety of appropriate strategies is a reflection of differing organisational structures and issues as well as personal and professional knowledge and skill, but included the following:

- having forums for sharing information
- celebrating and sharing success
- being passionate about issues
- involving potential saboteurs
- engaging other colleagues and leaders
- creating protected learning time

In addition to the leadership skills already highlighted in this chapter, a list of more specific skills needed to enable them to perform their unique role more effectively were identified. This list was complex and incorporated many of their existing skills but also highlighted the need to be:

- a speed reader of multiple and complex documents
- an advocate
- a strategic planner
- a wide networker
- analytical and critical

These skills were in addition to personal leadership attributes such as greater self-awareness, confidence, enthusiasm, integrity and being realistic.

The list of desired leadership qualities and attributes is long (Adair 2002a), but put into context, the potential for conflict between individuals when roles and responsibilities are unclear becomes a real possibility. However, when given opportunities to clarify roles, agree objectives and be clear about ways of working, professionals in primary care are better equipped to deal with challenges in a constructive and proactive manner.

Multiprofessional leadership training – service development and commissioning

One of the biggest challenges facing all health professionals, and organisations, is how to address identified health need to a changing local population of service users. The NHS plan for modernisation places individual and community health need at the centre of all activity. The Government expects that existing practice will be challenged and that leadership is needed to initiate and sustain this transformational change (DH 2000). For those working in primary care, there is an additional need to focus on:

- reducing health inequalities
- promoting health
- preventing ill health
- developing public health

It is recognised that this cannot be achieved by the health sector alone, but through creating partnerships and working collaboratively change will take place. In England, the abolition of area health authorities has demanded that PCTs take on this responsibility. There is an expectation that the closer decisions are made to the individual and the community, the more likely they are to meet identified need. For this to be successful, health professionals and their colleagues will need to work in different ways, working towards ending professional complacency and rising to the challenge of greater service user choice, flexibility and consumer-led services (DH 2000).

This could be viewed as an exciting opportunity for organisations and professionals to work together, to focus on existing services and to ensure they continue to meet the changing needs of the population they were designed to serve. Service review, redesign and commissioning are major activities within the PCLP and include exploration of the difference between purchasing and commissioning services as well as providing opportunities to identify gaps in existing services. Antrobus & Brown (1997) stated that nurses and their colleagues must understand the commissioning process and take part in discussions surrounding commissioning if they are to have influence over the development of services and patient care.

Participants are encouraged to work in small groups to discuss, identify and develop a service, using a nine-step model as a guide as follows:

(1) Assess the health needs of a population.
(2) Audit against current service provision.
(3) Compare need against provision in order to identify gaps or mismatch.
(4) Identify service development priorities to redress gaps or mismatch.
(5) Draw up service development plans for existing services.
(6) Identify and describe new services to be commissioned.
(7) Agree contracts for services to be commissioned.
(8) Introduce commissioned services and implementation of developments.
(9) Evaluate the changes implemented.

It is expected that this activity will underpin future proposals for service developments, which could be presented at board level to secure funding and organisational support. Not only does this ensure that nurses are involved in commissioning and service redesign, but also it enables the organisation to provide the services needed to meet the identified health needs of the population.

By looking at existing services, participants are able to review existing practice as well as translate a client perspective to the wider community. Taking a population focus for all healthcare delivery and review is most likely to change attitudes and culture (Gough 2001). During the training programme, groups of participants work together on real issues which could be developed in collaboration with their colleagues across services and organisations. By working in multiprofessional groups throughout the programme there is an increasingly greater understanding of the differences and similarities of roles and professional expertise. Greater awareness of their own and others' roles will ensure that the right person delivers the appropriate care in the right setting. This approach challenges existing professional boundaries, and questions the assumption that just because something has always been done or delivered in a certain way it is no reason that it should continue.

Over the three days of the programme, different small groupings allow the participants to mirror a multiprofessional approach to their work. A real willingness to share issues becomes apparent; there is less evidence of professional domination and a slow realisation that it is perfectly acceptable to challenge assumptions. Nurses and their colleagues are traditionally female and thus have a tendency towards the female characteristics of participation – understanding, collegiateness and collaboration (Gough 2001). In 1998, the Audit Commission highlighted the skills needed to establish effective partnerships. These qualities and skills sit very comfortably with those traditionally associated with the female psyche.

As this sharing culture between participants grows, each is encouraged to reflect on their preferred leadership style. As stated earlier, no one preferred style is necessarily the most appropriate for those working in primary care. However, taking into account gender issues, there is a greater tendency towards:

- engagement with others
- taking a team approach

- reflection
- a commitment to life-long learning
- recognition of the importance of self-awareness in the caring professions

It is essential to engage in our own development prior to engaging in the empowerment of others. Individuals on the programme complete a pre- and post-intervention leadership skills assessment as well as having opportunities to access other tools, enabling them to clarify their existing skills further and identify others they wish to develop. In addition, participants are encouraged to use situational stories to develop a statement of their preferred leadership style.

Stories are used throughout the programme to illustrate the importance of clearly articulating health need. This is especially relevant when trying to convey a message to key stakeholders who have little concept of the clinical roles of health professionals or the context in which services are delivered. This is a key influencing skill.

Sarah Mullaly (2001) states that 'visioning requires headroom, space for creativity, time for reflection' – key leadership skills to enable change. Nurses and their colleagues in primary care have been pioneering change in the health service for some time, but only recently has their hard work been recognised and their achievements celebrated (DH 2002). As a result of the shifting power base, nurses and their colleagues have embraced the opportunities presented to develop and deliver care that patients and communities really want. To enable this to continue, all those involved in delivering services need to review their work regularly, identify areas for change and influence those who can enable this change to take place within the local and national policy agenda. Understanding the structure and function of organisations is key to this activity. Not only do individual professionals need to understand this in relation to their own organisation, but also they need to be able to identify other individuals who can be influenced to support these developments. Identifying key stakeholders thus becomes an integral activity within the service redesign and commissioning process.

Shifting boundaries and changing practice – inter-agency leadership training and development

> During the PCLP I was able to reflect on my existing networks, but also to develop relationships with those who I only knew as names. (Community Nurse, 2003)

When an opportunity arose to work with groups of health and social workers in western Scotland the focus on teams, collaboration, networks and partnerships became important. Local Health Care Co-operatives (LHCC) are groupings of professionals from a range of disciplines who work together to provide services and to improve the health of populations (Scottish Executive 2000). Each LHCC has been given project management for traditionally vulnerable groups within the community in order to develop integrated care packages where assessments are shared, bureaucracy is reduced and thus referral, assessment and delivery of services are co-ordinated and simplified. The integration of services is intended to reduce duplication and promote greater efficiency for both those delivering and receiving services.

Bringing professionals from different backgrounds and organisations together provides an ideal opportunity to challenge existing assumptions, beliefs and practices. As one participant said 'Why hasn't this happened before?...you cannot expect practitioners to suddenly change their practice without a supportive framework in which this can happen'. These professionals, coming from different settings, bring with them distinct sets of skills, attributes and knowledge bases together with issues that may be specific or could be shared (RCN 2003). In order to form a cohesive working alliance, a skill set in itself, this training presented an ideal opportunity for participants to explore the barriers to adopting different ways of working.

Theoretical underpinning is vital, but sustaining change is equally important. To this end, the PCLP has an additional 2 days during which an action learning approach to problem solving is used. This not only allows the opportunity to explore problematic work-related issues but also concentrates on a solution-focused outcome. These action–learning sets consist of up to eight individuals and are facilitated by a programme leader. As Revans (in Pedler 1991) said 'there is no action without learning and no learning without action'. These sets offer participants the opportunity to present to their peers a work situation or issue that they find difficult, with the intention of identifying action that can be implemented in the workplace. Each person is individually responsible for feeding back progress on the final day. This final fifth day also provides an opportunity for further discussion of the issue. By sharing these difficulties and being asked questions relating to the issue, we develop a better understanding of ourselves, the issue and how we might work towards a solution. The learning sets provide a supportive yet challenging environment for this to happen away from the workplace.

During the programme the health professionals and social workers recognised similar issues relating to the general themes of people and environments, which included:

- behaviours relating to staff, managers and self
- managing conflict and avoidance
- environment and space
- equipment and IT

These two groups of staff had been brought together to form a local collaborative, yet the themes emerging from the programme were not dissimilar to those identified by other professionals who work in different organisations and cultures. Confusion over roles and responsibilities and a lack of understanding about the exact nature of the individual professional contribution to shared assessment and provision of services was evident. Bureaucracy was cited as one issue, exactly the reason for integrated working, which should reduce this very same bureaucracy. To maximise this learning opportunity, it is important to identify possible solutions to obstacles raised. This group identified the need for:

- devolving budgets to a locality
- pooling budgets
- making joint agreements
- having a supportive local governance framework in place
- an ability to use funding more creatively
- seeking stakeholder agreement

This work has made it clear that to achieve attitudinal change at all levels within organisations requires a shift towards effective multiprofessional working. This involves a real commitment to move away from uniprofessional approaches to service delivery whilst maintaining the primary focus of client or service user need. Effective leadership skills throughout the organisation and clarity surrounding roles and responsibilities are required for this to become a reality. However admirable these initiatives are they need support through joint training and development for professionals to develop their skills and to work in an effective manner together.

It has been suggested previously that partnership working builds on existing team working skills. John Adair (2002b) presents a useful three-circle model based on the role of the leader in relation to groups and teams. He calls this model 'functional leadership' and suggests it incorporates the core functions required of any leader. Each circle represents a function of leadership: task, team and individual. Adair claims that each circle exerts an influence upon the other two, with constant interaction and shifting. Transferring this model to collaborative and partnership working, it makes absolute sense that all three areas be addressed for a team or group to function effectively. This leadership programme enabled the participants to redraw and agree boundaries and adopt the flexibility to move in, out, around and within these groups. Theoretically, boundaries become more fluid, facilitating communication between professions, agencies and users and thus increasing awareness of each other's perspectives.

Conclusion – the changing roles of nurses and healthcare professionals

In conclusion, leadership training and development takes place within a context of change in both the health and social care domains. Central government expects professionals to embrace change, challenge existing professional boundaries and reflect on existing practice to enable change to happen. Additionally, those working in primary care and community settings need to become involved in commissioning and service redesign so that services are configured to meet the changing health needs of the local population. The

Box 11.2   The main elements required for leading change in primary and community care.

- An ability to apply current health and social care policy
- Taking a strategic view of health
- Having a broad understanding of the determinants of health and an ability to think in population terms about health and healthcare needs
- Skills for assessing need
- Understanding and recognising the skills, knowledge and expertise of other professionals and service users
- Tackling complex issues
- Developing sustainable partnerships and working collaboratively
- Developing networking skills to enable cross boundary partnerships to flourish
- Challenging existing ways of working and facilitating a willingness to work outside conventional boundaries
- Engaging in service redesign and commissioning
- Ability to articulate a vision for change which outlines the contribution of nurses to health and healthcare
- Identifying key stakeholders for influence
- Creating an environment for innovation and willingness to take risks
- Political astuteness

main elements that are required for leading change in primary care are summarised in Box 11.2.

The Primary Care Leadership Programme has been designed to address this issue by providing an action-oriented strategic leadership programme tailored specifically for primary care professionals. In a safe environment and away from the workplace, nurses and their colleagues are able to think 'outside the box', to be creative, develop new skills and create new alliances and networks.

That the future holds more changes is certain – we will continue to need leaders who can motivate and create conditions for this to happen.

References

Adair, J. (2002a) *Inspiring Leadership*. Thorogood, London.

Adair, J. (2002b) *Effective Strategic Leadership*. Pan Macmillan, Basingstoke.

Antrobus, S. (2000) Commissioning healthcare services: nurses as strategists, operating between policy and practice. In: *Nurses and Nursing: Influencing Policy* (eds P. Gough & N. Walsh). Radcliffe, Oxford.

Antrobus, S. & Brown, S. (1997) The impact of the commissioning agenda upon nursing practice: a proactive approach to influencing health policy. *Journal of Advanced Nursing*, **25**, 309–315.

Antrobus, S. & Kitson, A. (1999) Nursing leadership: influencing and shaping health policy and nursing practice. *Journal of Advanced Nursing*, **29** (3), 746–753.

Audit Commission (1998) *A Fruitful Partnership: Effective Partnership Working.* www.necc.org.uk/jum1.htm.

Crisp, N. (2001) *The National Nursing Leadership Project.* Modernisation Agency Leadership Centre, Manchester.

Cunningham, G. & Kitson, A. (2000) An evaluation of the RCN's Clinical Leadership Development Programme part 1. *Nursing Standard*, **15** (12), 34–37.

Department of Health (2000) *The NHS Plan.* The Stationery Office, London.

Department of Health (2001) *Shifting the Balance of Power.* The Stationery Office, London.

Department of Health (2002) *Liberating the Talents; Helping Primary Care Trusts and Nurses to Deliver the NHS Plan.* The Stationery Office, London.

Ewens, A. (2002) The nature and purpose of leadership. In: *Managing and Leading Innovation in Health Care* (eds E. Howkins & C. Thornton). Bailliere Tindall, London.

Gough, P. (2001) Changing culture and deprofessionalisation. *Nursing Management*, **7** (9), 8–9.

Hamilton, N. (2003) The engine room. *Nursing Standard*, **11** (17), 18–19.

Hayes, L. (2002) A Primary Care Leadership programme; why leadership skills are so essential to nurses working in primary care. *Primary Health Care Journal*, **12** (10), 22–25.

Howkins, E. & Thornton, C. (eds) (2002) *Managing and Leading Innovation in Health Care.* Bailliere Tindall, London.

Kets de Vries, M. (2001) *The Leadership Mystique.* Prentice Hall, London.

Mullally, S. (2001) Leadership and politics. *Nursing Management*, **8** (4), 21–27.

NHS Alliance (2002) *Listening to the Frontline – A Survey of Board and PEC Nurses in PCTs.* NHS Alliance, Nottingham.

Pedler, M. (1991) *Action Learning in Practice*, 2nd edn. Gower, Aldershot.

Royal College of Nursing (1999) *The New Primary Care Groups: The Knowledge and Skills Nurses Need to Make Them a Real Success.* RCN, London.

Royal College of Nursing (2001) *Primary Care Trusts in England: The Knowledge and Skills Nurses Need to Make Them a Real Success.* RCN, London.

Royal College of Nursing (2002) *The Community Approach to Improving Public Health: Community Nurses and Community Development.* RCN, London.

Royal College of Nursing (2003) *Voices from the Frontline.* RCN, Edinburgh.

Scottish Executive (2000) *Joint Futures.* Scottish Executive, Edinburgh.

12 Leading an Older Persons' Outreach and Support Team Through Transformational Leadership

Nadia Chambers

Introduction

> Truly transformational leaders, who are seeking the greatest good for the greatest number of people without violating individual rights, and are concerned about doing what is right and honest are likely to avoid stretching the truth or going beyond the evidence for what they want to set an example to followers about the value of valid and accurate communication in maintaining the mutual trust of the leaders and their followers. (Bass 1998, p. 174)

The arrival of *The NHS Plan* (DH 2000), hot on the heels of *The New NHS: Modern and Dependable* (DH 1997), heralded a new dawn for healthcare in the UK – a renewed system that had the core egalitarian values of the NHS (i.e. equality of opportunity and equity of access) at its heart.

Having spent more than 20 years in the NHS, watching the changing political scenery and wondering if anything ever truly changes, I felt that maybe now the time was right for change, or transformation, based on these fundamental core values, although this optimism was tempered by the underlying concern that changes in the NHS often seem to be no more than window dressing, a concern also expressed in the literature at the time. This chapter describes a somewhat precarious journey between the lands of substance and spin, and the leadership approach that helped to make it possible.

Transformational leadership

The notion of transformational leadership and its application in complex organisations, such as those exemplified in modern healthcare systems (Plsek & Wilson 2001), is based on four central components (Bass 1998):

(1)   Idealised influence (charisma)
(2)   Inspirational motivation
(3)   Intellectual stimulation
(4)   Individualised consideration

Transformational leadership has been the topic of much debate during the past three decades (Dixon 1999, Gaughan 2001, Goodwin 2000, Kark *et al.* 2003, Kunert & Lewis 1987), not least because these four components could reflect a potential for wreaking organisational harm and destruction if the leader in question does not have a strong moral framework, supported by high levels of what Goleman (2000a) describes as 'emotional intelligence' to guide them through the 'swampy lowlands' of organisational life (Schon 1983).

The current perspective on transformational leadership in healthcare has been largely positive, highlighting this approach as a force for beneficial change in organisational terms (Manley 2000) as well as team development and empowerment (Thyer 2003). Elsewhere, notably in North America, analysis of the key attributes demonstrated by those purporting to have adopted a transformational leadership style have shown qualities of integrity and honesty coupled with perseverance and the desire to improve things for other people, all underpinned by a strong core of moral and ethical values (Bashor 2000, Ward 2002). Jasper (2003) highlights the confusion that can surround those moving – often by default and with little, if any, preparation – from a clearly defined management role to a nebulous leadership role, and questions the availability of appropriate education and fast-track development to prepare the 'same heads' for 'new hats'. Meanwhile, Thyer (2003) is enthusiastic about the potential for transformational leadership to harness the creativity of nurses to bring about meaningful change.

Key principles for authentic transformational leadership

The key principles involved in applying transformational leadership in a healthcare setting centre around the need for as much openness and honesty as possible in all interactions. There needs to be congruence between the moral values of the leader and the aims and objectives of the organisation – all of which combine for the common good of the stakeholders involved. The use of personal attributes (such as charisma, communication and influencing skills) needs to be balanced by high levels of personal insight and understanding, often achieved through reflection on both self-perception and feedback from colleagues. The ability to inspire and motivate is centred around the process of visioning – being able to describe, with clarity and detail, what the future will look like. In order to do this in a constructive way it is necessary to temper 'future visions' with learning from 'past realities' and to work towards the vision of the future emerging from a collective process, where everyone has had the opportunity to participate in the creation (Fenton 2003).

Intellectual stimulation in transformational leadership requires the individual to maintain mental and intellectual alertness and acuity and, in doing so, encourage open debate and criticism of a wide ranging evidence base; this helps to form the foundation of substantive change as opposed to creating the illusion of 'spin'.

The development of all individuals towards their potential, be it in leadership, participation, personal and professional growth or health gain, is one of the goals of transformational leadership. This can only be brought about through the sharing, and sometimes the brokerage, of the power bases in both organisations and interpersonal relationships.

Learning to lead

In order to put transformational leadership into practice *effectively* I would suggest that the key framework for learning is reflective practice. Any leadership position is a precarious one and to achieve and maintain the principles outlined above requires constant and honest self-evaluation. The driving force that makes any change successful is trust: trust in the integrity of the leaders involved, trust in the vision and trust in the ability of the organisation to work cohesively. Learning to become, and remain, trustworthy is key to effective transformational leadership. This can have practical as well as philosophical implications; for example, 'walking the talk' – being seen to enact yourself the values you espouse to others. It is also important to 'deliver on promises'; this may sometimes mean admitting that you made a mistake or miscalculation but at the same time doing something positive to rectify the situation so that the realisation of the overall vision is not irretrievably damaged.

In short, learning about yourself, your strengths and weaknesses, and the impact that you have on your relationships with others must be what underpins transformational leadership.

Starting with the vision

An opportunity arose to bid for some money from the Modernisation Agency – Change Agent Team. One of my medical consultant colleagues had been lobbying both the NHS Trust and the Department of Health for financial support to implement standard four (general hospital care) of *The National Service Framework for Older People* (DH 2001). Since I had taken up post a little earlier we had both spent some time discussing the vague possibility of establishing an Older Persons' Outreach Team. It is important at this point to pause and analyse some of the key elements that took a casual conversation to a serious bid for funding.

- First, there is the notion of *shared values*. Both my colleague and I believed firmly in the principles laid out in the National Service Framework (NSF) for Older People; indeed we both commented that we felt it was one of the most coherent and genuine policy documents that we had read for some time. These core values are of central importance to the effectiveness of transformational leadership in this context. Although many colleagues expressed a degree of cynicism at the 'brave new world' outlined in the NHS Plan (DH 2000), none actually disagreed with the basic premises that underpin the NSF for Older People – namely the principles of person centred care, accessibility and service user focus. This was important because it implied a level of ownership that could be further developed as we planned our vision for the future.
- We had some *recent experience with a 'mini outreach' pilot*. One of the senior elderly care physiotherapists and I spent time in the general medical wards reviewing the older patients with complex needs in order to identify those who would benefit from a move to an intermediate care ward with a high nurse/therapy input.
- This '*shared experience*', which brought together nursing, physiotherapy, medical and management perspectives, laid the foundation for developing the proposal for a multidisciplinary outreach team. We worked collaboratively on defining the aims of the team, recognising the need for political expediency, i.e. tying the proposal into the implementation of government policy as well as blue-sky thinking (in an ideal world our wish list is . . .).

My first glimpse of transformational leadership in practice here was in two areas: articulating the vision and capturing hearts and minds. This involved utilising skills of influencing, inspirational motivation and intellectual stimulation. The core team, comprising consultant nurse, consultant geriatrician and superintendent physiotherapist, agreed that the overarching function of the Older Persons Outreach and Support Team (OPOST) was to improve the management of care of older people within acute clinical settings. This core function would be realised through a number of key aims:

- to improve the discharge planning process
- to improve the clinical management of older people through early identification of potential or actual complications using a range of multidisciplinary assessments
- to reduce length of stay associated with complications by working with clinical staff to plan and implement appropriate interventions
- to identify and maximise rehabilitation potential wherever this is appropriate
- to collaborate closely with other teams in order to reduce ward admissions from A&E; expedite timely and safe discharge from acute wards and follow up in the community whenever this is appropriate
- to develop the skills of clinically based staff in the management of care of the older person

We devised key objectives for each aim and a set of operational standards derived from the NSF (standard four) against which the OPOST could be measured. We outlined the component members of the team as:

- senior elderly care nurses
- senior elderly care physiotherapist
- senior elderly care occupational therapist
- speech and language therapist
- social worker
- audit facilitator and team administrator

The proposal was funded for one year. Neither my consultant medical colleague nor myself had been costed into the bid; this would have made it too expensive. However, we were both committed to making it work and therefore promised to give time to the project. This commitment has been central to the development of the team and the perceived success of the project.

A transformational approach to leading this project seemed to come about naturally; that is to say that I did not make a conscious decision to 'be a transformational leader'. However, because I was studying organisational dynamics and behaviour at the time and I was familiar with the literature on leadership, I recognised my own predisposition towards this style of leadership as well as the prevailing organisational context at the time that would have made transformational leadership the 'model of choice'. Transformational leadership has been described in terms of changing hearts and minds, not by coercion or manipulation but through fostering honesty, loyalty and fairness and aiming for justice, equality and human rights (Bass & Steidlmeier 1998). These terms sound very grand when rehearsed in an academic paper, but in reality they are not a million miles away from what we were (and still are) trying to achieve in our commitment to developing services for older people.

A self-managed team in a complex organisation

Once funding had been secured there was intense activity to try to recruit secondees to the posts and set up communication networks. It had been agreed that OPOST would operate across three directorates in the hospital – Medicine, Surgery and Accident & Emergency – and would provide three 4 hour sessions per week to those areas, taking referrals either in advance (by bleep, email or voice message) or face-to-face while visiting.

Once the initial team members had been identified we held a briefing to agree operational issues. Although each team member came into the OPOST as an 'expert' in their own right their immediate assumption was that I would be their manager. This is no doubt a reflection of the prevailing NHS culture. However, I felt it important that each of us was given the opportunity to be honest about why we were in this venture – and the 'what's in it for me?' section of our team meetings was born at this point! I ventured that my driver was to spend an increased proportion of my time in clinical contact with patients – exercising my nursing skills. I suggested that a team like this one would be an ideal template for self-management (Hurst *et al*. 2002, Yeatts & Seward 2000), where the team took collective responsibility for all decisions made, managed its own work schedule and each individual was accountable for their professional practice whilst engaged on team business and working to agreed team standards. This notion certainly appealed to those team members who felt they were being over-managed, and it was agreed that the team would have weekly meetings to effect decision making, review caseloads and discuss issues arising.

This proved to be the first real learning situation for the team. Everyone agreed that the professional empowerment and accountability engendered by working in a self-managed team was a 'good thing', but trying to find a day of the week that suited everyone was turning into a mission. I found that I had to work very hard to avoid adopting a didactic mode, which at this early stage in a transformational model was an extremely attractive short-term solution but would have proved to be a long-term disaster. If the team were unable to make a collective decision about something as simple as when to have a weekly meeting, how could they make complex decisions involving another person's health and well-being? Silence prevailed for a while and then someone suggested that we try a different day each week to maximise attendance. The team administrator provided a calendar of dates, times and venues for the meetings and attendance was abysmal! So the decision was made to select a day of the week that suited the majority, stick with it and make every effort to attend, send apologies if unavailable and take responsibility for reading the minutes and following up individual concerns with fellow team members. This seems very trivial even now, but it was a fundamental shift, a change and a transformation and it began the process of developing the team identity based on responsibility, accountability, respect and trust. I had outlined these concepts as the underpinning components of the OPOST before it had come into being and now the team had demonstrated in a small way that this, potentially, could be a real model for practice.

The development of the weekly team meetings has been a core component of the overall development of the OPOST itself and all four elements of transformational leadership have come into play during this process, especially the notion of individualised consideration.

Dealing with adversity

During the first 3–6 months of activity the members of OPOST were on a steep learning curve. They were discovering the responsibility that goes with multidisciplinary decision making in clinical areas away from their 'home turf', and to this end they encountered some hostility from colleagues. This was genuinely unexpected by most of the team members, the exceptions being those who had worked across agencies before or who had been involved in strategic work. It reflects the nature of a complex organisation where specialties often operate in isolation and subcultures develop quickly and easily. Members of the OPOST had not expected to be treated as outsiders by other members of their professional groups and they found themselves experiencing a real crisis of confidence. The transformational leadership role here was very much concerned with inspiring and motivating the team – reminding them about what they were doing and why it was important.

A key strategy that I adopted was one that I had recently learned from the Department of Health leadership course I was attending – to get the team members to provide a vignette of good practice each week at the team meetings. This was simple but invaluable and I was encouraged by the results. Each team member gave an example of where the OPOST had made a difference to a patient, and because of the different disciplines involved each example had a subtle but different perspective. However, the overall outcome was increased positivity based on fact, not fiction. By using a reflective format each week the team was enabled to get some perspective on the wider context and devise ways in which they could deal with the problem. On an individual basis team members resolved to operate strictly by the OPOST standards at all times and that they would be available for support for each other between team meetings.

Collectively, the team decided that it would be helpful if I, in my role as consultant nurse, gave a series of OPOST updates to all clinical areas, starting with the ones that were struggling the most with the concept. This reflects expedient use of my organisational position as well as more than a little political acumen from the OPOST members! They were not abdicating responsibility for tackling the issue, but they recognised the need for influencing and intellectual stimulation from the person in a leadership role whilst they demonstrated individual consideration and motivation in a team role. The team utilised my organisational networks and connections to bring together the key stakeholders and powerbrokers, in this case the ward sisters and staff and the senior physiotherapists and therapy managers. This engaged them in some hearts and minds work of their own using not rhetoric but evidence gleaned from the team's own reflective work. Another team member supported me in each presentation and as time has progressed OPOST members have given presentations themselves to small groups of fellow professionals. The outcome in operational terms has been that those areas that demonstrated difficulty with OPOST have had their concerns addressed and the team is now a welcome addition to resources. The team has also produced a newsletter to improve communications and is in the process of building an OPOST website.

The key to effective transformational leadership here lies in open and honest communications and establishing trust.

The growth factor

It would be very easy to simply concentrate on what I have learned through engaging in transformational leadership, but it is of much greater interest to see what members of the team have learned through its principles – in practical, professional and personal terms. Being a member of a team that is a new initiative may have its drawbacks, but it also has some benefits. Not least was the fact that part of the funding was for an education and development budget, some of which was used to support the team in attending an international conference where they had a poster presentation. This was the first time that any of the team members had given a conference presentation and the learning that took place was huge. This involved:

- developing and designing the poster
- monitoring it through the stages of production (using the hospital medical information and photographic service)
- organising the trip
- preparing support handouts
- deciding who would attend which concurrent sessions and how best to feedback to each other
- team members taking responsibility for organising cover on their own wards while they were away.

The precursor to the OPOST conference presentation had been a discussion around how best to give local feedback of the baseline OPOST audit results (carried out by a funded audit facilitator who did not work clinically on the team). Each ward that OPOST served was audited against the OPOST standards (derived from the NSF for Older People). The auditor favoured a blanket approach to disseminating the results, some of which were far from favourable for the clinical areas involved. I pushed for a more managed approach where the key stakeholders from each directorate would be invited to an open audit meeting to discuss the findings and plan actions to improve practice. This encouraged ownership of the results and, more importantly, the solutions to problems that were highlighted. It also enabled OPOST to realise a core component of its educational function and to provide support for improvements.

During this process it became apparent that OPOST has a much wider function than that of a clinical outreach and support service. Through audit it can highlight issues relating to older people and lead in the education and support required to resolve these. This realisation represented key learning for all team members, who now understood that they were role modelling best practice in the care of the older person for their colleagues. For most team members, especially the nurses, this recognition of their own expertise and 'body of knowledge' was a revelation. It was this level of intellectual stimulation that provided the driver for getting the whole team to be present at the conference. Each member of the team has been able to describe what it is that their own professional expertise brings to the whole in order to give the best possible outcome for the patients and provide a model for other clinical staff.

The physiotherapist and occupational therapist have recognised and described how they work on an interprofessional basis at times. The nurses have described distinct elements of the nursing care contribution such as supporting the patient in pain, assessing and preventing pressure injury and promoting adequate nutrition and hydration. The social worker has described the OPOST as a key vehicle for working across organisational boundaries to the benefit of the patient. The OPOST administrator has described being enabled to use previous knowledge of health and social care to support the team operationally.

Each team member has reported a degree of both personal and professional growth that has resulted from being an integral part of a larger whole – the OPOST is indeed greater than the sum of its component parts. Each team member also appears to have applied all of the components of transformational leadership in their relations with each other and, to a certain extent, colleagues. The nursing sisters have had to struggle with conflicting commitments – to OPOST and their wards – and have had to demonstrate transformational leadership skills of inspiration and motivation as well as individualised consideration to overcome these when they can, or manage the results when they cannot. The senior physiotherapist and occupational therapist have helped to transform the way their colleagues see multiprofessional teamwork in action, with many of the boundaries that are evidenced in ward-based work stripped away in a peripatetic team model. This has required high levels of influencing and intellectual stimulation. The social worker has successfully negotiated the most turbulent of organisational waters to continue to provide a fast accessible service for patients which really makes a difference to timely and safe discharge home, using all the components of transformational leadership to achieve this.

The ethical criticisms of transformational leadership may be well founded (Gini 1995, Howell & Avolio 1992), especially when one considers the issues related to the charismatic aspects of transformational leadership and its inverse relationship with sustainability (Fullan 2003). However, this is surely a reflection of any kind of extremism, especially one that is not tempered by ongoing personal development and insight acquired through reflection. Transformational leadership on a smaller stage, with clear ethical and moral frameworks to guide and support it, can be a catalyst for change for the good. It can be the key to *Making a Difference* (DH 1998) as long as those involved remain grounded and monitor their effectiveness, providing the checks and balances necessary to ensure that the 'what's in it for me?' factor does not override the provision of a service to others.

Quality control

In an analysis of *Why Change Doesn't Work* Robbins & Finley (1997) cite a number of reasons why a change initiative may fail, amongst them 'having the right idea at the wrong time', 'reality contradicts the change' and 'having the wrong leadership approach and/or a leader with the wrong motives'. It would seem to be reasonable to take these established reasons for failure, turn them around and use them as measures of success in the first instance, especially early on in the change process when outcomes are only just beginning to emerge (one year is a short time in which to set up a team from scratch and then totally transform the care of older people in an acute hospital setting!).

Research into what constitutes good quality leadership underpins the approach taken by the NHS Leadership Centre in the publication of its *Leadership Qualities Framework* (NHS Leadership Centre 2003) considered in greater detail in chapter one. This framework can be used by individuals, and with some adaptations whole teams, to rate their performance and effectiveness. The framework can also be used by key stakeholders to give feedback on their perception of team or individual effectiveness, using the 360° feedback mechanism that is a feature of many leadership courses (e.g. the RCN Clinical Leadership Programme). I have recently rated myself against this framework (and been rated by others) as part of the application process for an NHS Leadership Programme. Another useful device for monitoring leadership activities can be the Individual Performance Review framework, especially if this is coupled with mentoring in the workplace.

On reflection

One of the frustrations of working in the NHS is the somewhat unrealistic assumption about the nature of change and the most pertinent measures of success. The OPOST has been the subject of an ongoing service evaluation using both quantitative and qualitative approaches to establishing the effectiveness of the service provided. The quantitative element analysed two cohorts of patients' notes, using matched pairs, to examine the type, frequency and outcomes of assessments and interventions testing the hypothesis that the pre-OPOST cohort would have received fewer assessments or interventions (in terms of frequency and appropriateness) than the cohort to whom OPOST was available. The time intervals for the OPOST cohorts were at 3 and 6 months into the project. Although the results clearly demonstrated that the patients being seen by OPOST are the most complex, frail elderly population in the hospital (which suggests that the referrals are appropriate), we concluded that this was too early in the project to be able to measure such outcomes and that a full scale randomised control trial would be more appropriate at a minimum of 9 months. Early audit results of OPOST activity have been positive and would support this conclusion.

This is the point at which the perennial issue of sustainability arises. Change in the NHS is ultimately politically driven, but although the chief executive officer may have fiscal accountability for the Trust's financial performance and may leave the organisation when performance is poor, it is unlikely that an entire workforce will be made redundant and lose their jobs – although freezes on new and replacement posts are a common occurrence. Therefore it is the government that is 'measured' in terms of the number of changes it has introduced, not necessarily in terms of what these initiatives have actually achieved over a sustained period of time. At a local level the measurements of success revolve around such issues as service capacity, average length of stay and number of saved bed days – all of which can take time to demonstrate when dealing with complex cases in a complex organisation.

One of the key challenges I have faced as a leader has been to maintain OPOST's sustainability and to find appropriate measures of the team's effectiveness. It is important that a measure of effectiveness for OPOST can demonstrate the achievements made to date. The next step will be to propose that the OPOST members and key stakeholders rate themselves and the service against the components of the NHS Leadership Framework in order to gauge effectiveness in organisational and operational terms. This is entirely in line with the tenets of a self-managed team, but it could be perceived as a high-risk strategy if the team members view anything other than continuation of OPOST in its current form as a failure. At this point it is through reflection on the past 9 months that I can see a range of opportunities for the future which includes competing in the local development planning bids for continued funding to maintain the current format.

This is where I see a new phase of transformational leadership emerging. If a key component of this approach is influencing and motivating underpinned by honesty then it is critical that team members are enabled to see their achievements during the OPOST project as positive experiences, for both themselves and the patients they have cared for. It is critical that the ongoing vision for the future includes the sustainability of the skills, knowledge and expertise that have been developed and enhanced during the OPOST project – and to be creative in the ways in which these can be transferred to other operational models if necessary. It is critical that team members do not feel that they have wasted their time and effort. Although everyone has a full-time post that will absorb them back, each one has demonstrated a commitment to the core values and beliefs underpinning OPOST as well as achieving its aims and objectives. From my own perspective I have given a significant proportion of my time to leading the development of OPOST; this resulted in role overload for a while and I have had to take a conscious step back to regain some perspective about where this initiative may fit in the wider organisational and political picture. The NHS is an organisation that is in a state of flux at one level and remains static at others; the key challenge for any leader in this duality is to preserve the integrity of both others and him/herself and to search for ways to apply lessons learned in ever-changing contexts.

Transformational leadership as an approach is not without its drawbacks, especially if the leader becomes isolated and does not have the benefit of mentoring and feedback from others in the workplace. In order to ride the wave of change instead of drowning beneath it, I would argue that most individuals in leadership positions would benefit from learning about and applying a range of skills to improve their flexibility and build their emotional intelligence (Goleman 2000b). Perhaps more important though is the need to take a reality check from time to time to remember why we do the work we do – for the benefit of the people who use our services, and for each other.

Back to the future

The service evaluation in the first 9 months of OPOST utilised a theoretical framework derived from chaos, complexity and role theories to explore three perspectives on the service:

- team members
- key stakeholders (qualitative data from thematic content analysis of interview transcripts)
- documentary audit evidence on existing practice in care of the older person

The results indicated that OPOST has been developing as an emergent team within a complex adaptive system. This evolution was explored within six themes:

- issues with a new service
- communications
- life in a team
- benefits of OPOST
- a learning experience
- looking to the future

The findings highlighted that flexibility, creativity, leadership, responsiveness, good communications, consistent and easy access, the ability to develop sound working relationships and having a shared vision about care of the older person are all key to providing a person centred service which has contributed to improving clinical and multidisciplinary management in the following ways:

- by increasing the frequency and accuracy of nutritional, pressure injury and continence assessments and supporting staff to develop appropriate management plans for patients in their care
- supporting discharge planning by ensuring that all patients referred to the social worker were seen and assessed within 24 hours and that any

subsequent need for occupational therapist input was dealt with within 48 hours

- supporting safe and timely discharge – of 414 patients seen during this time there were no failed discharges (i.e. none was readmitted within 1 week)
- prevention of admission to hospital via A&E; the snapshot audit which took place over 2 months showed that 43 admissions to hospital were prevented as a direct result of OPOST intervention

These benefits helped the team to develop a successful bid to the Department of Health NSF for Older People standard four implementation fund and, as a result, a full-time team has now been funded for a further 2 years. In addition to this, the local Primary Care Trusts have agreed to consider commissioning the service on an ongoing basis.

References

Bashor, S.A. (2000) Transformational leadership and personal values for managers in the new millennium. *Home Health Care Nurse Manager*, **4** (1), 21–23.

Bass, B.M. (1998) The ethics of transformational leadership. In: *Ethics, the Heart of Leadership* (ed. J. Ciulia). Praeger, Westport, Connecticut.

Bass, B.M. & Steidlmeier, P. (1998) Ethics, Character and Authentic Transformational Leadership. http://cls.binghamton.edu/basssteid.html.

Department of Health (1997) *The New NHS: Modern and Dependable*. The Stationery Office, London.

Department of Health (1998) *Making a Difference: The Nursing Contribution to Healthcare*. The Stationery Office, London.

Department of Health (2000) *The NHS Plan*. The Stationery Office, London.

Department of Health (2001) *The National Service Framework for Older People*. The Stationery Office, London.

Dixon, D.L. (1999) Achieving results through transformational leadership. *Journal of Nursing Administration*, **29** (12), 17–21.

Fenton, K. (Chair) (2003) *Open Space Event*, Southampton University Hospitals NHS Trust, Sparsholt College, Hampshire.

Fullan, M. (2003) *Change Forces with a Vengeance*. Jossey Bass, San Francisco.

Gaughan, A.C. (2001) Effective leadership behaviour: leading the 'third way' from a primary care group perspective. A study of leadership constructs elicited from members of PCG management boards. *Journal of Management and Medicine*, **15** (1), 67–94.

Gini, A. (1995) Too much to say about something. *Business Ethics Quarterly*, **5**, 143–155.

Goleman, D. (2000a) Leadership that gets results. *Harvard Business Review*, March–April, 78–90.

Goleman, D. (2000b) *Emotional Intelligence*. Macmillan, Basingstoke.

Goodwin, N. (2000) Leadership and the UK health service. *Health Policy*, **51** (1), 49–60.

Howell, J.M. & Avolio, B.J. (1992) The ethics of charismatic leadership: submission or liberation? *Academy of Management Executive*, **6** (2), 43–54.

Hurst, K., Ford, J. & Gleeson, C. (2002) Evaluating self managed integrated community teams. *Journal of Management and Medicine*, **16** (6), 463–483.

Jasper, M. (2003) Nursing roles and nursing leadership in the new NHS – changing hats, same heads. *Journal of Nursing Management*, **10** (2), 1–3.

Kark, R., Shamir, B. & Chen, G. (2003) The two faces of transformational leadership: empowerment and dependency. *Journal of Applied Psychology*, **88** (2), 246–255.

Kunert, K.W. & Lewis, P.L. (1987) Transactional and transformational leadership: a constructive/developmental analysis. *Academy of Management Review*, **12**, 648–657.

Manley, K. (2000) Organisational culture and consultant nurse outcomes: part 1 – organisational culture. *Nursing Standard*, **14** (36), 34–38.

NHS Leadership Centre (2003) The NHS Leadership Qualities Framework. www.nhsleadershipqualities.nhs.uk.

Plsek, P. & Wilson, T. (2001) Complexity, leadership and management in healthcare organisations. *British Medical Journal*, **323**, 746–749.

Robbins, H. & Finley, M. (1997) *Why Change Doesn't Work*. Orion Business Books, London.

Schon, D.A. (1983) *The Reflective Practitioner: How Practitioners Think in Action*. Basic Books, New York.

Thyer, G.L. (2003) Dare to be different: transformational leadership may hold the key to reducing the nursing shortage. *Journal of Nursing Management*, **11** (2), 73–79.

Ward, K. (2002) A vision for tomorrow. Transformational nursing leaders. *Nursing Outlook*, **50** (3), 121–126.

Yeatts, D.E. & Seward, R.R. (2000) Reducing turnover and improving healthcare in nursing homes. The potential of self-managed work teams. *Gerontologist*, **40** (3), 358–363.

13　*Leadership for Practice Development*

Theresa Shaw

Introduction

Picture this...An acute ward of patients who are very unwell and highly dependent on nursing care. Bed occupancy for the ward is above average, staffing levels are low and sickness rates high. It is difficult to recruit new nurses and those who are recruited often leave soon after, leading to a heavy reliance on temporary/agency nurses. The ward is managed rather than led and it is acknowledged that the quality of patient care often falls below the standard expected. There is a constant demand from the top to 'change' and 'improve'. Everyone blames everyone else and staff feel they are constantly being told they are not good enough – in some instances they are not. However, looking in from the outside it is clear the practitioners are unable to make changes on their own.

There are many problems here, all of which have contributed to the development of a negative and ineffective culture. Competent leadership is the 'single most visible factor that distinguished successful cultural change' (Schein 1985). One of the problems with the above scenario is ineffective leadership, another the attitude toward development and change. Practice development offers an opportunity to begin to tackle these two problems. Whilst practice development needs effective and supportive leadership it also has the potential to enable the development of leaders. Initiating a systematic approach to practice development, facilitated by a skilled practice developer, would offer the opportunity to begin to transform the culture and leadership of the ward and result in improvements in practice and patient care (Garbett & McCormack 2002, Manley & McCormack 2003).

This chapter looks at the role of leadership in relation to practice development. Using relevant literature, my own experiences and real-life examples of practice-based initiatives (with permission) I attempt to illustrate and illuminate the influence of leadership on the process of developing and changing healthcare practice. I do not intend to propose one particular leadership style for two reasons. First, there is no 'one size to fit all'; second, the culture of healthcare practice remains diverse and challenging and so practitioners leading and/or facilitating development in practice need a repertoire of skills and experiences to adapt and modify their ways of working. However, I hope it will become clear that certain characteristics have a more positive impact on practitioners and practice, and influence the sustainability of change as well as the culture of healthcare practice.

The nature and purpose of practice development

Since the late 1970s there has been increasing emphasis on the development of nursing and advancing nursing practice together with a need to improve patient care. The establishment of nursing development units began to address these needs and whilst the number of units was small, evidence suggested they were positive environments which provided high quality nursing care and facilitated the development of the nursing staff (Griffiths & Evans 1995, Vaughan & Edwards 1995). Strong leadership was seen as a key to their success (Kings Fund Centre 1992).

During the last 5–10 years the concept of practice development has emerged as an activity aiming to change practice and improve patient care (Balfour & Clarke 2001, Clarke & Procter 1999, Garbett & McCormack 2002, Gerrish 2001, Kitson *et al.* 1996, McCormack *et al.* 1999, Unsworth 2000). There has also been a proliferation of so-called practice development roles (Garbett & McCormack 2001, 2002, Mallett *et al.* 1997). The nature and purpose of practice development (Box 13.1) has been illuminated by work exploring the concept of practice development and the experiences of practice developers (Garbett & McCormack 2001, 2002).

More recently, Manley & McCormack (2003) examined the 'means' by which practice development outcomes are achieved more closely. Whilst accepting that all practice development has the common purpose of improving patient care, they suggest that the approach we take to achieve improvement is underpinned by different assumptions and therefore by different methodologies. Drawing on critical social theory, in particular the work of Habermas (1972) regarding different 'knowledge interests' and Grundy's (1982) three modes of action research, they propose two 'worldviews': *technical practice development* and *emancipatory practice development* (Manley &

Box 13.1 The nature and purpose of practice development (Garbett & McCormack 2002).

Practice development:
- is a method of improving patient care
- is a means of transforming the 'context and culture in which nursing care takes place'
- uses 'systematic approaches to effect changes in practice'
- is a facilitated process

Table 13.1 A comparison of the two world views of practice development – technical and emancipatory practice development (PD). (Adapted from Manley & McCormack 2003.)

Shared characteristics and assumptions • Achieving 'better' or 'best' services for users *Differing characteristics and assumptions*	
Technical PD	**Emancipatory PD**
• PD is a technical or task focused process led by an 'expert authority figure' who directs a change in practice toward predetermined outcomes, i.e. the implementation of clinical guidelines.	• PD is a process that focuses on understanding of the social system of practice as well as empowering individuals and teams to understand their practice and to take action to change (rather than be led others). It also fosters a transformational culture.
• Staff development is viewed as a consequence (not purpose) of PD.	• Staff development is a deliberate and interrelated purpose of PD.
• Best practice is universally understood and static.	• Best practice is defined locally and is dynamic.
• Outcomes are more important than the process of achievement	• The process achieving development is valued as much as the outcome.
• Ideas for action arise from management and are management driven (top-down).	• Ideas for action arise from collective views and are practice driven (bottom-up).
• Knowing the evidence will ensure action.	• Evidence needs to be owned and seen as relevant.
• Evaluation of outcomes would focus on measurement, for example waiting times, length of stay, morbidity and mortality.	• Evaluation would additionally focus on process outcomes, cultural change and encompass stakeholder involvement.

McCormack 2003). As shown in Table 13.1, there are similarities between the two but each has differences in terms of purpose, facilitation and evaluation.

Manley & McCormack (2003) stress that their intention is not to present a 'good versus bad' approach to practice development. Rather, they wish to help practitioners engaged in practice development to consider their approach and the position of their organisation. This said, they do suggest that emancipatory practice development may be more 'sophisticated' and have more far-reaching outcomes. The impact of these two approaches in relation to the role of practice developers is more closely considered later in this chapter.

Influence of leadership on practice development and change

> We need nurse, midwife and health visitor leaders who can establish direction and purpose, inspire, motivate and empower teams around common goals and produce real improvements in clinical practice, quality and services. (DH 1999, p. 52)

This recognition of the value of leadership has been backed with a high level of resources and leadership training for health professionals.

Linked to this, effective ways of achieving change and improvement are also being considered. Policy documents, government papers and healthcare reports increasingly espouse the values of development and change that is multiprofessional, collaborative, in partnership across organisations and involves stakeholders. Undoubtedly, today's NHS is shaking off some of the traditional ways of working that have relied on charismatic leaders, hierarchy, rationality and control. However, there is still some way to go. Approaches to change in the NHS have been described as having a narrow focus and tending to ignore historical, contextual and process issues (Pettigrew *et al.* 1988). In my view, some of these problems remain and are perpetuated by the evidence-based practice movement, which continues to rely on a rational philosophy and attitude to change; for example, reliance on the assumption that practitioners will change practice because there is evidence of a better way.

Bennis & Nanus (1985) provide an overview of the differences between management and leadership. They see leadership as creating effectiveness and management creating efficiency. It concerns them that organisations are often top heavy with management and 'under-led', which might result in efficient routines, the effectiveness of which are never questioned (Bennis & Nanus 1985). Change should be enabled rather than managed. Fullan (1986) and Pettigrew *et al.* (1988), in exploring factors that facilitate change, include leadership and enabling the 'evolution' of ownership through examination of values, beliefs and practice (Fullan 1986). This said, some studies exploring the role of clinical leaders found that without some management responsibility the leaders lack the perceived authority to achieve change and development in practice (Christian & Norman 1998).

The important role of leadership for practice development is presented in the theoretical framework developed by Kitson *et al.* (1998). The framework includes three key elements that influence the use of evidence in practice: context, evidence and facilitation. Further refinement of the framework provides insight into the contribution these elements make to successful practice change and development. For example, McCormack *et al.* (2002) examine the contribution of leadership to the 'context' within which the use of evidence and change may (or may not) take place. Box 13.2 indicates the factors that characterise weak and strong leadership within organisations.

Box 13.2 Characteristics of strong and weak leadership within organisations (McCormack *et al.* 2002, p. 99).

Weak leadership
- Traditional command and control leadership
- Lack of role clarity
- Lack of teamwork
- Poor organisational structures
- Autocratic decision-making processes
- Didactic approaches to teaching, learning and management

Strong leadership
- Transformational leadership
- Role clarity
- Effective teamwork
- Effective organisational structures
- Democratic inclusive decision-making processes
- Enabling/empowering approach to teaching, learning and managing

Strong leadership clearly makes a difference to both the application of evidence in practice and the likelihood of change occurring and being sustained. A transformational leadership style is recognised and supported by a wide range of other literature on change and development (Cook 2001, Ewens 2002, Trofino 2000). With this in mind I now move on to look at some of the potential leadership roles in practice development.

Leadership roles in practice development: transformational leader, facilitator, practice developer

Transformational leaders

Other chapters have addressed in more detail the notion of transformational leadership. Here, the intention is to look at the characteristics of transformational leadership and its relationship with, and value for, practice development.

Traditional concepts of leadership in healthcare are primarily based on a 'transactional' model reflecting the hierarchy and authority within organisations (Cook 1999). Furthermore, this assumes that a vision for development and change is provided by a charismatic person who directs a team towards implementation (Manley 2001). In contrast, 'transformational leaders have the ability to clearly articulate a vision of the future ... like story tellers they capture our imagination with the vivid descriptions of the wonderful future we will build together' (Trofino 1992, p. ix). Being visionary and then being able to work with others to 'build together' a vision for future practice is a key attribute of an effective practice developer (McCormack & Garbett 2003).

Manley (2001) identified six transformational leadership processes:

- ability to develop a shared vision
- inspiring and communicating
- valuing others
- challenging and stimulating
- developing trust
- enabling

Using these processes, transformational leaders help those they are working with to become empowered and take ownership of practice challenges and solutions (Sashkin & Burke 1990). The impact of transformational leadership is more wide-ranging than just the development of individuals or single practice changes. It can influence organisational culture, thereby creating a context more receptive and conducive to the use of evidence, development and change (Schein 1985).

Facilitator

The role of facilitator may also be one of leadership, but not in the hierarchical sense that is so often seen in healthcare (Fullan 1986, Pettigrew *et al.* 1988). A facilitator needs to be an equal member within the team, whilst having a responsibility for enabling the team to be effective rather than directing or 'driving' (Fullan 1986, Pettigrew *et al.* 1988). Research by Dechant *et al.* (1993), focusing on team learning and organisational change, looked at the value of facilitating the development of cohesive and effective teams that become more able to effect change and result in the ability to influence the culture of the organisation. Their findings were not new. Indeed, they refer to other influential work such as how adults learn (Mezirow 1991), team/group dynamics (Mezirow 1991, Schon 1983) and learning organisations (Senge 1990). Dechant *et al.* (1993) highlighted that to be truly effective, teams need support and facilitation to help them examine their actions and to move forward.

Kitson *et al.* (1998) identified facilitation as an essential factor to achieving successful change, and further work by Harvey *et al.* (2002) exploring the purpose, role and skills of facilitation distinguishes it from other factors that influence change. For example, facilitation was felt to be an important and distinct role, which significantly influences the effectiveness of development and change in practice by helping and enabling rather than directing and persuading. However, they also recognised there was overlap between the facilitation role and other factors that enable change and development.

Practice developer

Practitioners working in practice development roles appear to take on a wide range of functions and activities. In their work exploring the characteristics, skills and qualities of practice developers McCormack & Garbett (2003) reviewed the literature and invited practice developers to take part in focus groups. Whilst from the literature they identified six categories of activity, their discussions with practice developers revealed that the primary focus of their work was facilitating and promoting change and communicating about their work. Further exploration of the skills and qualities of practice developers revealed the qualities that 'resembled' those of transformational leaders and facilitators.

The aforementioned work on practice development methodology (Manley & McCormack 2003) provided an overview of how practice developers might function within differing 'worldviews'. As they state, presentation of these is exaggerated to accentuate the characteristics. So, what might emancipatory and technical practice development look like in practice, how do the assumptions underpinning these two approaches influence practice developers and what are the consequences of different ways of working? The following two examples from my own journey as a practice developer attempt to answer these questions. With reference to Manley & McCormack's (2003) 'worldviews' they describe and reflect on my role as a practice developer in two different organisations, with different expectations and assumptions regarding development in practice. As you read the examples you may like to consider how they differ in terms of leadership and practice development.

Case study 13.1 Illuminating 'technical' practice development – working as a project manager.

The implementation of care pathways was a trust-wide activity. It was initiated by the Chief Executive and endorsed by the Trust Board as it was perceived as a more effective way of working that would ensure the 'implementation of evidence based practice'. Key clinical interventions and/or areas of practice were identified as targets for a variety of reasons, e.g. outcome of care perceived as poor, increased complaints, long waiting time, length of stay and increased complications. As a project manager, my role was to lead the development and meet the outcomes, which were the implementation of the care pathways. It was perceived that I would 'direct' rather than 'enable' development.

Multidisciplinary teams were established to support the development with the intention of increasing ownership, and whilst the team espoused interest in development and commitment to providing high quality care, there was little evidence of shared values. Some team members had limited involvement and felt like 'pawns'. Others expressed feelings of being 'manipulated'. There were attempts to consciously or unconsciously sabotage activities, for example, by not turning up for meetings or 'forgetting' to complete activities.

Continued

Case study 13.1 *Continued*

As a manager I took on full responsibility for making the change happen. Rather than challenge why people had not completed an activity or appeared resistant to an idea, I would complete the task. At times I would sit back and ask myself why I was doing all the work.

Once the care pathways were ready for implementation, I provided a range of information, and training sessions were held to help the process of change. Regular visits were made to the practice area to encourage use, but as the number of these visits reduced, the use of the care pathways became more sporadic. It was clear that change was not embedded in practice and therefore would not be sustainable.

Reflecting on the process overall, it was clear that there were willing supporters and some change had been achieved. There was also resentment by those who felt pressurised into change, and the longer-term sustainability could be questioned. I felt dissatisfied, as despite my personal desire to be supportive and enabling, it was clear that my role was perceived as delivering a management directive, and even though there were some clear benefits for patient care, practitioners resented being 'told' what to do.

Case study 13.2 Illuminating 'emancipatory' practice development – working as an external facilitator for practice development.

As an external practice developer I was invited to work with one ward to explore ways to improve practice and patient care. From the outset senior managers took a keen interest in what was happening. They asked to hear about the 'reality' of the work and wanted to know how they could support it. A small practice development team was formed for the ward and it was agreed that we would use action learning as a process for exploring practice and giving support. My role was to facilitate the learning set and enable the team to work towards changing practice. The learning set established clear ground rules, particularly relating to commitment and equality within the group, which was particularly important for me as facilitator. Individual values and beliefs were explored and shared values agreed.

The ward was a difficult environment and during the first 6 months the team explored the context and culture of the ward. This helped to identify the needs of patients and staff on the ward and it shaped our activities. It also revealed the 'messiness' of practice development and the team recognised that they needed to carefully consider what improvement meant

Continued

Case study 13.2   *Continued*

for them. There was an effort to involve 'stakeholders' including patients and other professionals in 'ongoing evaluation'. This has only been partly achieved, but the commitment is there. Progress has been slow but purposeful. Initially a small aspect of practice was tackled; however, this has led to a much larger focus which addresses fundamental attitudes toward patient care and in time could result in a significant culture change.

On reflection, the approach helped practitioners understand their own attitudes, knowledge and skills, and this has influenced how they want to work in practice. From the outset, the intention was to enable the team to be responsible for development and change. Several practitioners have become skilled and confident leaders of development in practice.

No two organisations and/or practice development initiatives are the same, so it can be difficult to make comparisons. However, the fundamental difference between these two examples in terms of leadership and practice development is the locus of control and ownership. In the first example, I was given control and was perceived to be 'in control'; the change was seen as mine. In the second example, the control was with the team. I was part of the team, with an equal role to play, but as an enabler rather than a director, the change and development activities were theirs. As I said in my introduction to the chapter, I am not intending to propose one approach or style of leadership; I believe that decision must lie with individual practitioners. However, I hope the examples have begun to challenge you to think how you are leading development in practice and the impact this is having on practice outcomes and other practitioners.

Reflecting on the influences of leadership and approaches to practice development in action: the realities of practice

At the Foundation of Nursing Studies (FoNS) our experience in supporting a wide range of practice development initiatives has given us much insight into:

- the range of strategies people use to develop practice
- the influence of leadership
- the difference these make to practice

The following three examples are completed projects that have all approached development in a different way and been influenced by leadership.

These three examples reflect differing approaches to development and change. They also show how practice developers work in different ways, drawing on both facilitation and leadership skills. The influence of leadership

Case study 13.3 Developing and implementing a family health assessment.

This practice development project aimed to develop a standardised approach to the assessment of family health needs.

Overview of the project
The impetus for the project came from a 'critical incident' from health visiting practice, which highlighted the need to be able to accurately identify vulnerable families in need of health visitor interventions. A small group of senior colleagues developed a project plan by looking at research evidence. A project leader was appointed to implement the project plan and she began by further reviewing the evidence, and from here the idea for developing an assessment tool emerged. The project leader recognised that involving the practitioners would help foster ownership of the tool and so a team was established. The assessment tool and guidance were developed based on the literature and input from the health visiting team. A pilot was then undertaken. At this point, uncertainty, discontent and resistance began to emerge. The health visitors either found reasons for being unable to use the tool or expressed discomfort about its implementation.

  This project was more closely aligned to technical practice development and, as found with this approach and the characteristics of organisations that have a tendency towards transactional leadership, the driving forces for change were top down. For example, following the identification of the practice problem a solution was identified at a senior level. There was a belief that this should happen and there appeared to be evidence from research that this was the 'right' thing to do. The project leader was placed in the position of 'leading' what was perceived to be a clearly defined change with predetermined outcome. The project leader's own opportunity for reflection enabled her to explore the consequence of being a 'technical practice developer'. This included the lack of a common purpose and vision within the team, the varied beliefs and values held about health visiting and the variability of implementation (Sanders 2002).

Case study 13.4 Rapid recovery from acute psychosis.

This project focused on promoting rapid recovery of patients with acute psychosis by developing practice in acute psychiatric wards. The project comprised two key activities: the development of a suitable training package and the establishment of a programme of training and support for ward nursing teams. The project was initiated by an academic

Continued

Case study 13.4 *Continued*

institution that appointed a project leader to work with clinical teams to implement the project plan.

Overview of the project
The first phase of the project involved gaining the support of senior practice colleagues. Meetings were initiated with consultants, managers and the heads of each professional group to inform them about the project. Several meetings were held with the ward managers to explain the training and its advantages, leading them in most cases to volunteer to participate. The project worker spent several shifts on the wards before starting the training, to get to know staff and to explain the rationale and benefits of the training. The training was provided on-site and sessions were repeated several times to allow all staff to attend. Staff attending outside normal shift hours were allowed to take the time back at a later date. Follow-up, on-site supervision was provided and the project leader role modelled good practice either by working on the ward or via time-tabled supervisory sessions for groups and individuals. Despite what appeared to be careful engagement with all those involved only two out of the seven wards trained continued to use the new skills in practice.

This project seems to sit somewhere in the middle of technical and emancipatory development. The project leader had a training role, but also made efforts to work with the nurses and enable them to use the new skills. On reflection, the project leaders identified a number of factors that hindered the development. In particular, they noted the impact of leadership at ward and middle management level. For example, in three wards, despite managers and staff making a positive commitment to the project, the ward managers either failed to secure venues for the training, or failed to allocate their staff to training sessions, or organise the off duty rota so that attendance was possible. In contrast, on the wards where the training was successfully implemented the ward managers had made a personal commitment to the project. They organised their staff to attend, attended themselves and facilitated the implementation of the skills taught. This success occurred within the context of a stable staff team and supportive managers (Bower & McCann 2003).

Case study 13.5 Enhancing partnerships with relatives in care settings for older people.

This project began as the second phase of a project that had validated guidelines for carer involvement and planned to apply the guidelines to

Continued

Case study 13.5 *Continued*

an identified practice setting. The overall aim was to implement guidelines that seek to involve relatives of older people in decision-making processes. A framework of work-based learning was used to facilitate the processes of developing practice.

Overview of the project

Two Clinical Development Nurses (CDN), who work with older people in the hospital setting, were nominated by the Trust on the basis of their eligibility and willingness to participate. Each CDN worked with a team of practitioners in the hospital setting to develop practice in relation to the guidelines. The project leader, an academic supervisor and an appointed workplace supervisor supported the CDNs. The CDNs began by collecting data about current practice and shared this with all the staff. From here ideas for change and development emerged. Action learning was used to help staff explore their work and their experiences of involving carers and enable development of new understanding about the issues they were dealing with in practice. The staff eventually decided they did not want to implement the guidelines; rather they developed and shaped their own standards for practice as a result of working with the guidelines.

This project is perhaps more closely aligned to emancipatory practice development and transformational leadership. Particular strengths of the practice developers (the CDNs and project leader) were their commitment to working with the staff and their ability to observe and listen to the feelings of staff and carers they worked with. This resulted in them recognising that pursuing the original aims of the work would not lead to implementation of the guidelines or changes in practice. The staff on the ward were instead enabled and empowered toward a practice change they felt was needed. In their report of the work, the project team highlight the complexity of practice change, the value of creating ownership and the importance of facilitated support (Dewar *et al.* 2002).

beyond the direct leadership of each project is also evident. In Case study 13.3, the evidence base was the driver for change and the project leader was expected to direct the change. In Case study 13.4, ward leadership influenced the likelihood of practice change. The commitment of the ward managers influenced the likelihood of practitioners continuing to use their new skills in practice. In Case study 13.5, the practice developers had some pre-planned aims for change but began by working with staff and looking at current practice. As leaders, they enabled the staff to explore their practice and identified areas for change. This, in some ways, was the most risk-taking and challenging approach to development but resulted in tangible change.

Transformational leaders and emancipatory practice developers are both prepared to take risks and acknowledge the value of challenge in successful development.

Conclusions

This chapter has considered the links between leadership and practice development. I began by providing an overview of the nature and purpose of practice development and introduced more recent literature proposing a practice development methodology. The methodology proposed by Manley & McCormack (2003) helped shape the remainder of the chapter, as I believe it sheds light on the way practice developers lead and support development. My review of the characteristics of three roles often associated with practice development (transformational leader, facilitator and practice developer) has indicated how each influence development and change. Both the literature and the practice examples indicate that effective practice developers use a range of skills but are particularly influenced by transformational leadership and facilitation. Finally, I used examples of practice development projects to illustrate and illuminate the influence of leadership on the process of developing and changing healthcare practice.

In today's so-called modern NHS, there is an urgent need for 'modern' and new thinking regarding the leadership of development and change which moves away from traditional and managerial approaches. Practice development has the potential to improve the care of patients, enable the development of effective leaders in practice and transform the culture within healthcare organisations.

To manage is to control; to lead is to liberate. (Owen 1990, p. 53)

References

Balfour, M. & Clarke, C. (2001) Searching for sustainable change. *Journal of Clinical Nursing*, **10** (1), 44–50.

Bennis, W. & Nanus, B. (1985) *Leaders: The Strategies for Taking Charge*. Harper and Row, New York.

Bower, L. & McCann, E. (2003) Rapid recovery from acute psychosis. *Foundation of Nursing Studies Dissemination Series* (eds T. Shaw & K. Sanders), **1** (6).

Christian, S. & Norman, I. (1998) Clinical leadership in nursing development units. *Journal of Advanced Nursing*, **27** (1), 108–116.

Clarke, C. & Procter, S. (1999) Practice development: ambiguity in research and practice. *Journal of Advanced Nursing*, **30** (4), 975–982.

Cook, M.J. (1999) Improving care requires leadership in nursing. *Nurse Education Today*, **19** (4), 306–312.

Cook, M.J. (2001) The renaissance of clinical leadership. *International Nursing Review*, **48**, 38–46.

Dechant, K., Marsick, V.J. & Kasl, E. (1993) Towards a model of team learning. *Studies in Continuing Education*, **15** (1), 1–14.

Department of Health (1999) *Making a Difference: Strengthening the Nursing, Midwifery and Health Visiting Contribution to Health and Health Care*. The Stationery Office, London.

Dewar, B., Tocher, R. & Watson, W. (2002) Enhancing partnerships with relatives in care settings for older people. *Foundation of Nursing Studies Dissemination Series* (eds T. Shaw & K. Sanders), **2** (2).

Ewens, A. (2002) The nature and purpose of leadership. In: *Managing and Leading Innovation in Health Care* (eds E. Howkins & C. Thornton). Bailliere Tindall, London.

Fullan, M.G. (1986) The management of change. In: *World Yearbook of Education: The Management of Schools*. Kogan Page, London, pp 73–86.

Garbett, R. & McCormack, B. (2001) The experience of practice development: an exploratory telephone interview study. *Journal of Clinical Nursing*, **10** (1), 94–102.

Garbett, R. & McCormack, B. (2002) A concept analysis of practice development. *Nursing Times Research*, **7** (2), 87–100.

Gerrish, K. (2001) A pluralistic evaluation of nursing/practice development units. *Journal of Clinical Nursing*, **10** (1), 109–118.

Griffiths, P. & Evans, A. (1995) *Evaluation of a nursing-led in-patient service: an interim report*. Kings Fund Centre, London.

Grundy, S. (1982) Three modes of action research. *Curriculum Perspectives*, **2** (3), 23–34.

Habermas, J. (1972) *Knowledge and Human Interests*. Heinemann, London.

Harvey, G., Loftus-Hill, A., Rycroft-Malone, J., Titchen, A., McCormack, B. & Seers, K. (2002). Getting evidence into practice: the role and function of facilitation. *Journal of Advanced Nursing*, **37** (6), 577–588.

Kings Fund Centre (1992) *Selection Criteria Used to Assess and Guide Applicants for Department of Health NDU Grants*. Nursing Development Programme. Kings Fund Centre, London.

Kitson, A.L., Ahmed, L.D., Harvey, G., Seers, K. & Thompson, D.R. (1996) From research to practice: one organisational model for promoting research based practice. *Journal of Advanced Nursing*, 23 (3), 430–440.

Kitson, A., Harvey, G. & McCormack, B. (1998) Enabling the implementation of evidence based practice: a conceptual analysis. *Quality in Health Care*, 7, 149–158.

Mallett, J., Cathmoir, D., Hughes, P. & Whitby, E. (1997) Forging new roles: professional and practice development. *Nursing Times*, **93** (18), 38–39.

Manley, K. (2001) *Consultant Nurse: Concept, Processes Outcomes*. PhD Thesis. University of Manchester/RCN Institute, London.

Manley, K. & McCormack, B. (2003) Practice development: purpose, methodology, facilitation and evaluation. *Nursing in Critical Care*, **8** (1), 22–29.

McCormack, B. & Garbett, R. (2003) The characteristics, qualities and skills of practice developers. *Journal of Clinical Nursing*, **12** (3), 317–325.

McCormack, B., Manley, K., Kitson, A., Titchen, A. & Harvey, G. (1999) Towards practice development – a vision in reality or a reality without a vision? *Journal of Nursing Management*, **7** (2), 255–264.

McCormack, B., Kitson, A., Harvey, G., Rycroft-Malone, J., Titchen, A. & Seers, K. (2002) Getting evidence into practice: the meaning of context. *Journal of Advanced Nursing*, **38** (1), 94–104.

Mezirow, J. (1991) *Transformational Dimensions of Adult Learning*. Jossey Bass, San Francisco.

Owen, H. (1990) *Leadership Is*. Abbot, Maryland.

Pettigrew, A., McKee, L. & Ferlie, E. (1988) Understanding change in the NHS. *Public Administration*, **66**, 297–317.

Sanders, K. (2002) Developing and implementing a family health assessment. *Foundation of Nursing Studies Dissemination Series* (eds T. Shaw & K. Sanders), **1** (8).

Sashkin, M. & Burke, W. (1990) Understanding and assessing organizational leadership. In: *Measures of Leadership* (eds K. Clark & M. Clark). Leadership Library of America, West Orange, New Jersey, pp 297–325.

Schein, E.H. (1985) *Organisational Culture and Leadership*. Jossey Bass, San Francisco.

Schon, D. (1983) *The Reflective Practitioner: How Practitioners Think in Action*. Basic Books, New York

Senge, P. (1990) *The Fifth Discipline: The Art and Practice of the Learning Organisations*. Doubleday, New York.

Trofino, J. (1992) Guest editorial: transformational leadership. *Journal of Nursing Administration*, **20** (4).

Trofino, A.J. (2000) Transformational leadership: moving total quality management to world class organisations. *International Nursing Review*, **47** (4), 232–242.

Unsworth, J. (2000) Practice development: a concept analysis. *Journal of Nursing Management*, **8** (6), 317–326.

Vaughan, B. & Edwards, M. (1995) *Interface Between Research and Practice*. Kings Fund Centre, London.

14 Leadership in an Interprofessional Context: Learning from Learning Disability

Janet McCray

The challenges of working in an interprofessional context

This chapter explores the leadership style and approach of the learning disability practitioner in the multi-agency setting, suggesting a model of practice applicable for all practitioners working together within modern interprofessional healthcare delivery. An empirical study by McCray (2003a) highlights evidence of the transformational leadership role and skills held by Registered Nurses for People with Learning Disabilities (RNLDs) in response to the changing contexts of services, and which have contributed towards the development of a conceptual framework for practice.

Valuing People (DH 2001), the first governmental review of learning disability services in England for 30 years, is now being operationalised. Areas under review are children and family care, supporting independence, health workforce planning and building partnerships. The White Paper focuses on valuing the differences and diversity of people with learning disability in line with the current government's policies.

Identifying the social exclusion, dependence and lack of rights and choice of people with learning disability as significant problems, the Government sets out its strategy for change based on collaboration between agencies and inclusion of people with learning disability. As Kinsey & Maguire (2001) note, one of the main areas to reward and penalise in regard to service quality will be that of accountability in relation to partnerships within health and social services, with the possibility of a 'joined up' approach to assessment. Furthermore, there is evidence of an increasingly broader set of multi-agency partnerships and networks in which professionals from health and social care are operating (McCray & Ward 2003).

One of the key areas identified for change is that of improving, promoting and facilitating better health for people with learning disability (DH 2001).

This has, in recent decades, been viewed as a significant practice role for the RNLD when wider health services have shown a lack of interest in this group of people (Hart 1998, Stanley 1998). However, this is gradually changing and some primary care teams are beginning to provide services. At the same time the number of agencies involved in health-promoting activities has broadened, resulting in a role shift for community-based RNLDs, where leadership skills and teamwork facilitation roles are increasingly at the forefront of their practice across the boundaries of health and social care.

The challenges of interprofessional practice

Loxley (1997, p. 24) writes that to 'achieve collaboration, then the word itself must be removed from political rhetoric and the world of common sense where it is too often found'. As Biggs notes (1997, p. 192), words like collaboration are used as a form of 'self evident truth' in all sorts of policy documents. In terms of policy, Biggs continues (1997, p. 194), current contexts include tendencies that are at one and the same time unifying and leading to diversity. For the professional working at the interface of health and social care, the policy and political agenda may seem fraught with ambiguity, and a paradox can be observed in terms of the calls for interprofessional practice on the one hand and the reshaping of professional structures on the other. Consecutively, the arguments in support of interprofessional practice are posited as efficiency in the use of resources, the removal of overlap in the delivery of services, the clarification of roles and responsibilities and, for the client, the delivery of comprehensive and holistic services (Hallett & Birchall 1992, p. 17). Yet such arguments occur when both financial and organisational boundaries act as barriers to good practice.

Whilst the facilitation of a dialogue between professionals is crucial, the more complex and far less specific issues of professional boundaries, contexts for practice, professional power, problem solving and responding to change often remain unaddressed.

Moves towards interprofessional partnership across all professions place individual practitioners in a dichotomous position. In striving for best practice for service users, their own professional identity may be perceived as at risk. Equally their role as a collaborator within a team may surpass outcomes for service users. Pietroni (1991, p. 3) summarises the still relevant issues: conflicts in values and procedures, resource and agency control problems, social defences, unresolved leadership issues and differences between professions mirroring conflicts.

Hudson and colleagues draw attention to the limits of organisational individualism. They argue that increasingly solutions to problems need to be addressed from a range of perspectives, as the incidence of clients with multiple needs rises (Hudson *et al.* 1999, p. 238). Further, from an agency point of view, collaboration may pose a threat, as agencies may lose some of their freedom to act independently. Additionally organisations may have to invest scarce resources when the return on investment may not be clear (Hudson 1987). Citing Huxham and Macdonald (1992), Hudson *et al.* (1999, p. 242) add that collaboration may mean having to share the credit for a particular outcome or even letting another organisation take all the credit. This may impact on the enthusiasm for collaboration in some small teams within particular sectors of health and social care organisations, who may be constantly at risk of usurpation both internally and externally. Ultimately the ways in which individual practitioners respond and deal with such challenges, in the decision-making process, impact on the likely success or failure of any future collaboration. These tensions and professional responses to them will be explored further throughout this chapter.

Leadership approaches used in this study

Throughout this chapter it is suggested that RNLDs are equipped to lead in the interprofessional or multi-agency setting within a definition of leadership which takes into account the key differences in Burns' (1978) transactional and transformative leadership styles (Trofino 1993). Transactional leadership is usually determined by a relationship with followers based on a short-lived exchange of resources. In contrast transformative leaders have a different type of relationship with followers, where there is a shared common purpose that can benefit the organisation. Burns (1978) highlights these leadership roles as being elevating, mobilising, inspiring and exalting. Boulter & Cook (1997) and Moore (1999) advocate the RNLD as the ideal person for the transforming leadership style, for whereas traditional transactional leadership is usually intent on the completion of tasks, this may no longer be a valid model in the health or social care services of the future (McDaniel 1997). Transforming leaders seek to seize opportunities, create change and empower others (Kanter 1983), which fits with the leadership role outlined and evidenced here. Further, Sofarelli & Brown (1998) argue that such transformational leadership is less concerned with management of the short term and more concerned with the holistic perspective. Moore (1999) writes of the leadership skills of the RNLD in dealing with the deceptive health and social care divide, and their ability to overcome marginalisation – both of people with learning disabilities and their own professional group. Boulter & Cook (1997) suggest that with their experiences of continuous change, RNLDs are ideal transformative leaders. For where there may be conflicting values in agencies, leading to different forms of power in operation along with a number of multiple power bases (Hudson *et al.* 1999), proposed change creates further complexities as those existing practices and values are further challenged. This can lead to ambiguity for professionals such as collaborative versus departmental loyalty and the need for a different emphasis on skills development as roles and boundaries shift.

Origins of transformational leadership roles

RNLDs are one group of nurses who have had to overcome many such barriers to change whilst maintaining the ability to make decisions and lead. This endows them with many of the attributes of a transformational leadership role. As Payne writes (2000), traditional models of interprofessional working based on primary care teams have been replaced by a set of more complex relationships, requiring different leadership at different times. In practice, RNLDs may be leaders when there is physical long-term care to be provided, as in the case of people with learning disabilities. Consequently their experiences have much to offer other professionals in health and social care.

The original source of transformational leadership skills and roles presented in this chapter came from a three stage research study, whose starting point was the broad research question 'How do professionals in the field of learning disability view interprofessional practice?' The study was set within a general grounded theory methodology, with the dialogue with participants being presented from two analytical perspectives (McCray 2003a, 2003b).

The participants

The ten participants had been professionally qualified in nursing or nursing and social work for at least 2 years. All were working in practice offering long-term support to people with learning disabilities. Areas of responsibility included disability and learning disability, with one person working across learning disability and mental health services.

When participating in the first stage of the research, which involved the completion of a questionnaire, individuals offered an applied practice account or response to interprofessional work. Those participants whose responses were embedded in practice, regardless of the positive or negative message accompanying them, were seen as significant partners in the continuing exploration of interprofessional practice and the development of theory.

The research process

Following questionnaire completion, a descriptive analysis of the individuals' experiences of interprofessional practice based on topic-focused semi-structured interviews was undertaken. This process identified key roles for the practitioner and identified significant practice-based knowledge. The impact of these roles and knowledge was explored in relation to professional and interprofessional confidence, teamwork strategy and subsequent use of power by the participants. The most significant of these in relation to the overall findings was the strength of the respondents' feelings towards creating change for the client group. Earlier in the research the motives of

225

professionals who might hide behind professional defences through role assimilation had been considered in order to offer an idealised vision of practice. In contrast, the data presented depicted dedicated practitioners offering a range of strategies to continue their intervention or to ensure the intervention of others with an unanticipated confidence and level of comfort despite a number of barriers at national and local level. Alongside this willingness to blur boundaries and remain involved in a particular situation, participants' dialogue set out their leadership strategies for the interprofessional setting. Participants' descriptions of creative, practice-level solutions were underpinned by a great deal of informal knowledge about interprofessional working. This commitment seemed to be based on reality rather than ideal or perfect practice. This was confirmed by the participant-driven exploration and acceptance of crisis as an integral part of their work.

The extent to which participants accepted crisis work was in itself to be expected given the nature of service delivery and a client group with profound learning disability. However, it was the maturity of responses to crisis that further confirmed the author's feelings about what this group of people could offer to others in terms of a blueprint or model for interprofessional practice and leadership. Responses and solutions were largely proactive, reflective and with an absence of hostility or cynicism towards the other professionals in teams. Participants' focus was centred on handling the conflicts that crisis could create, setting in place actions to sustain interprofessional relationships and acknowledging their own use of power in that process – the essence of transformational leadership.

There was a great deal of energy in participants' responses, with an absence of reliance on 'we have always done it that way' as a rationale for practice in the interprofessional context. This movement, motivation and receptiveness to new contexts and practice solutions, presented in the data, were captured as both accounts of what interprofessional practice was like, and a number of good practice guidelines founded on the practitioners' experiences.

These descriptions led to a further analysis of the data and the final stage of the research. This resulted in the construction of a framework for practice based on a detailed analysis of six concept analyses, which assimilated participants' activities in practice (the descriptive) with the prescriptive, i.e. their thoughts on how interprofessional practice should take place. The process resulted in the integration of the six concepts within a model for leading interprofessional practice in the field of learning disabilities. This is underpinned by knowledge of the continuously changing practice context, and ultimately offers a tool for practice of use to a wider range of professionals.

The conceptual framework for practice

The framework has six key concepts derived from concept analysis. For a detailed methodology of this process see McCray (2003a, 2003b) and Fig. 14.1. Box 14.1 summarises the development of the framework.

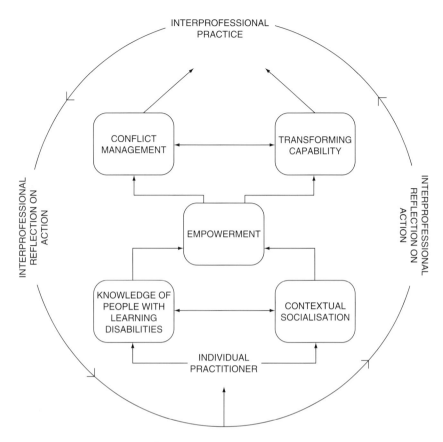

Fig 14.1   The conceptual framework (McCray 2003a).

Exploring the concepts and practice characteristics

In the earlier descriptive analysis, participants provided a detailed portrayal of the situation and environments in which practice occurred. From this vivid picture, evidence from the data in the form of *practice characteristics* was developed. This was then used to form the evidence for each of the concepts in the framework.

Findings during the research showed that healthcare relationships were only one aspect of the RNLD's role, collaboration with social workers and social work teams being another, with a more formal statutory link at its heart. When teamwork roles were discussed there was both an acknowledgement of a shift in practice in the role of the social worker and clarity with regard to the role boundaries of those involved in meeting the needs of this client group.

Box 14.1   The process of conceptual framework development.

Part One	From stage one, the descriptive to the conceptual analysis. A set of practice characteristics, drawn from the original categories in the descriptive data analysis, was used to identify the proposed concepts. These are contextual socialisation, knowledge of people with learning disability, empowerment, transforming capability, conflict management and interprofessional reflection on action.
Part Two	These proposed concepts are explored with the available literature; similarity and difference in meaning are explored.
Part Three	Clarity of meaning of each proposed concept is outlined.
Part Four	Defining attributes and case examples are presented to define concepts in this framework.
Part Five	Antecedents and consequences further refine the boundaries and meaning of the concepts.
Part Six	The interrelationship between proposed concepts (compatibility, congruence) is explored and concepts are formalised.

Concept one: contextual socialisation

These practice experiences underpinned the practice characteristics of *contextual socialisation* which were concerned with ongoing reclarification of the role of professionals in social care, particularly social workers, together with the significance of professional boundaries and a desire to recognise the positive elements of the reshaped professional roles. However, despite clarity of role being present where the statutory social work processes are concerned, at times relationships were ambiguous. This provided evidence of practice within an ambiguous context that was created by social and healthcare agencies being both accountable for the welfare of people with learning disabilities and yet constrained by resources, which may inhibit action. Often the practitioners described the influence of organisational tension and this led to the final practice characteristic, that of operating to meet desirable outcomes and change for clients within an environment centred upon protecting rather than challenging organisational action. Despite the complexities of collaboration, the RNLDs in the study frequently stressed the need for it and expressed the desire to work through tensions created. The main reason for this response was the position of the client.

Concept two: knowledge of the person with learning disability

The primary practice characteristic of the concept *knowledge of the person with learning disability* is that of ensuring that the person's needs are addressed. A range of strategies were described by the RNLDs in the study to ensure changes are made for people and the characteristic pro-active practice provided evidence of the commitment made. Practitioners highlighted the need for both formal theory and specialist knowledge of learning disability as well as the equally important knowledge of the person. This ensured that the individual client or the service user's understanding of the situation is at the fore. Emphasis on developing practice at service and organisational level was also a significant characteristic and an indicator of change for practitioners, who were prepared to act in the face of unacceptable practice and despite unfamiliar circumstances. Practitioners also described the need to acknowledge a different set of complex relationships within primary care where leadership roles were moving from a traditional approach to a more transformational one in order to work with clients and other professionals to design effective, flexible models of care.

Concept three: empowerment

Practitioners had a critical understanding of the uncertainty of some of the contexts of practice and suggested ways of challenging without hostility the failures of some service interventions. This formed evidence for the practice characteristics of the concept *empowerment*. This added to the motivation to work towards change and use expert knowledge to endorse the practice and personal contribution of others, not to undermine it. There was an understanding of the need to change one's own practice to meet contextual shifts and subsequent client need, based on an awareness of the contradictory nature and tensions of organisational goals; also a critical awareness of power and powerlessness as being at the foreground of practice for the client and the practitioner remained constant. Participants were skilfully managing the impact of power in both professional and interprofessional relationships whilst recognising when the inappropriate use of power can become controlling rather than facilitative.

Concept four: transforming capability

Practitioners' descriptions of their own roles acknowledged the applicability of their knowledge, skills and experience to function within the constantly changing practice arena. The concept *transforming capability* is built on evidence of characteristics that include actively engaging with the complexities of health and social care need. Such capability in practice is offered by practitioners who have the potential for knowledge and skill development underpinned by practice intervention, based on clarity and tacit knowledge.

Capability involves evidence of a creative element and the ability to change practice in different contexts. The RNLDs here have documented experience of marginalisation, which has resulted in professional self-awareness and assertiveness in order to move practice forward. In relation to leadership, participants described their motivation to confront the status quo and achieve real change. In the interprofessional context it is likely that their holistic view of the person means that other professionals are likely to identify the RNLD as the practitioner with a more developed knowledge of the individual person with learning disability and seek their advice and leadership in order to achieve change.

Concept five: conflict management

Nevertheless this does not mean that collaboration is without conflict and the practitioners acknowledge its presence, as demonstrated in the concept *conflict management*. Practice characteristics included evidence of the need for a balanced or impartial view of other professionals in a crisis situation whilst acknowledging the need for reflective learning in relation to their own and others' views in crisis-focused teamwork. As one Registered Nurse said:

> to gain a good working relationship, practice action is required. This may be a follow up action, or it may be a challenging action, that is not being afraid to have an exchange of thoughts with someone. If a person is closed up, so doesn't chase up what is happening, then what they are doing won't work, won't be so successful. (Rn 7)

Further, acting autonomously to improve communication and create change and staying with a problem to find a solution rather than withdrawing from the arena were seen as crucial. As collaboration becomes increasingly complex with the involvement of a number of different agencies in order to meet the needs of clients with multiple needs, contact is essential, as illustrated in the following quote from one Registered Nurse:

> It isn't helpful to be looking for scapegoats when things go wrong, but an honest discussion, maybe with some clearing of the air, can only help in future collaboration with that person. (Rn 6)

Consequently practitioners endorsed this through the characteristic seeking and maintaining a dialogue with other professionals despite the difficulties.

Concept six: reflection on action

Underpinning all of the other concepts was the concept *reflection on action*. Within this framework the concept emerged from the affirmation of interprofessional practice from the participants together with interprofessional thought and action. Throughout the descriptive analyses, participants presented examples of action that is doing, linked to problem solving. This was evidenced through examples of critical exploration and review of their own thought processes, knowledge and experiences in relation to each element of the framework and the other five concepts. A concern with challenging their beliefs and views was central and informed the characteristic prevention of professional insularity, and new approaches to problem solving. Whilst the attention to detail in relation to reviewing the social and environmental contexts of action and moving away from a rule-bound approach to interprofessional practice established the characteristic, this concept brings together all the elements of the framework, seeking as it does *to create a supportive element for practice* whilst not shielding inappropriate action and ultimately to bring about change.

The framework in practice

A framework offers a distinct frame of reference and is an approximation or simplification of reality, and includes only information that the author considers relevant to understanding (Reilly 1975). Additionally a framework should afford those using it room to question the approach together with a solution to practical problems.

This model will be used as an iterative tool for practice, enabling practitioners who are clinical leaders to critically reflect on their previous and next stage interventions using the *interprofessional reflection in action* concept throughout. This supports the practitioner to make practice thinking and action explicit by drawing on the other five framework concepts. The tool offers a structure for planning practice intervention, identifying areas of uncertainty, planning the next stages of action, and exploring the ongoing processes and their effect. As the practitioner works through each concept sequentially and reflects on their position at each stage, the nature of power and ambiguity within practitioner activity is openly addressed, and leadership is not seen as a separate decontextualised activity. Rather it is suggested that all six components are elements of a transformational leadership style.

Learning to apply the framework

At one level the framework could be used as a basic checklist or tool for practice to aid thinking in the interprofessional context. However, it is envisaged that it could be delivered as part of a formal module in interprofessional leadership or as an e-learning tool. Box 14.2 offers one route to achieving knowledge of the framework's application.

Box 14.2 Learning to use the framework.

Stage One
- Practitioner attends taught workshop on the framework as part of interprofessional leadership practice module.
- Concepts of the framework are explored, clarified and questioned.
- Framework integration and coherence are critiqued.

Stage Two
- Practitioner works through case example to solve practice problem, using the framework to determine professional action.
- Practitioner evaluates action, reflects on position and plans next stage of action.
- Throughout, the nature of power and its use in leadership are central to the process.
- Practitioner uses the framework in practice setting.
- Practitioner critically analyses use and reflects on own professional action.
- Practitioner questions outcome and experience and plans next intervention using the framework as a practice guide, and as a basis for supervision.

Example of practitioner use of the framework

Case example

The problem was how to gain better access to primary healthcare and education for a person with learning disabilities with type 2 diabetes living at home with family carers and in contact with the community learning disability team.

How the framework helps to facilitate practitioner thinking and learning in order to solve the problem

Initially contextual socialisation supported the practitioner to reflect (using the concept interprofessional reflection on action) on the impact of the context of the individual person. The practitioner questioned the economic and social circumstances of the person and his or her family and how it might impact on their general health. As the White Paper *Valuing People* (DH 2001, p. 30) notes, often parents with children or adult family members with learning disabilities have diminished earning potential because of care requirements. Knowledge of the context led the practitioner to contact colleagues in social care to check whether a full assessment of need had been undertaken. Having experience of the stages involved and the need to ensure that this is pursued over time and followed up is a key element of the facilitation role. Equally resource allocation may be at issue despite the best intentions of individual agency workers, and ultimately the practitioner may need to consider the wider political context. Interprofessional reflection in action included questioning:

- What is my role in this context?
- How shall I plan my leadership approach?
- What understanding of interprofessional leadership and roles will help in the balance of power in the practitioner and service user relationship?

Knowledge of the context also included being in contact with the local primary care practice to check the status of current GP services for this client group. Formal links were in place. However, in the absence of formal links and a lack of support the practitioner had to consider some of the following:

- The broader political issues at play in this practice situation.
- The focus of leadership intervention in this political context.
- Who needed to be influenced to impact directly on the practice outcome.
- When to intervene and how others were likely to respond.
- How to measure the practitioner's own effectiveness in this process

There was some disengagement of this client within a particular healthcare practice as a result of a lack of knowledge of the specific needs of people with learning disability by some of the primary healthcare team. Additionally the client did not have an annual review of her diabetes. This concept supported the practitioner to reflect on her own current knowledge of the individual person with learning disability and carers in relation to her perception of the person's current health status. She was then able to act as a facilitator in accessing primary care services.

Through actively considering her own knowledge, attempts to facilitate the health education needs of the individual were better informed, and from this position a relationship with the primary care team was pursued and supported. Further, as there were underlying concerns for the long-term health needs of this person in relation to type 2 diabetes the use of interprofessional reflection on action helped the practitioner to consider her own current level of knowledge. This process involved thinking about the issues shown in Box 14.3.

Additionally, the empowerment concept supported the practitioner to critically evaluate the nature of power and how it was operating for the person and the family. This also ensured that her own role as professional was assessed. The questions prompted by this concept are listed in Box 14.4.

Observing the role of change agents in a wider organisational context, Hudson *et al.* (1999, p. 251) refer to the key influence of the 'reticulists' in interagency working. Noting that a significant part of the reticulist role is operating from a sound position of power and legitimacy it was vital that the

Box 14.3 Issues involved in reviewing a practitioner's level of knowledge.

- What are the familiar parts of the practice situation?
- What knowledge and skills do I have in order to work in this type of teamwork role?
- Where are my knowledge gaps?
- Where can I gain the skills to take on this teamwork situation?
- Am I comfortable with any uncertainty present?
- Who else do I need to involve?
- Who should be leading this intervention?
- Am I happy to facilitate and lead?
- When should I challenge a specific approach that seems to be ineffective, if I am not leading in this teamwork intervention?
- How much involvement has the person with learning disability in the planning of care?
- How much credibility have I amongst fellow professionals as a leader in this context?
- How can I use my skills to ensure that the service user is empowered rather than disempowered in accessing this environment?

Box 14.4 Questions prompted by the empowerment concept.

- What indicators can be used to measure the extent of the individual's empowerment in terms of making decisions about her health as she had already been excluded from some vital health screening for her diabetes?
- Why have such decisions been reached? Are they based on evidence or anecdote?
- Where has the person been involved in any previous transition or care planning?
- Where does power lie? Is power being used to support the person with learning disability and her family?
- Broadly, where are local circumstances contributing to empowerment, for example in relation to the role of primary care trusts and their investment in facilitating education and screening for this group of people?
- Who is involved in facilitating more integration and additional models of intervention for this group of people?
- Why is the person being denied access to services? Is it, for example, because of a combination of learning disability and language barriers due to ethnicity? Who should be supported to address this?

Continued

Box 14.4 *Continued*

- When can I influence the balance of power? When might my position be powerful in creating and leading change here?
- How could interprofessional leadership influence outcomes for this individual?
- How can decisions about this be made?
- How can I ensure I am using professional power effectively?

---

practitioner was able to reflect on all contributory factors when assessing her individual capacity and ability to lead the change processes required to gain better access for the service user.

Therefore as the practitioner continued to engage with these issues, the concept of conflict management enabled the practitioner to question the appropriateness of potential interventions to create change. Questions prompted by this concept are listed in Box 14.5.

The concept of transforming capability also further directed the interprofessional leadership strategies used. For example, in relation to promoting the need for health education for this person a number of organisational as well as professional constraints needed to be overcome, in particular when working with different agencies that also impact on healthcare. Questions prompted within this concept are presented in Box 14.6.

Box 14.5 Questions prompted by the conflict management concept.

- If it becomes necessary what styles of conflict management should I use when seeking access to resources?
- Why might this influence outcomes for the individual in receipt of health care?
- Where in the teamwork process might it be appropriate for me to tackle any conflict that might arise?
- Who should I involve in addressing conflict and what are the likely longterm effects – on the team, networks, collaboration and the individual service user?
- When might it be appropriate for me to ignore conflict?
- Can this be validated?
- How would this impact on my future interprofessional relationships in this primary care team?

Box 14.6 Questions prompted by the transforming capability concept.

- What new networks might need to be created or accessed to achieve a more informed awareness from emerging professional agencies involved in health?
- What information in relation to resources might I need?
- Why do new agencies need to be influenced and supported to develop further strategies to include people with learning disabilities?
- Where might alternative agencies be accessed and by what means, if original plans are unsuccessful or inappropriate?
- Who else is supportive of my leadership interventions? Are these transparent and public statements of support? Could I use these to create change?
- When will I need to access other colleagues to lever further support for changes needed? Is this part of a planned strategy?
- How can I gain further support? How will I gain any additional skills I might need?
- How can I ensure continued influence across agencies?
- How can I measure change and evaluate success or failure?

Outcomes from using the framework

The case example above offers one very practical way of using the framework as a tool for practice. At a basic level it facilitated the practitioner to assess her knowledge and skill in relation to emerging new areas of practice, questioning her current motivation, strategies and interprofessional relationships. It offered a route to reflecting on the potential for shared leadership and decision-making which was able to be continuously evaluated through the use of the final concept interprofessional reflection on action. The success or failure of intervention and leadership strategies at each stage were determined, as other concepts in the framework were revisited and new strategies planned. This led to areas of strength being highlighted and further areas of new activity being considered.

The framework led to positive outcomes for the practitioner and the service user in a number of ways. These included the beginnings of a dialogue about appropriate health education for people with learning disabilities and type 2 diabetes involving the practice nurse responsible for diabetes, the GP, the client and her carer, along with the practitioner.

The practitioner gained an understanding about how local diabetes services operated and consequently how to influence more strategic local plans in relation to the heath education needs of people with learning disability and diabetes. The practitioner recognised that without this knowledge of the wider context which the framework facilitated no positive leadership could take place. Equally, although a formal assessment of needs had been undertaken with social services, as there were no urgent health or social care issues any future needs had not been addressed.

Fitness for purpose: a role in transforming services?

The conceptual framework has been tested for its current fitness for purpose using an adaptation of Fitzpatrick & Whall's (1996) criteria for analysis and evaluation of practice theory. This is presented in Table 14.1.

What can be learnt for learning disabilities practice?

The framework is particularly significant in relation to the White Paper *Valuing People* (DH 2001) because of the focus on building interprofessional relationships so central to its success. By offering a model of working that may strengthen the leadership role of the RNLD and creating change for people with learning disability, the framework sits well with contemporary policy goals.

One key factor is that the framework recognises the contextual and structural issues that impact on the lives of people with learning disability as well as the practitioner's own practice (Gilbert 1993). Equally it offers a place for values such as social role valorisation (Wolfensberger 1991) to be explored. However, it is not driven by any single theory that many other professionals and indeed service users and their families may be unfamiliar with.

In this sense it may represent a paradigm shift for the RNLD as it offers a set of global ideas about individuals, groups, situations and events of interest to a discipline (Fawcett 1995). This is because the framework encourages practitioners to seek formal theory and knowledge from a range of disciplines and sources. For example, in relation to promoting health, this might include accessing both the medical and the social models of care. The framework encourages a different perspective on practice, with a more formal concern for values as part of the concept knowing the person with learning disability. For instance, it may be more effective for a practitioner to reflect on the usefulness of social role valorisation as formal knowledge when seeking to address the needs of one individual at a specific point in time rather than as an unequivocal driver for every practice response.

More controversially, using the framework would mean that RNLDs may have to take a more critical and contemporary position in relation to the foundations of their values and knowledge, similar to that of other professional groups. This could be significant at a time when they are both overcoming marginalisation and gaining greater credibility as leaders. Equally by reflecting on their current values and knowledge the RNLD practitioner may become more articulate in expressing his or her role and action to others, at

Table 14.1 Evaluation of the theory using Fitzpatrick & Whall's criteria.

Assumptions of theory in framework
Are they congruent with interprofessional and learning disability practice history?

- Framework acknowledges the potential historically situated marginalisation of the client group and impact on professionals.
- Framework makes explicit issues of power in practice and its contested nature in interprofessional relationships and leadership interactions.

Are beliefs of framework consistent with existing ethical standards and social policy?

- Framework concepts address the ambiguous nature of policy implementation and professional roles.
- Framework facilitates the exploration of relationships with people with learning disabilities and other professionals in an ethically sensitive way.

External analysis and evaluation
Is practice theory consistent with existing standards of professional practice, and of external agencies?

Framework capacity
- Standards of care: there are no formal standardised protocols for interprofessional practice.
- Congruence with NMC and GSCC guidelines regarding antidiscriminatory practice.
- Use of external research agencies, the public domain and publication in peer-reviewed journals.

Is practice theory consistent with educational standards for interprofessional learning disability practice?

- It formalises, through the generation of research evidence, elements of pre- and post-qualifying educational requirements of professional groups of nursing and social work.
- It begins the process of formalising practice level theory in a new area of practice.

Is the practice theory supported by existing areas of research in interprofessional practice, learning disability practice and beyond?

- The development of concepts using concept analysis has involved the exploration of research in a wide area of subject disciplines, related and applied practice areas.

a time when a consensus on definition and purpose still remains absent (Stewart & Todd 2001).

In practice the RNLD's distinctive relationship with people with learning disability would not change. The framework facilitates a relationship that embraces the diversity and differences of people with learning disability in the twenty-first century, centred on interprofessional practice to create change. What may be in transition, however, is the ideological foundation of the learning disability nurse, and this framework both captures (through description of practice thought and action of participants) and facilitates (through prescription, in the analysis of possible practice action, i.e. 'what should happen', by participants) this process.

Wider application of the framework

Learning disability nurses have often been party to professional and interprofessional change created by a shift in policy, ideology and agency partnerships. Equally their role has been contested and challenged throughout the last three decades (Parrish & Kay 1998). On the other hand they have been at the forefront of facilitating change with service users and their families, for example in developing advocacy networks and in formalising individualised care packages with social care agencies. As a result of these experiences they are well placed to reflect upon and disseminate their knowledge and strategies for intervention (DH 1998) in the domain of leadership in the interprofessional context as described here. A consideration of both the individual and integrated components of the conceptual framework would benefit a number of professionals, particularly as boundaries for practice change and traditional strategies for leadership become obsolete. At this stage it is envisaged that with a shift in emphasis from 'knowledge of people with learning disabilities' to a more generic 'knowledge of the service user group' the tool has a far broader applicability, with much to be gained and learned from these initial experiences in learning disability. However, this is for the future when further testing is planned amongst a wider group of practitioners in the interprofessional field.

Conclusions

This chapter has presented the findings of an empirical study that led to a conceptual framework for practice in the interprofessional context of learning disability services. The components of the tool are underpinned by the very real practice experiences of RNLDs and subsequently describe and prescribe what is required for best practice and for change to take place. In highlighting the attributes needed for contemporary interagency teamwork, with reflection as a central element of change, the tool acts as an iterative mechanism for all those who wish to develop their skills as transformational leaders further. As a result of this it will appeal to those motivated to share power as health and social care contexts shift and who recognise the need to step out of their traditional pattern of working and leading in order to sustain the momentum of change.

References

Biggs, S. (1997) Interprofessional collaboration: problems and prospects. In: *Interprofessional Working for Health and Social Care* (eds J. Ouvretveit, P. Mathias & T. Thompson). Macmillan, London.

Boulter, P. & Cook, H. (1997) Leadership in learning disability nursing. *Nursing Management*, **4** (1), 12–13.

Burns, J.M. (1978) *Leadership*. Harper and Row, New York.

Department of Health (1998) *Signposts for Success*. The Stationery Office, London.

Department of Health (2001) *Valuing People: A New Strategy for Learning Disability in the 21st Century*. The Stationery Office, London.

Fawcett, J. (1995) *Analysis and Evaluation of Conceptual Models in Nursing*. F.A. Davis, Philadelphia.

Fitzpatrick, J.J. & Whall, A.L. (1996) *Conceptual Models of Nursing: Analysis and Application*. Prentice Hall, London.

Gilbert, T. (1993) Learning disability nursing: from normalisation to materialism – towards a new paradigm. *Journal of Advanced Nursing*, **18**, 1604–1609.

Hallett, C. & Birchall, E. (1992) *Coordination and Child Protection, a Review of the Literature*. HMSO, Edinburgh.

Hart, S.L. (1998) Learning disabled people's experience of general hospitals. *British Journal of Nursing*, **7** (8), 470–477.

Hudson, B. (1987) Collaboration in social welfare: a framework for analysis. *Policy and Politics*, **15** (3), 175–182.

Hudson, B., Hardy, B., Henwood, M. & Wistow, G. (1999) In pursuit of inter-agency collaboration in the public sector. *Public Management*, **1** (2), 235–260.

Huxham, C. & Macdonald, D. (1992) Introducing collaborative advantage. *Management Decision*, **30** (3), 50–56.

Kanter, R.M. (1983) *The Change Masters*. Simon and Schuster, New York.

Kinsey, P. & Maguire, S. (2001) Cultivating quality. *Community Care*, 30 August, 22–23.

Loxley, A. (1997) *Collaboration in Health and Welfare, Working with Difference*. Jessica Kingsley, London.

McCray, J. (2003a) Towards a conceptual framework for interprofessional practice in the field of learning disability. PhD Thesis. Department of Social Work Studies, University of Southampton.

McCray, J. (2003b) Leading interprofessional practice: a conceptual framework to support practitioners in the field of learning disability. *Journal of Nursing Management*, **11**, 387–395.

McCray, J. & Ward, C. (2003) Leading interagency collaboration. *Journal of Nursing Management*, **11** (6), 361–363.

McDaniel, R.R. (1997) Strategic leadership: a view from quantum and chaos theories. *Health Care Management Review*, **22**, 21–37.

Moore, D. (1999) A force to be reckoned with. *Learning Disability Practice*, **2** (3), 25–27.

Parrish, A. & Kaye, B. (1998) Exploring the NHS executive document *Signposts for Success*. *British Journal of Nursing*, **7** (8), 478–480.

Payne, M. (2000) *Teamwork in Multiprofessional Care*. Macmillan, London.

Pietroni, M. (1991) Right or privilege? Post qualifying training with special reference to child care. Collected Papers from a writing group, study 10. Central Council for Education and Training in Social Work, London.

Reilly, D.E. (1975) Why a conceptual framework? *Nursing Outlook*, **23**, 566–569.

Sofarelli, D. & Brown, D. (1998) The need for nursing leadership in uncertain times. *Journal of Nursing Management*, **6**, 201–207.

Stanley, R. (1998) The primary health care provision for people with learning disabilities: a survey of GPs. *Learning Disability Nurse Health and Social Care*, **2** (1), 23–30.

Stewart, D. & Todd, M. (2001) Role contribution of nurses for learning disabilities: a local study in a county of the Oxford Anglia region. *British Journal of Learning Disabilities*, **29** (4), 145–150

Trofino, J. (1993) Transformational leadership: the catalyst for successful change. *International Nursing Review*, **40** (6), 179–182.

Wolfensberger, W. (1991) *A Brief Introduction to SRV as a Higher Order Concept for Structuring Human Services*. Training Institute for Human Service Planning, Leadership and Change Agency, Syracuse University, New York.

Section Four

Challenges for Leadership in the Future

15 The Challenges for Leadership in the Future

Melanie Jasper

Introduction

This chapter is an opportunity to do what authors do not often get the chance to – to anticipate what the future holds and how we can prepare healthcare practitioners for leadership in the future. As the Editor of the *Journal of Nursing Management* I am in a privileged position of seeing the initiatives and innovations currently in progress in the UK and internationally, as well as being at the forefront of the ways in which practitioners are interpreting policy and government directives within their everyday reality. In addition, I see the publication of ideas, models and tools for leadership as authors, researchers and theorists gain confidence in their work and use the journals available for dissemination. Many more practitioners are willing to provide commentaries on a plethora of issues, and I am heartened that these are starting to come from practitioners working with the patient, as well as the opinion formers and leaders in exalted positions such as government and executive offices and academic institutions.

This chapter, then, will be different in nature from the others which have attempted to showcase leadership at the cutting edge across all levels within the NHS. Building on Chapter 1, and in reviewing the evidence from multiple sources, both within and outside of this book, I attempt to anticipate the challenges that need to be addressed if the Government's vision of 'leadership-for-all' is to become a reality in the next decade.

Challenge one: gaining hearts and minds – the challenge of culture change

The culture within public services tends to change very slowly due to the nature of services provided, employment practices and job security, and the inherent need for those services to exist within our society. Whilst the idea of having a 'job for life' once entering public service is not as ironclad as it once was, there is still a notion that people entering public service at all levels will spend their working lives there and live to collect their pensions.

Within the NHS this has tended towards a hierarchical culture, where the workforce is graded by jobs, and the work component of that grade is clearly identified – reminiscent of the military model after which the NHS was fashioned. This can be seen throughout all sectors of the health service, within the professions, technical and support staff and the management and administrative staff. Whilst this type of organisational structure enables the routine work to be done, it does not necessarily create a culture that enables every individual the freedom to contribute to change and development, or encourage an environment of creativity and acceptance. Many of the chapters in this book reinforce the government agenda of the need for existing culture and practices to be challenged if the health service is to be changed (DH 2001a). We need to move to a 'can do' culture and working environment, where people are encouraged to work within small teams with common objectives and shared values that are made explicit.

This culture will be one based on positivity, where there are no obstacles and no negativity, but challenges to be embraced and welcomed, where change is accepted as par for the course and actively welcomed, and good ideas are recognised, encouraged and rewarded; where everyone feels value as part of the organisation and as having a contribution to make. The Older Persons Outreach and Support Team (OPOST) case study presented in Chapter 12 is one example of where a long-standing problem was turned into a beacon of good practice using the combined ideas and experiences of an interprofessional team working together. This was clearly not an easy task, and in fact the major challenges seem to have arisen not from overcoming the environmental, organisational and professional constraints usually cited as impeding new developments, but from the interpersonal relationships between people within that organisation. Hence within this challenge there are three levels where there needs to be a culture shift:

(1) *The individual level* – at which every person needs to be encouraged to reflect on and explore their own attitudes, values and beliefs, the language they use, and the way they interact with other people. They need to consider their contribution to the organisation, what part they play in it and their motivation for working there. Finally, they need to consider how their lives could be enriched within their working environment, focusing on what they could suggest, initiate or achieve.

(2) *The team level* – at which teams of people working together perceive themselves as having some power and control over their own working lives, and that they play a valuable part in the organisation. Where each member of the team feels a part of that whole, and that they can contribute to the life and energy of that team.

(3) *The organisational level* – at which strategies are developed and enacted that enable everyone in the organisation to have a voice, structures are reviewed with fresh eyes to identify where the culture of the organisation is embedded, the practices that maintain that culture are identified and whether these need to be changed.

Of course these are ideals; utopian ideas that, many will claim, have already been part of many 'restructurings' in the history of the NHS (alongside drives for efficiency, the market economy and political expediency). However, is this really restructuring? Is it the structure that needs development, or is it the underpinning beliefs and values throughout the organisation that need fostering? The spectacular failure of successive NHS reorganisations since 1974 suggest that whatever model is imposed will be doomed unless the people within the organisation themselves are involved with and are part of the process of modernisation. Successive governments appear to believe that NHS reorganisation and restructuring will necessarily lead to an improved health service responding to the needs of the people it serves. This is, if recent history is to be believed, quite simply not the case. Amongst the rhetoric of change theories that have passed into common parlance is that of 'top-down' and 'bottom-up' approaches. Whilst the latter has been recognised as the most egalitarian (and possibly most successful) way for change to occur, it is often the strategy used for small-scale developments at local level only, with the arguably more important strategic changes still the preserve of the few individuals in the top echelons of the organisation.

One of the major barriers to 'bottom-up' approaches is the time it takes to truly enable everyone to be involved in the decision-making processes. Teamwork requires a commitment to creating and enabling that team; in a culture where work is target driven and objective measurements about 'productivity' abound, it may be perceived as inefficient to spend time creating a team when the people involved could be treating more patients, or filing more paperwork.

Modernisation of the NHS is dependent upon changing the culture throughout the whole organisation. The challenges for leadership at all levels in doing this are as follows:

- identifying the existing culture and questioning every aspect of it
- identifying the values that drive that culture and assessing whether these are shared, real and appropriate
- identifying clear statements of direction, objectives and values
- creating enabling strategies that empower individuals to contribute
- fostering a climate of trust
- accepting and valuing people's differences
- accepting that mistakes will be made
- embracing a 'bottom-up' change and developmental strategy
- using emotional intelligence across all levels of the organisation to enable others

Challenge two: leadership-for-all

The notion of leadership-for-all challenges the very idea of leadership itself as being vested in the few. Fundamentally though, it is a recognition of human potential – that there is a possibility for us all to lead in some way, however small, and that it is incumbent upon everyone to encourage individuals in striving toward this potential. This is reinforced with the creation of the skills escalator (DH 2001b, p. 18, shown in Box 15.1) and within the Government strategy *A Health Service for All the Talents: Developing the NHS Workforce* (DH 2000a) which recognises the need for the development of people at all levels of the organisation, and, moreover, for this to be supported structurally and systematically by the organisation.

Box 15.1 The skills escalator approach (DH 2001b, p. 18). (Crown copyright is reproduced with the permission of the Controller of HMSO and the Queen's Printer for Scotland.)

Category	Means of career progression
Socially excluded individuals with difficulties in obtaining employment ↓	Six month employment orientation programmes to develop basic understanding of the world of work
The unemployed ↓	Six month placements in 'starter' jobs, rotating into different areas of work, whilst undertaking structured training and development
Jobs/roles requiring fewer skills and less experience Cleaning, catering, portering, clerical, etc. ↓	Skills modules to support progression through to job rotation training and development programmes including National Vocational Qualifications (NVQs) and NHS LAs, appraisal and personal development planning
Skilled roles Healthcare assistants, other support staff ↓	Modules of training and development through NVQs or equivalent vocational qualifications
Qualified professional roles Nurses, therapists, scientists and junior managers ↓	First jobs/roles following on from formal preregistration education or conversion courses. Appraisal and personal development planning to support career progression. Achievement of a range of skills acquired at staged intervals

Continued

Box 15.1 *Continued*

More advanced skills and roles Expert practitioners, middle managers, training and non-training medical roles/grades ↓	Further progression, supported and demonstrated through learning and skills development as above. Flexible working and role development encouraged in line with service priorities and personal career choices
Consultant roles Clinical and scientific professionals, senior managers	Flexible 'portfolio careers' for newly appointed, experienced and supervising roles, planned in partnership with employers informed by robust appraisal, career and personal development planning processes

---

Fundamental to this will be the success of culture change that recognises and values each and every worker for what they can offer, the skills they have and that can be developed and the commitment they bring to the NHS (DH 2000a). However, what is also necessary is the development of the individual in recognising his or her potential and having the confidence to work towards achieving this. Initially, people need to believe in themselves and be encouraged by others in this belief. This may be very challenging for those at the early stages of the skills escalator whose previous life experiences may not have enabled them to develop confidence in their own abilities and a positive self-esteem. However, the first three stages identify this in terms of offering contracts that have a developmental component, recognising the need for a workforce that is secure in the knowledge that they have the skills to do the job required of them, and, perhaps more importantly, the support of the organisation in developing those skills. The latter stages of the skills escalator recognise the continuing professional development needs related to career progression and the need for these too to be supported from within the organisation as opposed to being the sole responsibility of the individual.

Key to this is the role that managers play in supporting and facilitating individuals within the constraints imposed by service requirements and resources. However, perhaps it is the *attitude* of the manager and his or her will to support others that is the most important requirement, as this does not cost anything in material terms, nor does it take a great deal of time, but it may have huge impact in terms of the development of the individual.

The challenges of leadership-for-all therefore are:

- enabling individuals to believe in themselves
- supporting initiative and creativity
- developing the individual
- facilitating and enabling across the workforce
- developing the role of managers
- the diverse workforce

Challenge three: overcoming traditional boundaries/barriers

The Government has already taken major, deliberative steps in starting to break down the inequity in power and influence between the different professions contributing their expertise to the health service. For instance, we have seen:

- consideration of the traditional boundaries in terms of 'who does what' and the blurring of accountability and responsibility for care, e.g. prescribing rights for nurses, pharmacists and some allied health professionals; nurse/therapist led clinics
- valuing of the specialist activity of individual professions, e.g. reduction of the need for general practitioners to provide 24 hour care, with the recognition that out-of-hours and walk-in surgeries can be an adequate substitute; the creation of consultancy posts for allied health professionals, nurses, midwives and health visitors
- the movement of major funding from secondary to primary care
- changes to the contractual basis of medical consultants' employment.

The effect of these and many other initiatives has been to start the process of valuing the skills and knowledge that all professions in the NHS bring to care and acknowledge that they are all vital within a patient's journey through a care episode. Whilst the intention of this is undoubtedly sound, it will inevitably take time for the traditional authority and power of the medical professions to move into a more equal relationship with the other professions, and this will clearly require facilitation and leadership. Whilst we are gradually witnessing the move to more interprofessional approaches to care, it is dependent to some extent on the culture change needed, as discussed above, and does need facilitation in tackling interprofessional barriers inherent within the previous power structures of the NHS.

Another challenge for leadership is the inequity between gender and ethnic groups within the health service. Many of the professions are female dominated, with others, such as medicine, having a disproportionate distribution of women in lower grades compared to the senior grades. There is still a great deal of work to be done in terms of enabling the skills and experience of women to be maximised by considering working practices, childcare facilities and continuing professional education.

Similarly, there are a disproportionate number of people from minority ethnic communities in the lower grades of employment in the NHS, and action needs to be taken in terms of attracting these groups into healthcare and into the professions.

In many ways, the job of breaking down professional boundaries has begun with the creation of the knowledge and skills framework in recognising that people need to be paid for the components of their job and what they do, and not necessarily the title of their profession.

The challenges for leadership in terms of interprofessional boundaries and barriers therefore relate to:

- the power of the professionals
- interprofessional boundaries
- traditional authority
- antidiscriminatory practices
- valuing people for their knowledge and skills rather than their profession or label

Challenge four: education for leadership

To some extent, the first three challenges outlined above are dependent upon the success of educational strategies for developing leadership. Without significant and effective investment in education and training for leadership, it will be difficult for the culture of the NHS to change, for individuals to develop the skills, confidence and professional experience to become leaders and for professional boundaries to be scaled. The Government report *Working Together – Learning Together* (DH 2001b, p. iii) establishes a framework for lifelong learning to ensure staff are: (1) equipped with the skills and knowledge to work flexibly in support of patients; and (2) supported to grow, develop and realise their potential.

The lifelong learning framework (DH 2001b, p. 5) summarises the Government's vision of a strategy for the educational strategies required to provide a workforce fit to deliver the NHS of the future, founded on the vision proposed in Box 15.2.

In terms of education for leadership, this needs to be instigated at all levels, as outlined in Chapter 6 of *Working Together – Learning Together* (DH 2001b, pp 45–52).

However, to some extent, preparation for leadership needs to begin before this; in terms of the professions it needs to be a component of pre-registration education, particularly given the changes to the roles likely to happen with the blurring of professional boundaries. The encouragement of individual initiative and recognition of innovative student work that is practice-based is the first important step to this, as opposed to the traditional approach to education that is theoretically led and focused on academic subjects, and where theory is assessed and valued more highly than learning in practice. The Government

Box 15.2 The Government's vision of lifelong learning (DH 2001b, p. 6). (Crown copyright is reproduced with the permission of the Controller of HMSO and the Queen's Printer for Scotland.)

The Government believes that:

- There is a set of core values and skills that should be central to lifelong learning in the NHS and healthcare more generally.
- NHS staff are entitled to work in an environment that equips them with the skills to perform their current jobs to the best of their ability, developing their roles and career potential, working individually and in teams in more creative and fulfilling ways.
- Access to education, training and development should be as open and flexible as possible – with no discrimination in terms of age, gender, ethnicity, availability to part-time/full-time staff or geographical location.
- Learning should be valued, recognized, recorded and accredited wherever possible.
- Wherever practical, learning should be shared by different staff groups and professions.
- Planning and evaluation of lifelong learning should be central to organisational development and service improvement, backed up by robust information about skills gaps and needs.
- The infrastructure to support learning should be as close to the individual's workplace as possible, drawing on new educational and communications technology and designed to be accessible in terms of time and location.

---

identifies the core knowledge and skills (DH 2001b, p. 7, shown in Box 15.3) that should be common to all staff as a basis on which to build.

This is to be enacted through the skills escalator presented in Box 15.1 above, recognising that all individuals can be encouraged to develop successively through various stages if they so wish and show the potential to do so.

A robust strategy for individual continuing professional development (CPD) needs to be made a reality through the use of personal development plans (PDP) (DH 2001b, p. 13) recognising the potential for every individual to progress and develop throughout their working lives. The publication *Continuous Professional Development: Quality in the NHS* (DH 2000b) outlines the Government's strategy for PDP provision. This needs to be supported through adequate resources for all in-house, local educational provision and funded external provision. It also needs reinforcing through staff management strategies where annual appraisals become the place where personal portfolios are reviewed and CPD requirements for professional registration are verified. The strategy of the professional bodies that devolve responsibility for achieving statutory or required CPD to the individual is flawed if safeguards fail to be

Box 15.3 Core knowledge and skills for NHS staff (DH 2001b, p. 7). (Crown copyright is reproduced with the permission of the Controller of HMSO and the Queen's Printer for Scotland.)

All staff should:

- fully understand and respect the rights and feelings of patients and their families, seeking out and addressing their needs
- communicate effectively with patients, their families and carers and with colleagues
- value information about, and for, patients, as a privileged resource, sharing and using this appropriately, according to the discretion and consent allowed by the patient and by means of the most effective technology
- understand and demonstrate how the NHS, and their local organisation, works
- work effectively in teams, appreciating the roles of other staff and agencies in the care of patients
- demonstrate a commitment to keeping their skills and competence up to date – including the use of new approaches to learning and using information – and supporting the learning and development of others
- recognise and demonstrate their responsibilities for maintaining the health and safety of patients and colleagues in all care settings

---

put in place to support the system. At present, it is the individual's responsibility to maintain the currency of both his or her professional registration and competence, whilst it is the employer's responsibility to ensure that his or her workforce is fit for practice. The missing link is a requirement for employers to ensure that minimal CPD requirements are achieved.

Similarly, a culture change needs to occur that recognises that staff development is an essential component of the NHS rather than being a luxurious extra. This will require a commitment to practice facilitator posts that are workplace based yet have robust links with educational providers in partnership agreements. The focus for the majority of CPD that goes on needs to be work based as opposed to classroom based. It also needs to be problem based, enabling people to focus on problems arising from their everyday practice, and enabling them to devise workable solutions suited to their own idiosyncratic environment. Bolted on to this, for added incentive, is a need for a system of academic accreditation of this sort of development. This already exists in many higher education institutions, where previous learning can be accredited into academic awards. However, this does not recognise the 'stand-alone' work that goes on, or could go on, in the practice arena, which could be built into a portfolio of work demonstrating achievements. This is particularly important given the drive towards evidence-based practice and the urgent need to build credible practice-based theory to support practice across all healthcare professions.

In addition, the future for developing leadership must be interprofessional, with practitioners encouraged to learn together in order to provide truly inter-professional care. Developmental projects need to ensure that cross-boundary perspectives are taken, and that all affected by proposed changes are given the opportunity to contribute opinions at the early stages. An awareness of a wider perspective will also arise from individuals being encouraged to study in different environments – these may be within the organisation itself, or perhaps through increased secondment opportunities or fixed term exchange programmes to other organisations. This also comes from enabling individuals to study formally at educational institutions where they will be exposed to a variety of people from other organisations with which they can share perspectives and work out solutions to common problems.

Finally, there are two overarching issues that need to be taken into account in providing education for leadership. The first is to enable everyone to develop critical and reflective practice that results in ethical decision-making. If we are encouraging 'leadership-for-all' there must be accountability for practice and decisions taken that are transparent and visible. Alongside this runs the need for effective interpersonal skills that enable practitioners to present their own viewpoint and defend their practice to others. Increasing responsibilities and recognition of individual potential through more inde-pendent working brings with it the dangers of unethical practice and rogue decision-making (e.g. the GP Harold Shipman). With increased independence must come robust strategies and techniques for establishing public safety as well as ensuring that those very individuals are practising within the public values espoused by their employers. There are various ways of doing this, including clinical supervision, appraisal systems, adequate record-keeping and requirements for the compilation of written portfolios of evidence that demonstrate practice-in-action.

The second issue is the responsibility placed on the employing organisation if the individual is to be given more responsibility for leadership. Inherent within developing and changing practice is a need for a culture that embraces educational development as a necessary component of any change. Hence, adequate resources need to be costed into developments and appropriate training provided before change is initiated. This will ensure commitment to development and change through leadership at all levels of the organisation.

The challenges for education for leadership are therefore:

- to establish lifelong learning as everyone's responsibility
- to develop learning strategies during pre-registration courses that are practice-based, problem-solving and encourage initiative, innovation and collaborative working, and develop leadership awareness and skills
- to ensure that within CPD, leadership skills as well as managerial skills are developed, and that these are accredited academically

- to build a managerial requirement into the strategy for verifying professional competence and fitness to practice
- to encourage work-based learning as a primary strategy for CPD
- to develop practice facilitators as central to CPD strategies
- to encourage interprofessional learning opportunities wherever possible
- to ensure that potential leaders are exposed to a range of environments and cultures in order for them to view the 'wider picture'
- to develop critical, reflective practice that involves ethical decision-making, autonomy and accountability in practice
- to ensure that adequate resources for education and training are built into all bids for developments, and that this is seen as essential to any change that occurs

Conclusions

This chapter has been a personal reflection and deliberation on what the future of leadership within the NHS means to me, and the challenges for leadership which are key to realising the vision of government policy outlined in so many documents relating to NHS reform since 1997. I spent many years training and working within the NHS before moving into education, and believe wholeheartedly in the principles that underpin its service. Arising from this background, and my own subsequent development as a social scientist and educationalist, I consider there are the dual imperatives of wholesale culture change and educational support of the workforce without which it is very unlikely that the Government's strategies for change will ever happen. The Government's policies spell out a clear vision, underpinned by coherent values and beliefs, for a new approach to providing and delivering healthcare for the future. Part of this vision is located within humanitarian principles of equality – both for employees and for service users. This involves recognising and valuing the importance of the individual at all levels, and providing leadership within a culture that maximises the talents of all those individuals.

References

Department of Health (2000a) *A Health Service for All the Talents: Developing the NHS Workforce*. The Stationery Office, London.

Department of Health (2000b) *Continuous Professional Development: Quality in the NHS*. The Stationery Office, London.

Department of Health (2001a) *Shifting the Balance of Power Within the NHS: Securing Delivery*. The Stationery Office, London.

Department of Health (2001b) *Working Together – Learning Together*. The Stationery Office, London.

Index